TAKE A WALK

IN QUEENSLAND'S
NATIONAL PARKS

Southern Zone

TAKE A WALK

IN QUEENSLAND'S NATIONAL PARKS

Southern Zone

John & Lyn Daly

Published in Brisbane by Take a Walk
March 1998

Cover design and photographic layout by Concept Australia Corporate Design Group, Brisbane.
Printed by Australian Print Group, Maryborough.
Distributed by Herron Book Distributors Pty Ltd., Brisbane.

National Library of Australia
Cataloguing-in-Publication Data
Daly, John, 1950-
        Take a walk in Queensland's national parks. Southern zone.
        Bibliography.
        ISBN 0 646 35105 2
Hiking - Queensland - Guidebooks. 2. National parks and
reserves - Queensland - Guidebooks. 3. Queensland -
Guidebooks. I. Daly, Lyn, 1951-. II. Title
796.5109943

Find us on the net: http://www.takeawalk.com.au
E-Mail us at: info@takeawalk.com.au

Front Cover: Mt Barney from Mt May, Mt Barney National Park.
Back Cover: Sunrise, Moreton Island National Park.
                 Ascending Spicer's Peak, Main Range National Park.
All photographs from the collection of John Daly.

CONTENTS

FOREWORD

National parks are special places. Queensland's 210 national parks protect the State's major ecosystems and places of cultural significance. They also provide much-needed habitat for our native wildlife and contain the State's best scenery.

Almost 4% of Queensland - more than 6 million hectares - is protected in national parks and other protected areas.

Parks belong to the people of Queensland. More than 100 national parks have facilities for nature-based activities, such as camping, picnicking and bushwalking.

The best way to see a national park and discover what makes it so special is to go bushwalking.

Walking tracks take you to the best spots in the park. If you are really adventurous, you might even head off the track to discover the wilderness.

If you want to go bushwalking in a national park in Southern Queensland, this is an excellent guide. Keen naturalists John and Lyn Daly have combined their years of bushwalking experience with the local knowledge of national park staff to help you decide where to go bushwalking.

Staff from the Department of Environment have praised the authors' efforts so I have no hesitation in recommending this book to you.

Take a walk in one of Queensland's beautiful national parks. Use this guide to help you choose the best place to go and discover the special attractions of the parks. The Ranger is also there to help you make the most of your park visit. For remote parks especially, you should contact the Ranger before you head to the park or go for a walk.

But, remember! Everyone has a special responsibility to care for our national parks. Please read the advice about minimal impact bushwalking carefully. Practise these commonsense ways to reduce your impact on the national parks so we can keep them beautiful for future visitors and for future generations.

Hon. Brian Littleproud, MLA
Minister for Environment

INTRODUCTION

This book is designed to introduce people to the wonders of Queensland's National Parks. Whether you prefer picnicking, camping, bushwalking, birdwatching, photography, or simply enjoy the solitude of sitting on a mountain top watching the sun rise, there is something in our national parks for you.

There are 51 national parks in Queensland below the 26th parallel that extends from Gympie, due west to the South Australian border and south to the New South Wales border. Comprehensive details covering history and major features, including flora and fauna are provided for 45 of these parks and for one conservation park, along with access directions, facilities available and ranger contact numbers.

More than 1000kms of walking tracks, trails and routes have been described. All have been personally walked by the authors between February 1997 and February 1998. Times and distances given for each walk are for the return journey, except for the Border Track in Lamington National Park. All walks have been graded as either easy, moderate or hard, providing options for both the beginner and experienced bushwalker.

It is not meant to be a technical bushwalking book, hence the more complex system of grading used by some bushwalking clubs to describe terrain, length and fitness level required, has been abandoned in favour of this simpler system. In some cases, the Ranger in Charge of a park may have suggested changing the grade of a walk from easy to moderate, or moderate to hard, based upon the typical visitor attracted to the Park. Whenever this has occurred the suggestions have been implemented.

Topographic map references have been supplied and Brisbane UBD Street Directory references are used where applicable. Reference is made to those parks where the Queensland National Parks and Wildlife Service (QNPWS) provide walking trail maps.

Every effort has been made to ensure that the information was correct at the time of publication, but be aware that conditions do change. Floods can alter the condition of creeks, landslides can close tracks and changeable climatic conditions may alter the terrain. What once was a relatively easy hike through the bush may change over time to a tough 'scrub bash' through lantana, lawyer vine or wild raspberry. The authors welcome your comments relating to changed conditions (or anything else) for possible inclusion in future editions.

Prior to publication, the Rangers in Charge of all Parks were invited to check the text to ensure there were no obvious errors. In many cases their associates also provided valuable information. Their input was greatly appreciated. Many of these Rangers spent time with us when we visited their park. We particularly wish to thank those mentioned in the acknowledgement section.

The vast library and archives of the National Parks Association of Queensland (NPAQ), available to all members, also helped us considerably. These archives dating from the 1930s provided us with information relating to the history and features of many Parks. The names of the individual members who gave assistance and encouragement are far too numerous to mention. However, special thanks must go to John deHorne, the President, and George Haddock for his assistance with archival information and for sharing his vast knowledge of national parks. Where the walks described were last reviewed during an NPAQ outing, reference has been made to the walk leader.

The six parks not included are Chesterton Range, Triunia, Sarabah, Mt Chingee, Mt Pinbarren and Pipeclay National Parks.

Chesterton Range National Park is extremely isolated and the Ranger in Charge suggested that we omit it from this edition. Because of its isolation, rescuing lost or stranded visitors would be particularly hazardous, time consuming and expensive.

Triunia National Park is a non visitation park protecting the *Triunia robusta.* This plant was considered extinct until recorded there in 1989.

Sarabah National Park, at only 1.4ha, was proclaimed in 1973 to protect an almost pure stand of black bean trees. Access to the Park is via private property and the Ranger in Charge feels Sarabah is best left in its current state.

Mt Chingee National Park also requires landowner permission to gain access. Much of the flora in this region could be used to regenerate areas in Lamington National Park in the event of serious fire damage. For this reason the Ranger in Charge prefers limited visitation.

Mt Pinbarren National Park is another small park, only accessed via private property. It contains some sections of sensitive vegetation amongst hoop pine rainforest and is *'protected'* by a dense barrier of lantana.

Pipeclay National Park protects an area of 2.5ha of particular Aboriginal significance and has also been excluded.

We encourage you to visit the parks described in this book. National parks are there for the enjoyment of all people. If nothing else, you should take the time to enjoy the fresh air, or simply get back to nature.

You've got the book, so why not do yourself a favour and, *'Take a Walk...'*

ABOUT THE AUTHORS

John and Lyn Daly have been keen bushwalkers for many years. They have walked extensively in Southern Queensland as well as many other areas of the State.

Interstate and overseas holidays are always planned in areas where good trekking is available; like Tasmania, New Zealand, Nepal and Peru. In fact, anywhere they go they always find time to *'Take A Walk'*, regardless of the season. Even if it's November in Cape York, or June in Tasmania!

Both are active members of the NPAQ and John is a walk leader with the Association.

After spending more than a decade in the computer business, they opted for a lifestyle change and now spend their time travelling, walking and writing.

The knowledge and enjoyment gained whilst visiting national parks to research this book has been one of the highlights of their life.

ACKNOWLEDGEMENTS

Alphabetically by Park

The following people deserve special thanks for their assistance and for checking the text relating to their parks.

Alton - Spud Thomas. **Bendidee, Erringibba, Southwood, Wondul Range** - Bob Lawes. **Blue Lake** - Leif Shipway. **Bribie Island** - Stephen Price. **Bunya Mountains** - Bernice Sigley. **Burleigh Head, Cougals section of Springbrook** - Peter Chapman. **Conondale** - Wyn Boon. **Crows Nest, Ravensbourne, The Palms** - Errol Ryan. **Culgoa Floodplain** - Saul Rankin. **Currawinya** - Danny McKellar. **D'Aguilar Range** - John Ravenscroft. **Eudlo Creek, Dularcha, Ferntree Creek, Freshwater, Glass House Mountains, Kondalilla, Mapleton Falls, Mooloolah River** - Mark Lythall. **Fort Lytton** - Peter Hodson. **Girraween** - Bernadette Carter, Jolene Spect, Ian Elms, Glen Elms. **Great Sandy. Cooloola Section** - Tony Monro, Greg Walker. **Lake Bindegolly** - Mark and Jenny Handley. **Lake Broadwater Conservation Park** - Bob Cameron, Colin O'Connor. **Lamington. Binna Burra** - Bill Flenady. **Green Mountains:** Andy Quirk. **Main Range** - Steve Finlayson. **Mariala** - Colin Dollery, Nick Swadling. **Moreton Island** - Chris Artiemiew. **Moogerah Peaks, Mt Barney** - Ross Buchanan, Keith Sullivan, Justin O'Connell. **Mt Coolum, Noosa** - Mick Cubis. **Springbrook** - Mike Hall. **St Helena Island** - Jenise Blaik. **Sundown** - Peter Haselgrove. **Tamborine Mountain** - Will Buch. **Thrushton** - Pat Bailey. **Tregole** - Colin Dollery, Greg Griffiths. **Venman Bushland** - Paul Hawthorne.

Thanks also to other Department of Environment staff. **Brisbane** - Alan Don, Kim Morris. **Charleville** - Clare Smith. **Roma** - Craig Eddie. **Toowoomba** - Nicola Moore, Sarah Walbank.

THE EVOLUTION OF NATIONAL PARKS

The first national park in the world was Yellowstone, established by the United States Government in 1872. The concept of national parks then gradually spread throughout the world.

The Royal National Park in Sydney was Australia's first, and the world's second national park, but when it was conceived in 1879, it was definitely not intended to preserve large tracts of virgin land. Trees were felled along the river banks, and lawns and European trees were planted. Deer were bought in and exotic birds and fish were released. It was simply called, *'The National Park'* for three-quarters of a century.

You could be excused for thinking that the Government of the day did not intend to have *'too many'* national parks.

A year prior to the proclamation of *'The National Park'*, Robert Collins, a grazier from Queensland's Beaudesert area visited the USA. Collins was impressed with the concept of national parks.

After being elected a Member of Parliament in 1896, he began campaigning actively for the creation of a national park in the McPherson Ranges, which form part of the eastern boundary of Queensland and New South Wales.

Unfortunately, very few people felt the need to preserve specific parcels of land because Australia had millions of acres of undeveloped land.

In 1906, the then Queensland Minister for Lands introduced an act *'...to provide for the reservation, management and protection of state forests and national parks'*. This provided the first legal opportunity for a national park reservation, and in 1908, Queensland's first national park was proclaimed at Witches Falls on Mt Tamborine.

Forestry officials at the time claimed the land was *'unfit for any other purpose'*.

Bunya Mountains National Park, between Dalby and Kingaroy, was proclaimed in August of the same year.

In 1911, Romeo Lahey, a timber miller from Canungra joined with Collins and continued lobbying for the creation of a national park in the McPherson Ranges.

In 1915, two years after Collins' death, Lamington National Park was finally proclaimed.

Several more parks were gazetted over the next few decades, but in those early days national parks were generally established to protect their scenic qualities and provide recreational opportunities. They were often considered worthless lands or useless scrub. They were also relatively small.

There are several national parks in Queensland whose original boundaries covered an area of only one square mile (259ha). It was not uncommon to draw a boundary this size around a waterfall, a mountain top, or some other scenic location and call it a national park.

In 1930, The National Parks Association of Queensland (NPAQ) was formed. This small group of enthusiasts saw a need to educate the public about the value of national parks and to liaise closely with the Government of the day to create new national parks and promote conservation ideals.

With ongoing lobbying by NPAQ and the assistance of various departmental members who were sympathetic to the national park ideal, sound management policies for the protection of national parks evolved.

By the 1960s there was a gradual realisation that we needed to preserve representative samples of the diverse ecosystems and habitats found within Queensland.

The Mines Department and the Lands Department objected to many early submissions and land of high conservation significance was used for other purposes.

During this time, NPAQ members conducted field trips to many areas considered worthy of protection as national parks and made appropriate submissions to the Government.

Gradually, more technical specialist staff were employed by the Government to handle national park matters and a more scientific approach began to emerge for the evaluation of areas selected for gazettal as national parks.

But what is a national park and why do we need them?

There are many different descriptions of national parks but this lengthy definition, adopted at a conference of Australian Ministers responsible for national parks, tends to sum it up:

"A national park is a relatively large area set aside by legislation, for the conservation of flora and fauna, the protection of scenic, landscape and special cultural values, permanently dedicated to these purposes and for education, inspiration, scientific research and public enjoyment and managed so that it's natural attributes are retained and restored."

National parks are living museums and natural laboratories. Many of our medicines come from natural sources.

Scientists are currently investigating the possibility of Australian plants providing a cure for AIDS and Barrier Reef corals providing protection from skin cancer.

We rely on biological resources for many life sustaining processes that we tend to take for granted – oxygen supply, soil formation, nutrient recycling, flood preservation, climate regulation and waste cleansing.

National parks are important as scientific base lines and gene pools for the future.

They are areas where the human species can gain inspiration and learn to appreciate and value the processes of nature.

But how are areas for new national parks selected?

The present underpinning philosophy for the establishment of national parks is the conservation of areas representative of biological diversity, or biodiversity.

Biodiversity is the variety among and within living organisms and the ecological systems in which they occur.

It's all about preserving as many different species of flora and fauna as we possibly can.

As well as biodiversity other criteria include the conservation of uncommon and threatened species, the protection of cultural and historic sites, the preservation of outstanding natural features and opportunities for education and passive recreation. Queensland is the most naturally diverse state in Australia.

There are 114 amphibians (about 60% of the national total), 396 reptiles (50%), 581 birds (80%), 180 mammals (70%) and 1 600 species of fish.

A further indication of Queensland's natural diversity is its major vegetation communities.

The State has now been divided into 20 different terrestrial biogeographic regions. These distinct regions are:

Cape York Peninsula	The Gulf Plains
Gulf Coastal	Gulf Fall Uplands
Wet Tropical Rainforest	Einasleigh Uplands
Mount Isa Inlier	Mitchell Grass Downs
The Brigalow Belt North	The Brigalow Belt South
Central Queensland Coast	Desert Uplands
Channel Country	Simpson-Strzelecki Dunefields
South-East Queensland	Mulga Lands
Darling-Riverine Plain	Nandewar
New England Tableland	NSW North Coast

To determine the site of a new national park, scientific studies are undertaken in each biogeographic region. These studies identify areas where at least 30% of the vegetation communities or landscape types occur, within that region.

If necessary, a number of smaller areas are also selected to conserve rare or endangered species.

The key areas are ranked and then targeted for acquisition.

Areas can be vacant crown land or other crown reserve, leasehold or freehold properties and funding for purchase is generally required.

How much land is needed for national parks?

There is an International Convention, formed under the auspices of the United Nations that calls for national parks and nature reserves to make up 5% of any country's territory. These parks are also meant to represent every kind of biological community. In Queensland, sadly, we fall far short of that recommendation.

In 1987, the then Queensland Government committed itself to double the national park estate in its first term, with the ultimate aim of achieving the total of 5%.

A concerted effort was made to select areas of the State where there was little or no protection of specific vegetation types or landforms.

These areas included; the Brigalow Belt, Mulga Lands, Channel Country, and the North-West Highlands.

Significant progress has since been made in these areas. Thrushton, Erringibba, Currawinya, Lake Bindegolly, Mariala, Wondul Range, Culgoa Floodplain,

Tregole and Tarong National Parks, all covered in this book, have been gazetted since 1990.

Even with all this progress we have fallen far short of the 5% required to ensure biological diversity.

Currently, only 3.8% of Queensland has been preserved and approximately one third, or 297 of a total of 968 different ecosystems in the State, are under threat.

The management philosophy for national parks has changed considerably over the years.

There was a time when the approach was *'let nature take its course'*. This approach has now been abandoned in favour of more positive steps to preserve and protect biodiversity.

Controlled burning is undertaken to minimise the risk of wildfires. Cleared and trampled areas are regenerated with plants grown from locally collected seed. Fencing is used to protect endangered species from predators and cattle grazing. Non native species competing with natives are removed and human impacts like firewood collection are controlled.

National parks belong to all people and everyone has a responsibility to assist with the maintenance and preservation of our Parks. In most cases this simply means adhering to minimum impact bushwalking practices whenever visiting a national park.

In this book several environmentally sensitive areas, along with areas of particular Aboriginal significance, have been excluded in an effort to protect our unique environment.

NATIONAL PARKS ASSOCIATION OF QUEENSLAND

The National Parks Association of Queensland (NPAQ) was formed in 1930 by a small group of dedicated people committed to the creation of more national parks. In fact, over the last 65 years nearly all national parks in Queensland were either gazetted or extended following recommendations made to the State Government by NPAQ, after inspection and assessment of the areas concerned.

Another proud achievement of NPAQ was the original concept of Marine National Parks. All those Island National Parks off the coast of Queensland are protected from unbridled development because of the National Parks Association.

NPAQ is a non-profit, non-government organisation. It is managed by elected, non-party political council members who give voluntarily of their time and expertise to promote the ideals of the Association. A scientific officer is employed to conduct research and provide facts for inclusion in submissions to the Department of Environment, on the management and selection of national parks. The Association receives some funding from State and Federal Governments but most of its revenue comes from membership fees, donations, some fund raising and earnings from bequests.

Several different committees have been established within the organisation and are responsible for much of the work associated with membership, public awareness, library, social activities and outings.

The objectives of NPAQ include the irrevocability of gazetted national parks, the permanent protection of all flora, fauna and geology within them and the reservation of further areas that warrant protection. Members combine pleasure visits with inspections of existing and potential national park sites and make recommendations to Government.

NPAQ representatives actively serve on Government committees and are invited to comment on draft management plans and issue papers.

The ideals of the Association are promoted amongst its members and the general public through education and example. Information on newsworthy issues is produced for the media and members staff displays at various venues.

Member's meetings are held monthly at Mt Coot-tha auditorium and interesting guest speakers provide details on topical issues, or perhaps even a recent visit to national parks throughout Australia and abroad. Potential new members are very welcome at these meetings.

NPA News is a monthly magazine informing members of both current issues and Association activities.

Over the years, NPAQ members have assisted QNPWS with walking track maintenance, planting of native species, and eradication of noxious plants.

In 1996 NPAQ was awarded the John Herbert Award by the National Trust of Queensland for work done in eradicating lantana at Boombana, in D'Aguilar National Park.

An important and very enjoyable aspect of NPAQ membership is its outings. Almost every weekend there is a day walk to some interesting feature within driving distance of Brisbane. These could be to places as well known as Lamington, or to areas where landowner permission is required to access isolated mountain tops.

But NPAQ is definitely not just another bushwalking club. The Association is conscious of the needs of all its members, as well as its ideals. Specialist outings are organised with an emphasis on wildflowers, birdwatching, and photography, especially during weekend camps. The impact of these outings on the environment is considered and where possible car-pooling is used to reduce the number of vehicles on the road.

NPAQ generally organises one mini outing of around two weeks duration and an extended outing of around four to six weeks duration every year. They have also organised trips to national parks overseas at very reasonable cost.

But there is no pressure to participate in a given number of outings to remain a member. Participation is purely voluntary. Some members attend weekend camps purely for the social interaction. Some members find it difficult to attend meetings while others always attend meetings, but seldom participate in walks. The choice is yours!

You may ask, *'How can I help to assist in promoting Queensland National Parks Association ideals?'*
If you feel that NPAQ's ideals are in line with your own, then they invite you to join the Association.

You would be doing something constructive to assist with the protection of our environment. At the same time, you could learn a great deal, meet some interesting people to *'Take a Walk'* with and generally have a good time.

**For more information about the National Parks Association of Queensland:
Telephone (07) 3367 0878 or Fax (07) 3367 0890**

GENERAL BUSHWALKING INFORMATION

SAFETY AND NAVIGATION

Let a responsible person know where you intend walking and when you intend to return. Rangers from some heavily visited parks require a bushwalker's safety form to be completed prior to the commencement of your walk. Try to walk in a group of at least three. If a person is injured, one member of the group can go for help while the other stays with the injured party. In this age of modern technology a mobile phone is considered by many to be a useful addition to your pack. Precious hours may be saved in an emergency, but maintain the serenity of the bush by leaving them turned off unless needed!

On all day walks a *'turn-around time'* should be established at the start of the walk. As a general guide divide the number of available daylight hours from your starting time by two, leaving one hour spare at the end of the day. Even if you have not reached your destination by the agreed *'turn-around time'* be disciplined enough to turn back. You can always try again later. Learn to take note of prominent features on the way to a location to aid navigation on the return journey.

If at any time you are feeling uneasy, tired or uncomfortable with the terrain, then turn back. **Remember, there are too many good walks to be done to risk injury to yourself or any member of your party.**

Everyone who attempts off track walks should be equipped with a compass and topographic map and know how to use them. Large scale rescue exercises for lost or stranded bushwalkers are expensive and in many cases they also place rescuers in danger, as well as having a marked effect on the local environment.

Whilst a pool or a creek may look inviting after a hard, hot walk, take extreme care if cooling off. Submerged logs, rocks and other snags can cause potentially fatal injuries. Heed any warning signs and do not dive into swimming holes.

MINIMUM IMPACT BUSHWALKING

Minimum impact bushwalking is an *'ideal'* rather than a hard and fast set of rules. However, there are several accepted principles that should be practised by all bushwalkers to help preserve and maintain our natural environment.

These guidelines should not be seen as posing unnecessary restrictions on visitors to national parks or other wild places, rather a set of ground rules that make for *'common sense in the bush'*.

Always take care to leave no sign of your visit, and remember: *'take nothing but photos, leave nothing but footprints'.*

Tracks

In areas where graded tracks exist, use them. Don't cut corners on zigzags, it causes erosion. Stay on the track rather than walking parallel to the track, even when the track is muddy.

Where there are no graded tracks, follow existing trails where possible to avoid the proliferation of *'goat tracks'*. Skirt around sections of scunge rather than trying to blaze a trail through. In delicate areas or on coastal sand dunes look for a path that will cause the least damage to fragile vegetation.

Track Marking

As a general rule, track marking is frowned upon. Some purists claim that track marking makes people dependent on the markers and they will never develop their own navigation skills. They also claim that if a person can't follow a natural feature like a ridge or a creek, then they should not be out in the bush.

Whilst there is some truth in this argument, there are some defined routes in South-East Queensland where effective marking with rock cairns and tape has led to a more defined route being used by bushwalkers. Many good bushwalkers have also developed their navigational skills in areas where track markers were prevalent.

Perhaps the day will come when the major bushwalking clubs will agree to use and perhaps even maintain a standard set of markers for a selection of *'off track'* walks, leaving other more remote, pristine areas totally unmarked.

When checking current conditions prior to leading a group of walkers into unmarked areas, it is sound practice to mark the trail with tape tied to trees, then remove the tape when completing the return journey with the group.

However, machete blazes should never be used. Apart from being unsightly, the tree becomes susceptible to attack by fungi and termites. Whenever necessary, tape markers should be used sparingly.

Camping

When bush camping, always try to use an established camp site rather than make another. Carry in tent poles - don't cut them from trees. Don't dig trenches around tent sites. Leave machetes and tomahawks at home. In pristine areas, try to erase any sign of your visit by ruffling up the grass where your tent was pitched and replace any logs or rocks that were moved to make way for your tent.

Permits are required for camping in all national parks. These are available from the Ranger's station, self-registration booths or by contacting the Ranger in advance.

Cooking fires

Wherever possible use portable stoves for cooking. They are safer, cleaner, faster and much more efficient than wood fires. They are also much easier to use in wet conditions. If you are in an area where camp fires are permitted, use an existing fireplace. Keep the fire small and clear flammable material well back from the fire's edge. Never cut trees or collect fire wood in national parks. Even fallen trees provide a home for many reptiles and small mammals and should be left where you find them. Douse all fires thoroughly with water when finished.

Rubbish

'Pack it in and pack it out.' Whilst in the bush, put lolly papers, orange peel, cigarette butts (if you must smoke), and any other rubbish in a garbage bag and carry it out with you. Years ago the philosophy was, *'burn, bash and bury'* all rubbish, but this leads to litter around popular camp sites and walking trails and should no longer be practised. If you see rubbish left behind by environmental vandals, pick it up and pack it out with you. Orange peels may be biodegradable,

eventually, but the unsightly mess is offensive to many people.

Sanitation

Always use a toilet site at least 100m from the nearest creek. Dig a hole in the ground at least 15cms deep and cover it after use. Unless you are in an area of extreme fire danger toilet paper should be burned to prevent animals digging it up and scattering it through the bush. Carry out all sanitary items.

Leave your soap at home. Even biodegradable soaps are pollutants and should not be used. Never use shampoo in creeks or waterholes.

YOUR EQUIPMENT

Bushwalking does not have to be an expensive sport. A pair of sturdy sneakers, comfortable clothing, a hat and a basic backpack will get you started.

The most important item to be carried in your backpack is WATER. As a general rule you should carry two litres of water, per person, per day. On extremely hot days in Southern Queensland, up to three litres may be needed.

Other essential items include a first aid kit, snacks and lunch, compass, map, whistle, torch, raincoat, sunscreen and insect repellent.

Many specialist books have been written about bushwalking equipment and specialty bushwalking shops are only too happy to provide information for novices.

NATIVE ANIMALS AND BIRDS

All native animals and birds are protected in national parks. Although it may seem appealing and fun for children, please refrain from feeding the wildlife. It makes them aggressive and is particularly bad for their health. Constant feeding encourages larger birds and animals to inhabit areas otherwise inhabited by smaller species. All wildlife have a natural diet and hand feeding by humans discourages hunting.

DOMESTIC ANIMALS

Domestic animals are prohibited in national parks and should not be taken into the bush. Even if they don't manage to kill birds or reptiles, their scent will disturb the native fauna.

BEACH DRIVING

Permits are required for driving along the beaches at Stradbroke, Moreton and Bribie Islands. If you do drive, please observe the tide times, don't drive on the dunes and adhere to recommendations relating to reduced tyre pressure.

Anyway, walking is by far the most pleasant way to appreciate our beaches.

19

Park Locations

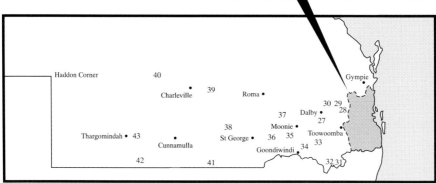

1	D'Aguilar Range NP	16	Glass House Mountains NP	31	Girraween NP
2	Freshwater NP	17	North Coast Rail NP's	32	Sundown NP
3	Venman NP	18	Kondalilla NP	33	Wondul Range NP
4	Fort Lytton NP	19	Mapleton Falls NP	34	Bendidee NP
5	Mt Barney NP	20	Conondale NP	35	Southwood NP
6	Main Range NP	21	St Helena NP	36	Alton NP
7	Moogerah Peaks NP	22	Blue Lake NP	37	Erringibba NP
8	Burleigh Head NP	23	Moreton Island NP	38	Thrushton NP
9	Lamington NP	24	Bribie Island NP	39	Tregole NP
10	Springbrook NP	25	Ravensbourne NP	40	Mariala NP
11	Tamborine NP	26	Crows Nest NP	41	Culgoa Floodplain NP
12	Mt Coolum NP	27	Lake Broadwater CP	42	Currawinya NP
13	Mooloolah River NP	28	The Palms NP	43	Lake Bindegolly NP
14	Noosa NP	29	Tarong NP		
15	Great Sandy NP	30	Bunya Mountains NP		

THE PARKS AND THE WALKS

BRISBANE PARKS

D'AGUILAR NATIONAL PARK

HISTORY
Allan Cunningham named the D'Aguilar Range in 1821, after Sir George D'Aguilar, a British Army Officer.
Brisbane Forest Park, situated on the southern portion of the Range, encompasses areas of national park, state forest, scenic reserve, water catchment and some freehold land, making it the largest and most accessible reserve of its type so close to a major city, anywhere in the world. Referred to as *'the Park on Brisbane's doorstep'*, Brisbane Forest Park celebrated its 20th anniversary in October 1997. At 28 500ha, it is the second largest park in South-East Queensland. (The Cooloola section of Great Sandy National Park is the largest at 40 900ha.) A scenic road winds its way over the D'Aguilar Range, through the rainforest and private landholdings, connecting the eastern and western sides of Brisbane Forest Park.
The D'Aguilar National Park holding within Brisbane Forest Park totals 3 270ha and consists of six separate areas, four of which were originally gazetted as individual national parks.
Jolly's Lookout was the first of the D'Aguilar National Parks, being proclaimed in 1938 and named after William Jolly, Brisbane's first Lord Mayor. Here, you are afforded magnificent views over the Samford Valley, all the way to the Islands of Northern Moreton Bay. Mt Tempest, the highest stabilised coastal sand dune in the world is easily identified on Moreton Island, along with the Island's Big and Little Sandhills. A geological interpretive display, showing various rock formations found in the Park was the first of its kind in Australia, when installed in 1985.
The site of the Maiala picnic area was once home to a flourishing sawmill, processing timber cut from the surrounding rainforest. Due to its close proximity to Brisbane, Maiala is one of the most heavily visited national parks in Queensland and a popular destination for family outings. It was proclaimed in 1940, but parts of this section of the Park have been preserved for *'public enjoyment'* since 1901.
Boombana National Park was proclaimed in 1948. NPAQ has been conducting regular clearing of weeds, including lantana, in the Boombana area for many years and in 1996, the Association received the John Herbert Award from the National Trust of Queensland, for their efforts. This work is all done on a voluntary basis and is a further indication of the Association's participation in the management and maintenance of our national parks. Boombana is an aboriginal word meaning 'place of flowering trees'.
Many trees in Manorina National Park fell to the timber getter's axe prior to it's gazettal in December 1948.
The two other areas making up D'Aguilar National Park are west of Mt Nebo and west of Mt Glorious. They are undeveloped and have limited public access.

FEATURES
The D'Aguilar Range is the result of relatively recent volcanic activity. It forms the connection between the Border Ranges in the south, the Conondales in the north, and the Bunyas to the west.
About 20 different types of eucalypts have been identified in Brisbane Forest Park. Open forests cover about 90% of the Park, and the remainder is made up of rainforests, closed forests and grassed clearings. The rainforest patches tend to be on the southern slopes in sections that have resisted bush fires.
Maiala region supports an example of a fast disappearing subtropical rainforest ecosystem with rare and vulnerable animal and plant species.
Red bloodwood and small-leaf fig are a feature of the lush eucalypt forest and rainforest of the Boombana area. The rainforest in Boombana is one of the closest patches of rainforest to Brisbane.
Cabbage tree palms are prominent in the Manorina area of the National Park as they raise their majestic heads amongst the open eucalypt forest and subtropical rainforest. Spectacular brush box and tallow wood are common throughout the Park, with some trees reaching 50m in height. Yellow flowering wattles and red lillypilly fruit are particularly evident during the summer months.
Because of the diverse habitat of the area, many different types of fauna live in the forest. Colourful finches, parrots and honeyeaters flit amongst the trees. Visitors may spot scrub turkeys, noisy pittas, regent bowerbirds and paradise riflebirds, as well as dingoes, brushtail and glider possums, koalas and echidnas. Lizards and snakes are also common.
The vulnerable Mount Glorious spiny cray is found only at Mt Glorious. It inhabits the running waterways in the Maiala section and survives only in unpolluted water with temperatures below 20°C.
The endangered southern dayfrog, once inhabited the waterways along the rainforested areas of Mt Glorious. The Kondalillas is the only other area to support this frog, now considered an *'endangered species'*. It has not been sighted in either area for a number of years.

ACCESS
D'Aguilar National Park can be reached by travelling to The Gap, one of Brisbane's western suburbs. Journey via Waterworks Road, following the signs to Brisbane Forest Park. Waterworks Road becomes Mount Nebo Road. Distances to the four developed sections of the Park are taken from Brisbane Forest Park Headquarters, just inside the Park boundary.

ACCESS - JOLLY'S LOOKOUT
Jolly's Lookout is only about 45 minutes from the Brisbane GPO.

0.0kms	Brisbane Forest Park Headquarters.
14.3kms	*D'Aguilar National Park* and *Jolly's Lookout* signs.

15.7kms   Car parking area at the start of the walking track. (From this car park you can continue up the hill to the left, to the Jolly's Lookout car park and picnic facilities.)

EGERNIA CIRCUIT TRACK
Distance: 1.5kms, allow 45 minutes. Easy grade.

This pleasant stroll starts just after the head of the walking track. Turn left down some steps at the first track junction, then left again and walk gradually downhill through the open eucalypt and casuarina forest that is typical of this section of the Park. The track is paved and well maintained all the way. As you swing left on a stone bridge over a small gully, look for a strangler fig that is just beginning to wrap its roots around the host tree. Even though you are never far from the sounds of traffic, you can't help but hear the birds as soon as you drop below the level of the road. The track continues gradually downhill and swings right, crossing several wooden footbridges before climbing back to the starting point.

Last reviewed: 9 November 1997

THE THYLOGALE TRACK
Distance: 8kms return, allow 2.5 hours. Easy grade.

From the start of the walking track continue straight ahead, ignoring the turn off to the Egernia Circuit described above.
This well maintained track initially contours along the side of the ridge in a south-easterly direction, before turning right and heading west towards Boombana. After about 10 minutes, the forest canopy opens up providing good views down to the valley below. As you walk back into vine forest, look for the burnt out trunk of a tree on the right. You can see notches on both sides of the trunk, cut by timber getters to hold the springboard platforms they worked on to fell the tree.
You soon pass an area where several trees have fallen, pulling the canopy down with them. The gully to the left is filled with piccabeen palms. Thirty minutes from the start, cross a service road. The moss-covered stump of a felled tree on the left is more evidence of early logging in this part of the State Forest. The track enters Boombana about five minutes from this road. Look for a tall tree that has fallen parallel to the track. Nature is taking its course and the tree is gradually decomposing. Listen for the screech of cat birds as you head towards Boombana. Whip birds are also common in this area. Continue past a track junction leading to the road and walk a further 10 minutes to the Boombana picnic area. From the picnic area, retrace your steps back to Jolly's Lookout to complete the 8km walk. Alternatively, shorten the return journey by walking 1.5kms back along the road.

Last reviewed: 9 November 1997

ACCESS - BOOMBANA

Continue along Mount Nebo Road from the lower car park at Jolly's Lookout.

16.5kms   *Boombana National Park* sign.
17.1kms   Turn left into Boombana Picnic Area.

THE PITTA CIRCUIT

Distance: 1.1km, allow 30 minutes. Easy grade.

This short walk through examples of open eucalypt forest, transition forest, and subtropical rainforest provides many day visitors with their first glimpse of the vegetation once dotted throughout the area. Commence the walk on the left side of the shelter shed in the picnic area and pass a section closed for revegetation. NPAQ members have cleared lantana from much of this area and replanted native trees. Try to identify the different forest types as you head towards an elevated boardwalk. Just after the start of the boardwalk, look for an old gnarled vine hanging from the canopy. The boardwalk completely circles a giant strangler fig whose host tree died and rotted away, leaving the twisted, hollow trunk of the fig.

The steps from the boardwalk lead down past a smaller strangler fig to an area where lantana has been cleared. This track winds through the forest, eventually reaching the road, near Mt Nebo village.

To complete the Pitta Circuit, return to the boardwalk and follow the main track past a massive fallen tree on the left. Note how this tree has started decaying. Eventually it will totally rot away adding nutrients back into the soil. The track ends at the picnic area.

Last reviewed: 9 November 1997

ACCESS - MANORINA
Continue on from Boombana Picnic Area.

19.3kms	Mount Nebo Road swings right towards Mt Glorious.
20.7kms	*Manorina National Park* sign on the right.
22.0kms	Turn right into Manorina Bush Camp and car park.

THE MORELIA TRACK
Distance: 6kms return, allow 2 hours. Easy grade.

Locate the start of this track on the right of the toilet block, at the rear of the car park. The track immediately leads uphill through eucalypt forest and past the Atrax Circuit junction. Five minutes from the start you reach a small grove of cabbage palms, interspersed with piccabeens. Continue uphill, past some massive Sydney blue gums with bark hanging in strips from their lower trunks, to another section of rainforest. The gully on the right is filled with piccabeen palms. Keep walking uphill through more open eucalypt forest to the top of the ridge. The track now descends a short distance to a service road. Turn right and walk 100m to the rocky outcrop of Mt Nebo Lookout. On a clear day Mt Tempest and the sandhills on Moreton Island are clearly visible.

On the return journey, extend the walk by turning right when you reach the Atrax Circuit junction. This 1km circuit has interpretive signs placed along the track to assist with identification of many mammals that inhabit the area. It is ideally suited to walking at night, using a torch to locate nocturnal animals. Reflective markers have been positioned below the signs. The track climbs gently uphill through forest, then descends, passing through the burnt out stump of a large tree, before returning to the car park.

Last reviewed: 9 November 1997

ACCESS - MAIALA
From Manorina Bush Camp, Mount Nebo Road continues on to Maiala picnic grounds. Even though this is the furthest section of the D'Aguilar National Park from Brisbane, it is only a little over an hours drive from the Brisbane GPO.

27.0kms	Continue straight ahead. The turn off to Samford is on the right.
29.7kms	Travel through the village of Mt Glorious.
30.5kms	Turn right into Maiala picnic grounds and parking area.

THE RAINFOREST CIRCUIT AND GREENE'S FALLS
Distance: 5kms return, allow 2 hours. Easy grade.

This attractive walk is one of the most popular in D'Aguilar National Park. The 1.9km Rainforest Circuit can be completed without walking all the way to Greene's Falls and is ideal for families with young children.

The track starts at the bottom of the picnic area. The first thing you notice when you enter the rainforest is the change in temperature. This provides a welcome relief on hot days. An old steam boiler used by saw millers lies half buried to the left of the track.

If going on to Greene's Falls, ignore the Rainforest Circuit junction soon after the start and continue walking ahead, on the left fork. Interpretive signs placed along the track explain different features of the rainforest. After a few minutes you reach a wooden boardwalk protecting the area around the massive buttress roots of a Watkins fig. Follow the track past a giant Sydney blue gum. Seven hundred metres from the start the track reaches Browns Road.

To walk to Greene's Falls, cross the gravel road and follow the track as it leads downhill. Boardwalks and footbridges have been constructed along much of the track. These prevent erosion and provide vantage spots as the track follows the creek through attractive sections of rainforest, to a lookout platform at the head of the falls.

On the return journey turn left on the Cypress Grove track. This short detour leads through an isolated grove of bush cypress before meeting the gravel road. Cross the road and turn left to complete the Rainforest Circuit. The track now descends along the right hand edge of a palm filled gully. As the track swings left you pass a 2m moss-covered rock slab that appears to weep water into the head of the gully. Continue past a tree splattered with white, yellow and green lichen to a boardwalk over another gully. From here it is only a short walk uphill to the main track. Turn left and walk back to the picnic area.

Last reviewed: 9 November 1997

MAP REFERENCE
Jolly's Lookout UBD Brisbane Street Directory - Map 135
Boombana   UBD Brisbane Street Directory - Map 135
Manorina   UBD Brisbane Street Directory - Map 105
Maiala   UBD Brisbane Street Directory - Map 85

FACILITIES

An excellent though sometimes winding road through the Park, to Wivenhoe Dam and back to Brisbane via Ipswich gives the motorist an interesting and particularly attractive scenic drive.

If stopping at any of the Parks visitors can enjoy picnicking, bushwalking and birdwatching.   Picnic tables (shelter sheds at Jolly's Lookout, Boombana and Maiala), barbecues, tap water that is suitable for drinking, garbage bins and toilets (wheelchair access at Jolly's Lookout and Maiala), are located at all four sections of the National Park.   There are camping facilities at Manorina Bush Camp that provide an ideal spot to practice your camping skills, while still in reach of civilisation.   Try spotlighting at night - you will be surprised by the number of creatures inhabiting the forest so close to Brisbane.

Contact the helpful people at Brisbane Forest Park headquarters to arrange participation in the outdoor activities, such as the Go Bush Program. Activities are offered throughout the year and include bushwalking, camp-outs, birdwatching, spotlighting, stargazing, craftwork and specialised children's programmes.

RANGER CONTACT - (07) 3300 4855

FRESHWATER NATIONAL PARK

HISTORY

A little north of Brisbane lies an area of 93.5ha that was gazetted as a national park in 1973.   The region is mainly of scientific value and contains an almost undisturbed sample of natural vegetation. Xanthorrhoea (grass trees) and scribbly gum woodland, a combination rarely seen in South-East Queensland is quite evident to motorists as they travel along Deception Bay Road. Freshwater National Park was formerly a scenic reserve, and odd as it may seem, Freshwater Creek does not traverse the Park.

As part of their ongoing commitment to preserve natural bushland in our national parks, several members of NPAQ spent the day removing rubbish and small exotic pines from the Park on *'Clean up Australia'* day in 1996.

FEATURES

Surprisingly, little evidence of past logging and grazing is visible in the open grassy forest and woodland.

Koalas, wallabies and possums are a regular sight amongst the grass trees, scribbly gums, banksias and melaleucas. An early report from QNPWS files states *'a'* platypus was sighted in a small creek that runs through the Park, but there is no evidence of recent sightings.

ACCESS

The Bruce Highway skirts the Park, 35km north of Brisbane. If travelling north from Brisbane take the second Deception Bay exit.

0.0kms	Turn right and pass over the Bruce Highway.
1.2kms	Turn left into Priests Road.
1.6kms	An area on the left is a suitable car park.

XANTHORROEA WALK

Distance: 0.5 to 1km return, allow 1 hour. Easy grade.

From the car park follow an old 4WD track for about 500m into the Park. When it fades out, make your own way amongst the grass tress and eucalypts. Take the time to photograph this unique combination of vegetation, or just enjoy a walk through this small parcel of bushland, so close to Queensland's capital city.

Last reviewed: 6 June 1997

MAP REFERENCE

UBD Brisbane Street Directory - Map 79

FACILITIES

There are no facilities in this undeveloped national park. The park can be enjoyed at any time of the year, although the vegetation is at its best during the cooler months of spring and autumn. Carry your own water.

RANGER CONTACT - (07) 5494 3983

VENMAN BUSHLAND NATIONAL PARK

HISTORY

Mr Jack Venman sold 102ha of land near West Mt Cotton to the people of Brisbane for $1.00 in 1975. It was to be kept as a nature reserve. The trusteeship of the reserve was transferred to Redland Shire Council in 1978 and Mr Venman remained the resident caretaker of the Flora and Fauna Reserve.

The area was extended to 300ha in 1991 and became an Environmental Park. Controversy erupted when in 1994 Venman Environmental Park was amalgamated with parcels of adjacent land, gained national park status and was named *'Koala Bushland National Park'*. In less than 12 months the Venman name was officially restored and the 415ha park was renamed, Venman Bushland National Park in 1995.

During this decade, concerned residents and members of the public became embroiled in a heated dispute with the State Government. The Government of the day decided that a toll road between Brisbane and the Gold Coast was far more appropriate than protecting an area containing one of Australia's most concentrated koala populations.

Although koalas are not endangered, continual land clearing does threaten their habitat. Thankfully, the outcome of the toll road debate was a win for the koalas and caring Australian's, but not before many angry protests were waged against the Government who paid the ultimate price - lost electorate seats. The message was loud and clear - Australian's do care for their national icons, and for their environment!

FEATURES
Part of shrubby Tingalpa Creek meanders through this area that consists of both wet and dry habitats. Open eucalypt forests contain beautiful scribbly gums, rusty gums and pink bloodwoods. Bloodwoods and brushboxes grow on the lower slopes. Grey ironbarks, scribbly gums and spotted gums line the gravelly ridges. Koala colonies favour forest red gum, smooth-barked apple and smudgee that grow along the banks of Tingalpa Creek and its tributaries. Melaleucas (paperbarks) are also common around the creeks. These types of vegetation once covered a widespread area, but rapid urbanisation has meant that many species are becoming restricted to this location.

Native animals and birds seek refuge here from encroaching urban development. Along with the much debated koala population, red-necked and swamp wallabies, brushtail and ringtail possums, gliders, bandicoots and marsupial mice are relatively common. Platypus live along the creek banks but are more elusive.

Listen for frogs around the waterholes, particularly following rain. Goannas and various snakes represent the reptile species in the Park. Large St Andrews Cross spiders and golden web spiders, who spin webs around 2m wide, along with lots of stick insects provide tasty meals for many animals and birds that inhabit the Park.

Willy wagtails, black-chinned honeyeaters, rufous whistlers, spangled drongos, kookaburras, butcherbirds, magpies, galahs, painted quail, spotted quail thrush, little cuckoo shrikes and black-faced cuckoo shrikes are just some of the 80 species of birds recorded in the Park.

Because of heavy visitation, the wallabies and many of the birds have become accustomed to visitors in the picnic ground. BUT, please resist the temptation to feed them. It makes them aggressive and it's bad for their health.

ACCESS
Venman Bushland National Park is situated in the Redland Shire. It can be reached via Mt Cotton Road from the north, or if travelling south on the South-East Freeway, take the Bryants Road exit at Shailer Park, and follow the directions below.

0.0kms	Intersection of Bryants Road and Mandew Street.
1.2kms	Veer left into Beenleigh-Redland Bay Road.

2.0kms	Turn left into California Creek Road. A sign post points to *Venman Bushland National Park 6km.*
3.4kms	Continue along California Creek Road, turning left, and left again into West Mount Cotton Road.
8.0kms	Turn left into Venman Bushland National Park.
8.2kms	Car park.

The two walks described give a good overview of the terrain and vegetation types found in the Park. There are no good or bad locations to sight koalas. Although they favour the trees along the creek banks, they have been sighted in the trees adjacent to the car park. But even if you don't see any koalas, you are sure to enjoy your walk and you will certainly see many different species of birds. Mr Venman built many fire break roads that cris-cross the Park, so it is advisable to collect your map from the car park and take a pencil to mark your trail as you proceed. All the walks are along the firebreak roads.

THE WESTERN LOOP
Distance: 6.5kms, allow 2 hours. Easy grade.

Start this walk at the north-western end of the car park, to the right of the toilet block. Ignore the road leading to the right, 100m from the car park. This is the

start of the Eastern Loop walk.   Continue down the road in a north-westerly direction for about 10 minutes and cross Tinglapa Creek, ignoring roads to the left and right, prior to the crossing.   Turn left over the creek and follows the bank in a southerly direction.   The creek banks are lined with bracken fern amongst the eucalypts.   The ground cover on the ridges is predominantly grass.   The road swings around to the right, where paper barks and casuarinas grow amongst the taller eucalypts.   Turn right after passing the power lines and walk uphill to the top of the first ridge, then turn left.   Keep walking west along the ridge until you reach the Park boundary.   Turn left and walk downhill to a 'Y' junction and veer left, and then right at the next junction and walk southwards, keeping the creek on your left. As you walk uphill, take the time to stop and listen to the different bird calls.   Ten minutes later, take the left fork at a 'Y' junction and walk uphill.   Then turn left downhill on a faint track towards the creek.   You pass the Park boundary prior to reaching the creek.   The creek is easily forded about 10m downstream.   Walk steeply uphill and turn left, walking in a northerly direction, with the creek on your left.   Keep walking to a 'T' junction and turn right, continue under the power lines, and walk down to the creek.   Head straight uphill to the car park, ignoring all tracks to the left or right.   There is a picnic area on the right as you cross the creek.

Last reviewed: 29 July 1997

THE EASTERN LOOP
Distance: 2.5kms, allow 1 hour. Easy grade.

This walk also starts from the north-western end of the car park.   Turn right at the road 100m after leaving the car park and head downhill.   After a few minutes, veer downhill to the left.   Continue over the creek and turn left again.   The road follows the creek and heads uphill.   You will notice that there are melaleucas growing alongside the creek and the gully contains patches of rainforest.   The road climbs steeply to the top of the ridge, levels out and then descends left towards the creek before turning right again past a large termite nest.   You soon reach the Park boundary where you turn right.   Follow the road to the top of the ridge again before descending left through a patch of lantana, then swinging right along the boundary fence.   A few minutes later you reach the section where West Mt Cotton Road bisects the Park.   Turn right along the fence, parallel with West Mt Cotton Road until you reach a road heading right, near a gate.   This road takes you back to the creek crossing.   From here retrace your steps to the car park, turning left past an old eucalypt with its trunk hollowed out by fire.

Last reviewed: 29 July 1997

MAP REFERENCE
UBD Brisbane Street Directory - Map 244
A map showing the various tracks in the Park is available at the Park.

FACILITIES

Large picnic areas complete with tables, barbecues with wood supplied, water and toilets (suitable for the disabled) make this an excellent family destination for those wanting to escape city life without travelling too far. Any time of the year is ideal to visit Venman Bushland National Park, but ensure you have a hat, sunscreen and water, particularly if walking during summer.

RANGER CONTACT - (07) 3299 1032

FORT LYTTON NATIONAL PARK

HISTORY

Fort Lytton, a pentagonal shaped 19th century fortress, lies at the mouth of the Brisbane River. Built in 1880/81, it protected the port of the developing city of Brisbane. Although not as prosperous as the ports of Sydney and Melbourne, the port of Brisbane was only three days sail from the French Naval Base at Noumea. Being part of the British Empire, attacks on the fledgling colony from the French, the Germans and the Russians, who all maintained fleets in the Pacific, were a real possibility.

Situated behind grassy embankments and a deep moat, the fort was equipped with a large arsenal and manned by the Queensland Defence Force. The Force, formed in 1860, consisted mainly of volunteers who were the mainstay of Queensland's defence system until Federation in 1901. Annual camps were held at Lytton where permanent defence staff trained the volunteers. Those early military ceremonies were a highlight on the social calendar for the citizens of Brisbane.

To further fortify the port, a minefield and timber boom were placed across the Brisbane River to deter and/or sink any vessels that may have tried to continue upstream. Today, visitors are able to visit the secret tunnel from where the minefield and the boom were observed, and the mines could be detonated. This minefield was in use until 1908.

Lytton was the main training base for the Queensland Defence Force before World War I. The fort's guns were only fired twice in defence during this time; first to warn a Dutch steamer and secondly to warn a fishing vessel attempting to travel upriver without observing the official protocol.

During World War II the fort became a secondary defence station to those on Bribie and Moreton Islands.

The Fort was abandoned in 1945 and Ampol Oil Refineries acquired it in the early1960s, along with other land they purchased for a refinery.

Public interest in the area was increasing and it was decided that the protection of this historic site was best put in the hands of the Department of Environment. Ampol generously handed over the 12.6ha site in 1988.

Many people do not realise they are visiting a national park when they explore our past at Fort Lytton, Queensland's second historic national park.

FEATURES
Definitely a national park with a difference, the buildings set amongst mown grass and a man-made moat depict part of our early heritage. It is a sobering thought to picture young boys from the local reform school providing labour to help dig the moat and foundations for the buildings. During Ampol's ownership, part of the moat was filled in to enable trucks to have access to the buildings for storage. Some of the remaining buildings are gradually being restored or rebuilt by QNPWS, with voluntary help from members of the Royal Australian Artillery Association, many of whom were stationed at the Fort during World War II. It is an interesting and humbling experience to participate in a guided tour led by these old *'diggers'*, as they recount their experiences.   The voluntary organisation receives a small grant from the Government, but relies on revenue generated from the canteen for many of their activities. Here you can have the best and cheapest *'cuppa and bickies'* in Brisbane.

ACCESS
Located 18km from the Brisbane city centre, Fort Lytton National Park is reached by travelling east along Lytton Road.

0.0kms	Lytton Road overpass above Gateway Arterial Road.
6.3kms	Continue on Lytton Road, following the *Fort Lytton National Park* signs.
6.7kms	Entrance, sign posted *Fort Lytton National Park.*

FORT LYTTON HERITAGE TRAIL
Distance: 1-2kms, allow at least 2 hours. Easy grade.

You can join a guided tour or collect a self-guiding walk map from the QNPWS office where your admission fee is paid.
Begin at the picnic grounds or at the gate behind the canteen and amble past the searchlight emplacement point, original fort guns, arsenal stores and barracks, to the moat which gives access to the fort. Marvel at the restored *'disappearing guns'*, loading galleries, ammunition storage sites and parade ground before visiting the secret tunnel mentioned earlier. No tour is complete without visiting the museum, which once housed the blacksmith's and carpenter's workshops. Here, a collection of memorabilia and military artefacts is on display.

Last visited: 30 July 1997

NB. Due to firearms and other weapons on display the museum is only open to visitors on guided tours.

MAP REFERENCE
UBD Brisbane Street Directory - Map 142
A self guiding walk map is available at the Ranger's office.

FACILITIES

A picnic area with tables and toilets is located behind the Information Centre. Drinking water is available in the Park.

Fort Lytton is open every day, except Saturdays, from 10am-4pm. It is an excellent venue for families. Chartered buses bring many interested groups of people, ranging from senior citizens parties to classes of school children.

Guided tours are available on Sundays and public holidays at 10.30, 11.30, 12.30, 1.30 and 2.45. Tours for groups can be arranged during the week.

RANGER CONTACT - (07) 3893 4647

SCENIC RIM AND FASSIFERN VALLEY

MT BARNEY NATIONAL PARK

HISTORY

Mt Barney holds special significance for the Yugambeh Aborigines, the original inhabitants of the area.

The first recorded climb to the 1 359m summit of Mt Barney, the second highest but most significant peak in Southern Queensland, was in 1828 by Captain Patrick Logan, when he was Commandant of the Brisbane settlement. He was accompanied by two well known botanists and explorers, Alan Cunningham and Charles Fraser. The climb became too difficult for Cunningham and Fraser so they turned back, leaving Logan to complete the climb alone.

A July 1937 report from the Courier Mail, told of a group of 17 NPAQ members, including *'three girls'*, who scaled the Mountain over ice-encrusted crests to reach the peak and gather information requested by the Queensland Government, prior to the National Park being gazetted. Two other parties from NPAQ were also climbing the peak from separate approaches and collecting information. One party discovered a stand of Antarctic beech trees estimated to be 2 000 years old. The diverse terrain and features of the countryside led to the National Park being proclaimed in 1947.

The park now covers 13 000ha and includes the peaks of Mts Barney, Ballow, Ernest, Lindesay (to the state border), May and Maroon, and countryside to the McPherson Ranges. Mt Barney National Park includes three of the six highest peaks - West Peak, East Peak and Mt Ballow - and 10 of the 24 highest peaks in South-East Queensland.

FEATURES

The terrain surrounding Mt Barney is some of the most rugged in Queensland. Precipitous ridges, steep cliff-lines and rocky gullies with creeks cascading into deep pools are typical of the region. The mountain is made up of granophyre, a granite-like substance formed well below the earth's surface. This rock and the overlaying sandstone was pushed up to a height of 2 000m, 350 million years ago. Over millions of years, the sandstone has eroded leaving the mountain formation we see today. Mts May, Maroon and Ernest were formed in a similar manner, however, they are composed of rhyolite.

Much of the Park is covered with open eucalypt forest. Some of the species found in the lower regions include box, gum and native apple. Many of the creeks and cascades are lined with red flowering bottlebrush, golden silky oak and river she-oak. Amongst the rocky slopes are patches of montane heath which provide a beautiful display of wildflowers in the spring. The heath on Mt Maroon makes a particularly impressive show. Over 20 species of orchids grow on the drier eastern slopes of Mt Barney.

Birds of prey nest along the higher rocky slopes and kingfishers, honeyeaters and robins can be seen around the lower reaches of the creeks. Platypus breed in the lower creek areas, but are rarely seen. Kangaroos and wallabies, including the brush-tailed rock wallaby are common throughout the Park.

ACCESS - MOUNT BARNEY
From Brisbane, follow the Mt Lindesay Highway 1km past Rathdowney and turn right on the Boonah-Rathdowney Road. Travel 7kms to Barney View-Upper Logan Road turn off. From Boonah, take the Boonah-Rathdowney Road south for 39kms to this road.

0.0kms	Enter Barney View-Upper Logan Road.
3.0kms	Continue straight ahead at 'Y' junction, following the signs to *Lower Portals, Yellow Pinch* and *Mt Barney Lodge.*
7.7kms	Continue straight ahead on Upper Logan Road. (If travelling to the Lower Portals turn right here.)
8.1kms	Gravel road begins.
10.8kms	Continue straight ahead, or turn left to reach Mt Barney Lodge and private camp ground.
11.7kms	Locked gate at Yellow Pinch camp ground and boundary of Mt Barney National Park.

MT BARNEY: UP SOUTH-EAST RIDGE AND DOWN SOUTH (PEASANT'S) RIDGE
Distance: 16.5kms, allow 10-12 hours. Hard grade.

The precipitous ridges of Mt Barney have attracted many climbers and bushwalkers. For a long time, an ascent of the Mountain was considered the ultimate in Queensland bushwalking. There are many different routes to the summit of Mt Barney, the *easiest* being via the South Ridge. This ridge was named *Peasant's Ridge* by bushwalkers in the late 1960s because of its relative ease, compared to other more arduous routes. *However, this ridge is still steep and should **not** be attempted by inexperienced walkers. It would be irresponsible to attempt this climb without a topographic map, a compass and the appropriate skills.* There have been several serious accidents on the ridge, including one fatality. Countless instances of bushwalkers being lost on the Mountain and spending a cold, uncomfortable night in the bush, have resulted in expensive rescue operations.

The walk starts from a locked gate at the south-western end of Yellow Pinch camping area. Follow the rough 4WD track up and over Yellow Pinch and along the Logan River flats before entering the forest about 2.3kms from the start. Cross a shallow ford and follow the road as it heads up Cronan Creek Valley. Continue past *'Camp Site 10'* and locate a disused 4WD track leading uphill on the right, a little more than 3kms from the main camp ground. This is the start of the South-

East Ridge Track and approximate timings to East Peak are given from this point. The 4WD track turns left at the top of the ridge and becomes a well-worn footpad. Continue uphill through open eucalypt forest with grassy ground cover and swing right at a rocky outcrop, then uphill, keeping the rocks on your left. At the next cliff-line, veer left and then right uphill, again keeping the rocks on your left until you reach the top of a narrow ridge, about 1 to 1.5hours from the start. From here you get good views beyond Mt Ernest to Mt Lindesay. In the valley below you can see where Campbell's Creek flows towards Logan River. After scrambling over some large boulders you reach a deep gully with sheer cliffs. Walk down to the right and then climb left, up a crack in the rock to the top of a narrow razorback section. The views are now getting better. As you continue uphill, the ground cover consists of low heaths, wattles, banksias and grass trees, with she-oaks scattered amongst the eucalypts. Some of the yellow flowering banksias are tipped with crimson, making them particularly attractive.

The track heads to the left of the next rocky outcrop and continues steeply uphill. About 2 to 2.5 hours from the start you reach a steep gully with a seemingly impassible cliff directly opposite. The track swings steeply down to the right, then left across a shallow gully before heading back up on the right of that seemingly impassible cliff. You soon reach a section where you need to scramble up a steep rocky slab. This slab is very slippery, especially when wet and a rope is recommended. The track skirts to the right of some more rocky slabs, descends into another shallow gully, then to the left of the next cliff and heads straight uphill. You will find some strategically placed yellow arrows painted on the rock. Keep scrambling for another hour, and after passing a spot where you get good views towards the summit, you reach the second steep pinch where a rope is recommended. About 15 minutes from here, after passing a section that is sometimes boggy, you can look up towards the summit as you swing to the left of some more rocks before turning right and scrambling uphill. Another 20 minutes slogging uphill and you reach a rocky knoll. Cross a small gully and continue uphill. The vegetation is now very thick along the edge of the track. The ridge almost flattens out before finally reaching the summit of East Peak, about 4 to 5 hours from the start. The 360° views from the summit are spectacular and make the climb worthwhile. From Mt Lindesay, look right to Mt Ernest and the Organ Pipes. Edinburgh Castle and the Obelisk rise above the plains in NSW and Mt Ballow is off to the west. On a clear day you can see Main Range. Maroon Dam, Mt May and Mt Maroon are to the north.

After lunch and a well earned rest on East Peak, locate the South (Peasant's) Ridge Track by walking west towards West Peak. The track leads through some thick vegetation, turning right before starting to descend. A relatively easy scramble over some large boulders and rock slabs leads you down towards Barney Gorge Creek. If you loose sight of an obvious track, just keep heading towards West Peak in a south-south-westerly direction (to the left) and not a north-north-westerly direction (to the right). Turn right when you reach the creek and walk downstream for a few minutes, then cross the creek towards the Saddle camp site. Caution is required here not to continue descending Barney Creek Gorge. If you start descending into the gorge, you have gone too far! Walk uphill through Rum Jungle rainforest to a larger camp site. The track swings to the left and climbs out of the rainforest. Many people have become lost and headed into Egan Creek, looking for the descent track from the Rum Jungle camp site, instead of climbing first. About 15 minutes from the Saddle, after passing to the right of a rocky outcrop, the track finally begins to descend. Keep heading downhill with the rocks on your left until you reach a narrow rocky ridge. The rocks get larger but there are several orange arrows painted on the rocks and the scrambling is relatively easy.

About one hour after leaving the Saddle, you reach a small clearing. Follow the arrows right, then left and continue to descend for about 15 minutes to another small clearing. From this clearing you get good views back up the valley towards the summit. Continue downhill through a channel in the rocks for another 15 minutes until you reach an exposed rocky slab. This slab requires extreme care if wet, but is the last difficult section of the track. From here, the track is very well defined as it follows the ridge-line. The understorey is now grass and there is some wild raspberry and lantana. You soon reach a palm filled gully and the track continues to descend along the left of this gully before emerging onto the remains of an old logging road. Follow the road down to a sign at the start of the South (Peasant's) Ridge Track, about 3.5 to 4 hours after leaving East Peak. Turn left and walk back along the road. After 400m you pass the start of the South-East Ridge track. Continue along the road, back to Yellow Pinch camp site.

Last reviewed: 26 July 1997 with NPAQ members. Leader: Geoff Sear.

ACCESS - LOWER PORTALS
Follow the directions towards Mt Barney, turning right from Upper Logan Road at the **7.7kms** point.

0.0kms	Turn right on the gravel road.
0.6kms	Lower Portals Road veers left over a grid.
1.5kms	Pass through quarry.
2.0kms	Cross over grid and enter Mount Barney National Park.
2.2kms	Lower Portals parking area.

LOWER PORTALS
Distance: 7.4kms return, allow 3 hours. Moderate grade.

The track leaving from the car park is coated with gravel to the top of the first ridge. The terrain is open eucalypt forest with grassy ground cover and lots of grass trees. From the first ridge the track is heavily eroded and logs have been used to make steps. After about10 minutes, cross a rocky creek bed, turn right and then left up to a stile at the top of the next ridge. The track winds up and down, crossing another three gullies. At the start of the fourth gully, look for a large spotted gum on the left of the track. You can tap the trunk of the tree and hear a hollow sound. It is this hollow sound that saved many forest giants from the timber getters axe.

Fifteen minutes from here, you reach a bare sandstone ridge. The soft sandstone has eroded exposing veins of red, yellow, white, brown, mauve and ochre. Ignore a footpad leading off to the right at the top of the ridge and continue straight ahead. As you emerge from the next boulder-strewn gully, take note of the attractive stand of grey gums along the ridge. Ten minutes from here you pass another stile at Mt Barney Creek. You can rock hop across the creek onto a wide rocky slab. Turn left on the slab and follow the creek to the Lower Portals camp sites. Visit the Portals by climbing through a hole beneath a balancing rock just before the river's edge, and walk 100m upstream.

Return via the same track, to the car park.

(Mt Barney Waterfall is approximately three kilometres return, from the Lower Portals camp ground. Turn right at the last camp site and head up and over the hill. Locate an obvious footpad that bypasses the Portals leading to the creek and rock hop up to the falls.)

Last reviewed: 28 July 1997

MAP REFERENCE
Sunmap - MT LINDESAY 1:25 000

FACILITIES
Yellow Pinch camping area has tables, barbecues and bush toilets. Bush toilets are also provided at the Lower Portals parking area. Private camping facilities are located at Bigriggen on the Boonah-Rathdowney Road entrance, or Mt Barney Lodge at the end of Upper Logan Road. Mt Barney Lodge also has accommodation ranging from self-contained budget cabins to fully catered bed and breakfast facilities.

A permit is needed to camp in all national parks on the Scenic Rim. Mt Barney is a fuel stove area and as such, wood fires along with machetes are prohibited.

Autumn, winter and spring are the best times to climb the Mountain, but be prepared for changeable weather conditions and always carry plenty of water. The Lower Portals provide a great swimming spot during the hot summer months.

ACCESS - UPPER PORTALS
From Brisbane, follow the Mt Lindesay Highway 1km past Rathdowney and turn right on the Boonah-Rathdowney Road. Travel 19kms to Newman Road. From Boonah, take the Boonah-Rathdowney Road for 27kms to Newman Road.

0.0kms	Enter Newman Road. (Mainly gravel).
4.2kms	Grid.
4.8kms	Grid.
5.2kms	Sharp turn left, past farm house.
5.8kms	Gate. *Dry weather road* sign. They really mean it!
6.2kms	Mt May camp ground. 4WD required from this point.
6.6kms	Gate.

8.7kms	Gate.
9.7kms	Gate. Road to left is towards Mt May walk.
10.9kms	Gate.
11.5kms	Clearing at top of the ridge. Turn sharp left, past self-registration booth.
11.9kms	Locked gate. Leave vehicles here.

UPPER PORTALS CIRCUIT
Distance: 10kms, allow 4 hours. Moderate grade.

This relatively straight forward circuit walk presents little navigational difficulty and provides an interesting perspective of the area around the Upper Portals. From the locked gate, follow the old road across the grassy ridge, directly towards the imposing peaks of Mt Barney. After descending for about 10 minutes, you reach a sign pointing to the right, towards the Upper Portals. (The road straight ahead is the return track.)

Follow the 4WD road as it descends steeply to the right, towards Yamahra Creek. A sign at the creek points left, to the *Park Boundary 400m* and the *Upper Portals 2.7km.*

(The track to Montserrat Lookout leads to the right, over the creek, then swings left at the cattle yards and follows the ridge, all the way to the lookout. However, this is private property, and you need the land owners permission to traverse the property. Contact the Ranger for details.)

The track follows Yamahra Creek downstream and enters a cool section of forest where you normally hear lots of birds, before crossing the creek, just prior to the Park boundary.

Cross the creek several times before reaching Yamahra Creek camp site, 150m from the junction of Yamahra Creek and Barney Creek. Cross Barney Creek and follow a well worn footpad downstream, past the Upper Portals camp site (closed for regeneration when last reviewed), a few hundred metres to the wide rocky slab that marks the start of the Upper Portals. If the water level is low, you can scramble down stream about 40m, past several cauldron shaped depressions in the rock, eroded by the swirling water over thousands of years, to a section where steep sided rock slabs lead down to the creek. A short swim through the Portals takes you to a large pool with a stony beach. From here, you can skirt around to the right of a 4m waterfall and explore further downstream, before making your way back the start of the Portals.

(If the water level is high, the Portals become exceptionally dangerous and it would be extremely difficult to make you way back upstream. However, they can be bypassed by a track high on the northern bank.)

To complete the circuit walk, cross to the northern side of the creek at the start of the Portals and locate a well worn track leading very steeply uphill. Scramble up the ridge and follow the track as it turns right and look for a round boulder at the highest point on the track. A footpad leaves the track here and heads left, then right, up the steep ridge. (The Portals bypass track continues straight ahead from the highest point.)

The route up the ridge passes through open eucalypt forest with patches of thick heath and several grass trees. About half way up the ridge you reach some large granite boulders and the view of Mt Barney begins to get better. Another 15-20 minutes takes you to the top of the stony ridge. This is a good spot to rest and enjoy the views. From the ridge, the well worn track descends to a saddle and the start of a disused road, adjacent to a wire fence. This road follows the ridge-line, eventually passing through a locked gate before meeting the road where you turned right towards the Portals, at the start of the walk. Follow the road back uphill to your vehicle.

Last reviewed: 27 October 1997

MAP REFERENCE
Sunmap - MT LINDESAY 1:25 000
              MAROON 1:25 000
A partial walking track map supplied on QNPWS brochure.

ACCESS - MT MAY
Follow the directions for the Upper Portals to the gate at **9.7kms**. This is the third gate from the Mt May camp ground.

0.0kms	Turn sharp left.
0.2kms	End of 4WD track.

MT MAY
Distance: 3kms return, allow 1.5 hours. Moderate grade.

The short but steep climb to the south peak of Mt May provides spectacular views of Mt Barney. The climb is ideal for those wishing to photograph the soft hues of sunrise across the northern faces of the Mountain.

From the end of the 4WD track, locate a well worn trail leading straight up the ridge-line through a stand of tall eucalypts. About 10 minutes from the start, climb under a barbed wire fence and head uphill. Continue past a small knoll to a scree-covered slope at the base of a small saddle. The trail now becomes steeper and leads to the striated face of a 5m cliff. Obvious wear marks on the cliff face outline the route to the right of a small shrub, at the base of the cliff. At the top of the small cliff, there are uninterrupted views extending in a huge arc from Mt Maroon in the north, around to the grassy ridge at the start of the Upper Portals walk, (Montserrat Lookout is behind this ridge), and south towards Mt Barney.

It is only about five minutes from this point to the summit. Take the time to sit and enjoy the panoramic view across to the rugged face of Mt Barney before using the same track to return to your vehicle.

Last reviewed: 27 October 1997

MAP REFERENCE
Sunmap - MAROON 1:25 000

FACILITIES
Mt May camp ground has no facilities, but is still very popular. Camp sites should be chosen well away from Waterfall Creek as flash flooding can and does occur.

Swimming in the Upper Portals is very enjoyable during the summer months. Some bush camping is permitted, but check with the Ranger first.

ACCESS - MT MAROON
As for Mt Barney, travel via Rathdowney or Boonah from Brisbane. Take the Boonah-Rathdowney Road 16kms from Rathdowney or 30kms from Boonah to the Cotswold Road turn off.

0.0kms	Enter Cotswold Road (gravel).
17.0kms	Cross grid.
18.2kms	Cross another grid.
19.2kms	Turn right into a clearing by the lagoon and park here.

MT MAROON
Distance: 6kms return, allow 6-7 hours. Moderate grade.

The track to Mt Maroon starts at the western end of the lagoon. Follow a well worn footpad, through a fence and head towards several old corrugated iron tanks. The track turns left before the tanks and climbs to the top of a grassy ridge, leading towards the Mountain. From the top of this ridge, the track becomes very rocky and eroded. After walking for about 30-45 minutes, the gradient increases and you reach some large rounded boulders, just before a rocky bluff. Scramble over these boulders, left of the bluff to a rocky ridge. From here you get good views of the striated cliffs on the face of the Mountain. You can also scramble to the top of the ridge on the left for views to the east.

The track now sidles around the right side of the ridge, descends and climbs twice before reaching the base of a steep gully, leading to the saddle between the two peaks. The sheer cliffs of the east face of north peak now tower above you on the right. The scramble up the gully is relatively straightforward with plenty of hand-holds, but care is required not to dislodge loose rocks onto climbers below. After a few minutes, the track swings to the right, then left over a fallen tree. (Note this point for the descent, to avoid following a track straight ahead to a short steep cliff that may present some difficulty.) From the top of the gully, follow a well worn track to a flat cleared section. Turn right and follow the track up a shallow, dry gully, past another cleared area off to the right. The main track soon swings around to the left and another track (leading to the north peak) continues straight ahead. Continue on the main track to a large rocky slab and veer right. The top of this slab makes a good morning tea spot. The track starts again from the top right hand corner of the slab and winds through tall shrubs before reaching another rocky outcrop. Scramble to the top of this section. There are some faded red markers on the rock, but the route to the summit is relatively easy. The rocks in this area are speckled with patches of white, grey, green, yellow, orange, brown and red lichen. Swing left and walk through the tea trees and grass trees to a faint track leading straight up through a short cleft in the rock. There are some more faded red markers on these rocks. Remember this spot for your descent and walk straight up towards the summit. During late winter and early spring, the wildflowers are in full bloom. On a clear day, the view extends east towards the Lamington Plateau and the cleared section below Green Mountains (O'Reillys) can be seen. Mt Lindesay is to the south, then Mts Ernest, Barney and Ballow. To the west, the Ramparts of the Scenic Rim lie behind Maroon Dam. The foreground includes Mts Moon, Greville, Alford and Edwards, then across to the flat top of Mt French. Immediately in front of you to the north is the bowl shaped depression below the north peak of Mt Maroon.

After lunch, descend via the same route to the start of the track towards the north peak. This track leads up a gully and is relatively indistinct until it passes some large boulders blocking the entrance to a narrow section of the gully, and veers right. Follow this track along the dry creek bed, ignoring a gully off to the left, until you reach some rocks. Scramble up these rocks, on an obvious trail leading to a ridge. Remember this spot for your descent, and follow the ridge to the summit.

To return, follow the summit ridge westwards towards a small saddle below the summit, turn left (south) and make your way down to the edge of the normally dry depression known as the *'swampy area'*. Take note of the stained parallel fissures in the rocks. Either skirt around this section or walk straight through it towards the area where you start the descent, then follow the same route back down the Mountain.

Last reviewed: 21 August 1997

MAP REFERENCE
Sunmap - MAROON 1:25 000

FACILITIES
Late winter, spring and autumn are the best times to climb the Mountain. Summer days can be extremely hot. A vast array of wildflowers covers the peak during August, September and October. Carry sufficient water and be sure to have suitable clothing. It can become very windy and cold on the summit.

There are no facilities at all on the Mountain and camping is prohibited. A lone picnic table is the only convenience at the car park.

Private camping areas with full facilities are located at Bigriggen and Mt Barney Lodge.

RANGER CONTACT - (07) 5463 5041

MAIN RANGE NATIONAL PARK

HISTORY
Several parks have been amalgamated to form this 18 400ha national park. This World Heritage listed park now stretches from Mt Mistake in the north, along the western part of the scenic rim to Cunningham's Gap, through the Mt Roberts section to Wilson's Peak on the Queensland-New South Wales border, and west to Queen Mary Falls.

The Scenic Rim was once an impassible barrier between the coast and the Darling Downs. In 1827, the explorer Alan Cunningham sighted a gap in the mountains from the west. Some historians believe that the gap originally seen by Cunningham was in fact Spicer's Gap, 2.5kms to the south. He located Cunningham's Gap in August 1828, and named the two sentinel peaks Mt Mitchell and Mt Cordeaux, after the Surveyor-General Sir Thomas Mitchell and his assistant, William Cordeaux.

Local Aborigines called Mt Mitchell, *Cooyinnirra.* Mt Cordeaux was known as *Niamboyoo* and the gap was called *Cappoong.*

The route through the gap proposed by Cunningham proved too steep to be used by drays. Cargo needed to be lowered over a cliff-line with ropes.

Henry Alphen, a stockmen working on Canning Downs, the first property established on the Darling Downs, was the first European to discover Spicer's Gap, in April 1847. A road was then constructed through Spicer's Gap providing the first access route between Moreton Bay and the Darling Downs. There is now a self-guiding walk along the old road showing the different construction methods of that era. Bullock drays were used to carry supplies and wool to and from the Darling Downs. An inn was built across from the current camping ground and was a welcome sight for many thirsty travellers. Use of the road declined in 1871 following the construction of the railway linking Warwick to Moreton Bay, via Toowoomba.

At least 13 early pioneers are buried in a small cemetery, a short walk from the Spicer's Gap picnic ground. Words on the epitaph have been inscribed by hammering nails into the concrete. Moss's Well, just south of the camping area at Spicer's Gap is believed to take its name from Edward Moss, the first road contractor. The well provided the only water for travellers making their way over the range. The water is now unsuitable for drinking.

The Rocky Creek Falls area, just east of Warwick was surveyed and gazetted as a Reserve for Recreation Purposes as early as 1892. This small 64ha area was given national park status in 1945.

Much of the area now contained within Main Range National Park was heavily logged during the early 1900s. Timber getters soon felled almost all the red cedar and then began harvesting hoop pine, carabeen, tulip oak, purple laurel and pigeon berry. Logging was carried out in the open forest and rainforest of Mt Mistake until the 1960s. The remains of an old timber jinker, a winch and old logging chutes lie in the state forest, just outside the National Park boundary.

In the early 1930s, Jack and Boyd Walton sold their assets to fund a search for gold after being deceived with samples of 'fools gold'. They spent several years digging fruitlessly near the top of Mt Cordeaux before the fraud was exposed and the mine was abandoned.

Cunningham's Gap was declared a national park in 1909. A dirt road through the Gap was completed in 1927, giving better access between Brisbane and the areas west of the Dividing Range. This road was sealed in the 1940s and is now part of the Cunningham Highway. The walking tracks were constructed between the late 1930s and the 1950s.

Mt Superbus, in the southern section of the Park, was the site of a tragic air crash in 1955. A Lincoln bomber, flying from Townsville to Brisbane with a sick baby on board, strayed off course in bad weather and crashed 50m below the summit, killing all on board. Remnants of the plane remain on and around the Mountain.

Early settlers to the Queen Mary Falls area, on the western slopes of the Great Dividing Range, came in search of cedar. Much of this section of the Condamine Valley has since been cleared for cattle, but the forest is still intact along many of the high ridges. A 78ha park was originally proclaimed to protect the falls, the gorge below the falls and sections of Spring Creek above and below the falls. An area known as Blackfellow Falls, 5kms north of Queen Mary Falls, is also protected under the umbrella of Main Range National Park.

Main Range National Park was declared part of the Central Eastern Australian Rainforest Reserves of Australia in December 1994 and is a very popular bushwalking destination.

FEATURES

Main Range consists of an almost unbroken line of peaks, ridges and escarpments following the edge of the Scenic Rim in a north-south direction. Many of the peaks are over 1 000m, with Mt Superbus, the highest in South Queensland at 1 375m. A spur leading to the 940m Mt Mistake, leaves the Dividing Range north-west of the northern end of the Ramparts. Early explorers mistakenly thought this area was part of the Great Dividing Range, hence the name, Mt Mistake.

The eastern escarpment of Main Range National Park is extremely steep. There are a succession of ridges and valleys leading to the crest, from the west.

Water erosion formed many of the deep gorges in the Queen Mary and Blackfellow Falls areas of the Park. Water has eroded layers of basalt and trachyte from the Main Range, leaving deep gorges, steep escarpments and long waterfalls. At Queen Mary Falls, the headwaters of Spring Creek tumble 40m over a gorge before flowing west to join the Condamine River. The Condamine becomes the Balonne, eventually flowing into the Darling and Murray, before reaching the sea near Adelaide, a distance of over 3 000kms. This is Australia's most extensive river system.

North of Queen Mary Falls, Blackfellow Creek tumbles 45m and then 60m into a gorge to form Blackfellow Falls.

Rocky Creek, a tributary of Emu Creek drops 120m and then 16m to form another twin drop waterfall in the area that was originally Rocky Creek National Park. Hoop pine rainforest grows on the steep gullies and in the gorges of Rocky Creek.

Vegetation types in the eastern section of Main Range National Park include rainforest in moist, sheltered areas, with open eucalypt forest on the exposed drier slopes. Mountain heath vegetation grows along the cliff-lines and rocky outcrops and brush box trees line the creeks. The giant spear lily, a restricted plant species can be seen in the Park, especially on the Mt Cordeaux walk. The lily produces vivid scarlet blooms on spikes up to 4m tall. The peak time to enjoy the flowering spear lily is mid-September to mid-October.

Lantana and wild raspberry have encroached upon many of the old logging tracks.

At Queen Mary Falls, mist creates an ideal atmosphere for tree ferns, bracken ferns and vines, with staghorns and orchids flourishing on the trees and rocky areas of the gorge. Forest red gums, Sydney blue gums, silky oaks and hoop pines are also prevalent. As you leave the rainforest areas near the falls, open eucalypt forest is predominant. The canopy consists of forest red gums, brush box, stringybarks, wattles and kurrajongs, finally giving way to shrubby undergrowth.

The Mistake Mountains are the most northerly habitat of the rarely seen Albert's lyrebird. Also difficult to spot are red-tailed black cockatoos, eastern bristlebirds and black-breasted button-quails that live around Cunningham's Gap. Yellow-tailed black cockatoos and glossy black cockatoos, along with bellbirds, satin bowerbirds and crimson rosellas are much easier to spot around Cunningham's Gap.

A small population of koalas inhabit the Mt Matheson region. Brush-tailed rock wallabies can be encountered during the day, but are hard to spot, taking cover in the tall grasses of the Mt Cordeaux area. Nocturnal greater gliders and brushtail possums are best seen with a spotlight as they feed at night. Large goannas are commonly seen around Spicer's Gap camp ground.

Platypus live in the area below Queen Mary Falls and may occasionally be spotted with a torch after dark. Other animals likely to be seen include ringtail and brushtail possums, gliders, quolls, wallabies, pademelons, bandicoots, native rats and marsupial mice. Red spiny crayfish also inhabit the creek below the falls. It would be quite hard to spot the brush-tailed rock wallaby, even though it does live around the steep gorges, as this shy creature sleeps throughout the day and is one of the rarer animals of the Park.

More than 100 different birds have been recorded in Main Range National Park and visitors to the Queen Mary Falls section are sure to see kookaburras, king parrots, rosellas, cat birds and satin bower birds. Listen for the mimicking call of the Albert's lyrebird - like the brush-tailed wallaby it is also shy and difficult to spot.

ACCESS - CUNNINGHAM'S GAP
Drive west from Brisbane on the Cunningham Highway to Aratula.

0.0kms	Aratula Hotel
15.8kms	*Main Range National Park* sign.
19.3kms	Cunningham's Gap parking area. Walking tracks begin on either side of the Crest car park.

MT MITCHELL
Distance: 10.2kms return, allow 3 hours. Moderate grade.

The track begins on the southern side of the Crest car park and immediately climbs uphill through rainforest. After one kilometre, the terrain changes to open eucalypt forest. Half an hour from the start, you reach some steps, just prior to the site of a massive land slide. The track was closed in May 1996 when tonnes of mud slipped down the hill following a period of torrential rain. National Park Rangers had the enormous task of removing the debris and recreating 350m of walking track that included more than 56 rock steps. The track was reopened in December that year.

From the landslide, the track winds steadily around towards the western side of the Mountain at a fairly gentle grade, through numerous grass trees. As the track re-enters a small patch of rainforest, note some shallow grottos on the left with delicate ferns growing near the bank. The forest opens out again as the track passes some cliffs, then heads east back into the rainforest and starts to climb. Just inside the rainforest, look for an old gnarled vine, hanging down near the track. The vine looks like a massive plaited rope and is twisted like a pretzel. Continue walking steeply uphill and you reach some stone steps beside a large hoop pine, covered in moss and lichen. The track now leaves the rainforest and emerges on the northern side of the west peak. Follow the track past some cliffs and up some steps to a saddle. Warning signs have been erected here to inform people that there are cliffs ahead, so take particular care and strictly supervise young children.

Continue uphill along the saddle to a track junction. The left track leads to a cairn on the 1 168m summit of the east peak, but there are no views. The right track leads through an avenue of grass trees to a narrow rocky spur with superb views. Over the years, more than 30cms of soil was eroded from this razorback ridge, by countless feet. To prevent further erosion, the track has been paved. Please conserve the Mountain by not walking beyond the paved area.

Looking north, the view is across the face of Main Range Ramparts towards Mt Castle. To the east you see Mts Edwards and French, Moogerah Lake, Mt Greville, the humps of Mt Moon, the twin peaks of Mt Maroon, then Mts Lindesay, Barney and Ballow. Spicer's Peak is to the south. The view to the west is towards the Darling Downs. Look for the remains of the old Spicer's Gap road in the valley.

Descend the Mountain via the same route. (On the return trip, as you reach the saddle and the steps, you pass a footpad that leads steeply down into the valley on the southern side of the Mountain, and across to Spicer's Gap road. Here, you can follow the road back to Governors' Chair car park. This makes an interesting round trip, but should only be attempted by people with good navigational skills.)

Last reviewed: 17 May 1997

MT CORDEAUX AND BARE ROCK
Distance: 12.5kms return, allow 4 hours. Moderate grade.

The climb to Mt Cordeaux starts at the eastern end of the car park and passes the memorial to Allan Cunningham before reaching Fassifern Valley Lookout, 400m from the start. Follow the Rainforest Circuit for a further 300m to the next track junction and take the centre track leading uphill through lush rainforest. About 15 minutes from the start, a small waterfall cascades down a fern filled gully and over the track. Light reaching the forest floor allows a complete ground cover of ferns and mosses to flourish on either side of the track. Zigzagging up hill, you pass a gully filled with piccabeen palms on the left and a large rocky outcrop covered with mosses on the right. This track is particularly appealing after rain when water bubbles down almost every gully and adds a lustre to the foliage. After about 45 minutes of steady climbing, you pass a large clump of spear lilies as the track winds along the edge of the cliff-line. Continue climbing past the base of the old gold mine to a lookout near the head of the shaft.

Five minutes from the gold mine you reach a track junction. The right branch heads 65m to Mt Cordeaux Lookout, an exposed rocky slab below the 1 135m summit. This is where the graded track ends. Take particular care around the cliffs and don't leave any children without supervision. The sheer cliff-line below the summit is covered with spear lilies creating a brilliant red display in spring.

From the Lookout, head back down to the junction and follow the track west towards Bare Rock. The track hugs the southern cliff-line of Mt Cordeaux and leads through more spear lilies before emerging on an exposed narrow ledge offering good views back towards the summit of Mt Cordeaux. Head uphill through a section of rainforest to another track junction, 5.5kms from the starting point. The left track towards Bare Rock climbs 680m through moss-covered trees before reaching the wide exposed slab of Bare Rock. There are good views along the Ramparts to Mt Castle in the north.

On the return journey, the first left hand track junction leads 350m down to Morgan's Lookout. Trees have obscured most of the view from the Lookout but you do gain a different perspective of Mt Castle before retracing your steps back towards your starting point.

A track junction 700m from the car park leads to the right, along the Rainforest Circuit before reaching the car park.

Last reviewed: 17 May 1997

GAP CREEK FALLS
Distance: 9.4kms return, allow 6 hours. (It is a long, steep climb back from the Falls.) Moderate grade.

The track to Gap Creek Falls branches off the Mt Cordeaux track at Fassifern Valley Lookout. The track descends quickly through rainforest before emerging into open eucalypt forest dotted with grass trees, along the right side of a steep, fern filled gully. About 30 minutes from the start, as you pass some lily-like clumps of native ginger you can see Mt Cordeaux towering above you to the left and Mt Mitchell to the right. You soon reach a sign post, 2.2kms from Fassifern Valley Lookout. It is now 2.1kms to the Falls. Descend through an area previously burnt in a bushfire. The eucalypt and casuarina regrowth is thin and woody. The track crosses a rocky creek bed and swings around to the right where you get good views of the ridge from Mt Cordeaux, to Morgan's Lookout. A few minutes from this point you see the spear lily covered cliffs below Gap Creek Falls. A steep track leads down to a wide rocky slab at the top of the Falls. Extreme caution is required as this slab would be very slippery if wet. Very little water flows over the Falls in dry weather, and on hot days you can feel the heat radiating in waves from the slabs. In these conditions you must ensure you carry plenty of water.

It is worth exploring the small creek leading into Gap Creek from the east. A clump of relatively rare green hooded orchid grows about 50m up this creek and a hollow tree at the head of the creek houses a hive of native bees.

Return to the car park via the same track.

Last reviewed: 20 July 1997 with NPAQ members. Leader: Mary Reid

MAP REFERENCE
Sunmap - CUNNINGHAMS GAP 1:25 000
Walking track maps are available at the Ranger's station, just west of the Crest car park on the Cunningham Highway.

FACILITIES
Toilets with wheel chair access are located at the Crest car park. A camp ground and picnic areas are situated west of here. Tables, barbecues (firewood supplied), water and toilets are provided.

ACCESS - MT MISTAKE
Take the Cunningham Highway to the Crest car park at Cunningham's Gap and continue west.

0.0kms	Cunningham's Gap car park
21.6kms	Turn right. Sign posted *Goomburra 10km*.
31.3kms	Turn right towards Inverramsey. Sign posted *Goomburra State Forest 25kms.*
50.9kms	Cross grid and continue on the dirt road past several camping spots named, Platypus, Black Cockatoo, Wallaby Flats, etc.
56.5kms	Y junction. The road ahead leads to the Goomburra camping area. The *'dry weather road'* to the left is marked *Sylvester's Lookout 5kms*, and *Mt. Castle Lookout 7kms*.
56.8kms	Pass through a gate, which is closed during wet weather.
60.4kms	Araucaria Trail on the left takes visitors on a 3km, 2 hour return walk in the State Forest.
61.1kms	The walk to Sylvester's Lookout is 750m to the right.
62.8kms	End of the road. Park here to take the 600m walk to Mt Castle Lookout.

NB. Conventional vehicles can use this road in dry conditions.

MT CASTLE LOOKOUT
Distance: 1.2kms, allow 30 minutes return. Easy grade.

This short track leads uphill through rainforest towards the Lookout. Along the heavily eroded track are good examples of large buttress roots, tall hoop pines and vine forest. As you near the Lookout platform, look for the remains of an old hoop pine that has fallen across the track. You can see nature taking its course. The trunk has crumbled to a mass of sawdust near the track, but it is identifiable further off to the right. Note how the bark has lifted away from the trunk in *'hoops'*.
This short walk is not in the National Park, but it has been included because it provides good views towards the cliffs of Mt Castle and down the Laidley Creek Valley.

The track to Sylvester's Lookout is in the National Park, but the lookout is closed due to concerns regarding its structural safety. There are no plans to repair or replace it at this stage.

Last reviewed: 20 July 1997

MAP REFERENCE
Sunmap - GLEN ROCK 1:25 000
              TOWNSON 1:25 000

FACILITIES
Mt Mistake is a wilderness park. There are several unmarked bushwalking trails but these should only be attempted by experienced walkers who must be self sufficient and contact the Ranger prior to a visit. There is only limited space on the steep slopes for bush camping.
Camping facilities with barbecues (firewood provided) and toilets are located in Goomburra camping area. This is a State Forest Reserve and campers should register at the self-registration booth.

ACCESS - SPICER'S GAP
Drive west from Brisbane on the Cunningham Highway to Aratula.

0.0kms	Aratula Hotel.
4.2kms	Turn left at Moogerah Dam Road.
10.0kms	Turn right into Spicer's Gap Road.
12.8kms	Gravel road. This road may be closed following wet weather. It is not suitable for caravans.
16.3kms	*Main Range National Park* sign.
16.8kms	Camp ground on left.
17.0kms	Pioneer Picnic Ground on left, and entrance to Mt Matheson Trail on the right.
19.0kms	Governor's Chair car park.

SPICER'S PEAK
Distance: 6kms return, allow 6-7 hours. Hard grade.

Don't be misled by the short return distance for this walk. Parts of the ridge are extremely steep with loose dirt and rocks, and few hand holds. Do not attempt this walk unless you are an experienced, competent scrambler, with no fear of heights.
The climb to Spicer's Peak starts at Governor's Chair car park. Follow the walking track 150m to the Lookout. This wide rocky slab provides good views over the Fassifern Valley towards the coast and is popular with day trippers. The Lookout is believed to have been a popular resting spot for various Governors as they travelled through the Gap.
From the Lookout, walk south towards the peak and locate a well defined footpad. This footpad leads through open eucalypt forest with grassy ground cover towards a

fence-line. If the footpad is obscured by grass, follow the fence as it crosses a small gully and continues to ascend. After climbing for about 20 minutes, there are good views across to the knob on top of Mt Mitchell. Where the fence-line ends, a track leads left to a clearing at the edge of the cliff. The view extends from Mt Edwards on the left, around to Mt Greville, Glennies Pulpit, Mts Moon and Maroon and right towards Mt Barney.

Back on the track, and it gets steeper as it continues uphill past remnants of an older fence. There are more grass trees, she-oaks and clumps of paper daisies and you are likely to startle quails as you continue upwards. Skirt around a rocky outcrop and then up towards the first cliff-line. The original route to the summit was straight up the edge of the cliff, close to the eastern face. This route is still used frequently, however, it is very steep and the dirt and rocks are loose and slippery. There has already been one fatality on this mountain and it is best to avoid the original track.

Turn right along the cliff-line, following a track for 10-15 minutes to a section where the cliff gives way to a rocky slab, and the next cliff-line comes into view. Scramble over boulders, heading towards the base of the next cliff. Note this point for your descent, turn left and walk along the base of the cliffs to a section where you can climb to the top of the ridge, near the eastern face. A trail now leads towards the final set of cliffs, below the summit. About 20m from the cliffs, veer right and walk diagonally towards the rainforest. The grass along this section of the route is loose and slippery with clumps of stinging nettle near the top. The steep trail through the rainforest is also loose and crumbly. When you reach a track junction, turn left towards the 1 222m summit. (The right track leads to the west peak.) Views from the top include the obvious peaks seen below, as well as Mts Doubletop, Huntley, Asplenium, Panorama Point, Steamer and the Steamer Range. Descend via the same route. Extreme care is required on the grassy verge between the base of the rainforest and the track near the eastern cliff face.

Last reviewed: 13 August 1997

Alternatively, a less precarious but much longer descent route is possible by following the track along the ridge towards the west peak. From the saddle, turn right (north) and descend through the rainforest to a point below the cliff-line. Then contour east until you reach the ascent ridge and follow the track back to the car park. This descent route would add 1-2 hours to the return trip.

Last reviewed: 25 April 1997 on NPAQ walk. Leaders: John Bristow, Ron Owen.

MT MATHESON CIRCUIT
Distance: Mt Matheson Trail: 4.6kms, allow 1.5 hours return. Easy grade.
　　　　　　　 Mt Matheson Circuit: 8.1kms, allow 3 hours. Moderate grade.

This track starts opposite the Pioneer Picnic Ground. The walking trail climbs steadily through eucalypt forest and passes a section of lantana and wild raspberry, but the track is well maintained and the scunge does not encroach on the track. Notice the black bean pods on the ground. The track swings to the right and after about 15 minutes reaches a barbed wire fence and turns left, up the ridge. You may be lucky enough to spot a koala in the trees as you walk towards a track junction at the 752m Mt Matheson summit. Continue straight ahead to the end of the ridge for views of Mt Mitchell and Mt Cordeaux, and along the Ramparts towards Mt Castle. It is easy to identify the feature called *'The Sleeping Assyrian'*. On a clear day, you can see *'The Hole-in-the-wall'*, just to the left of Mt Castle and a dip in the ridge-line.

Return to the track junction and either retrace your steps to the picnic ground (Mt Matheson Trail), or turn right to complete the circuit as described.

Follow the track along the top of the ridge, past some moss-covered rocks. There are several sections that provide uninterrupted views of the face of Mt Mitchell. Early morning light provides excellent photographic opportunities. The track continues to ascend towards a rocky bluff. Look for a large staghorn fern and a clump of orchids clinging to the side of the bluff. The track contours around the rocks to the right, through a shallow gully and steeply uphill again to the ridge top.

This ridge is higher than the summit of Mt Matheson and continues uphill to a small clearing near the start of the rainforest. The track immediately descends to the left through the rainforest and passes several large strangler figs. There is also evidence of early logging in the forest.

After leaving the rainforest, cross an open grassy paddock before reaching the remains of an old bullock drawn timber jinker. The track ascends slightly and then contours around the side of the hill, reaching the road 1.1kms from the jinker. This historic road was completed during the 1860s and interpretive signs explain the *'sophisticated'* construction methods used. Walk left towards Governor's Chair car park and head down the road 2.1kms to the picnic ground. A large colony of bell birds inhabits the area along the sides of the road.

Last reviewed: 13 August 1997

MAP REFERENCE
Sunmap - CUNNINGHAMS GAP 1:25 000
QNPWS Visitor Information sheet.

FACILITIES
Camping area, picnic area, tables, water, limited barbecues (firewood supplied) and toilets are at Spicer's Peak camp ground and Pioneer Picnic ground. It is wise to bring alternative cooking equipment if you intend camping in this area.
Picnic tables are located at Governor's Lookout car park.
The best time to attempt the off track walks on Main Range is during crisp winter days, although night time can prove very chilly for camping. Always carry plenty of water.

ACCESS - WILSON'S PEAK

Travel from Brisbane to either Boonah or Rathdowney, then take the Boonah-Rathdowney Rd to the sign post reading *Carneys Creek, Croftby* and *The Head*; 14kms from Boonah or 33kms from Rathdowney.

0.0kms	Turn into Carneys Creek Road.
14.5kms	Continue ahead at the sign post marked *White Swamp 19.* The road to The Head and Queen Mary Falls goes off to the right at this point.
16.0kms	Gravel road - suitable for conventional vehicles.
23.6kms	Cross grid.
28.0kms	Boonah Border Gate.

WILSON'S PEAK

Distance: 11.5kms return, allow 6 hours. Hard grade.

There are three accepted routes to the summit of Wilson's Peak. This route is the longest and provides the most variety. The hard grade has been assigned because the final climb through the rainforest is very steep. Rain would make this part of the track extremely slippery, so it is definitely a dry weather walk.

From the Boonah Border Gate, walk along the service road on the left (NSW) side of the rabbit fence for about 10 minutes. This avoids the first steep climb along the fence. Find a suitable spot to climb over the fence and continue on the Queensland side through open eucalypt forest. The track soon starts to ascend towards a locked gate. The ridge gets steeper as you follow the fence. Listen to the bell birds as you head towards another gate about 30 minutes from the start. A few minutes further on the fence veers to the right and you start to descend. The eucalypts and grass trees have been scorched by bushfires. You get your first glimpses of Wilson's Peak off to the left. Continue along the fence as it climbs again, through another gate to the top of a ridge, before descending very steeply with the imposing cliffs of Wilson's Peak directly in front.

After about 1.5 hours, the ridge almost flattens out near a large clump of grass trees just before entering the rainforest. At a point where the fence veers left, look for the trunk of a large tree felled years ago by timber getters. The slots used to place spring board platforms in the trunk are still obvious. The terrain now becomes steeper! There are several sections where the track levels off before climbing steeply again. The trees at this point are covered in old man's beard and crows nest ferns cling to the upper branches. After climbing through the rainforest for about 15 minutes you reach a large crows nest, clinging to the side of a moss-covered rock. Keep climbing for another 10 minutes past more boulders to a section where the forest opens up. The views south-east to the cleared valley provide a stark contrast to the tree covered slopes of the mountains. It is easy to visualise what this land was like prior to European settlement.

Another steep 10 minute climb from this point and you reach the cliffs at the base of Wilson's Peak. Spare a thought for the workers who originally built the rabbit fence all along this section of the State border! To reach the summit, locate a well worn track to the right of the cliffs. This track contours around some fern and orchid covered cliffs, past some shallow caves. When you reach the remains of an older rabbit fence, at a point where the track starts to descend the north ridge towards Teviot Gap, look for an obvious cleft in the rock leading left uphill. Follow the wear marks through a clump of woody tea trees towards the summit. This climb is relatively steep, but not as difficult as the previous final climb along the rabbit fence. There is a trig point and a rock cairn on the summit. Follow a track from the summit towards the cliff-line for good views towards the Fassifern Valley. Moogerah Dam is to the north and the view arcs to the right towards the distinctive knob of Glennies Pulpit at Mt Alford and around past Maroon Dam, Mts May and Maroon. The prominent peak of Mt Lindesay is seen just above the ridge between Mts Ballow and Barney. After lunch, return to your vehicle via the same route.

Last reviewed: 23 November 1997

MAP REFERENCE
Sunmap - WILSONS PEAK 1:25 000
              MOUNT CLUNIE 1:25 000

FACILITIES
There are no facilities in this section of the Park. Be sure to carry adequate water.

ACCESS - QUEEN MARY FALLS
From Brisbane follow the directions to Carneys Creek Road, as detailed in the access notes for Wilson's Peak.

0.0kms	Beginning of Carneys Creek Road.
14.5kms	Turn right at the sign post to *'The Head 21'.*
22.6kms	*Main Range National Park* sign on left.
25.4kms	Teviot Falls Lookout on right. Note adjacent landslip.
25.6kms	Gravel road.
31.2kms	Continue towards Killarney. The road to Boonah, via White Swamp is to the left.
32.0kms	Veer left towards Killarney.
35.7kms	Gravel road.
38.0kms	Carr's lookout. From here you receive excellent views of The Head Valley, Mt Superbus and Wilson's Peak.
45.5kms	*Queen Mary Falls National Park* sign on the right.
46.1kms	Turn right into Queen Mary Falls car park and picnic area.

NB. The winding, steep road, although offering magnificent scenery, becomes very slippery following rain and may become impassable. It is not suitable for caravans. An alternate route is via Warwick, then to Killarney and on to the Queen Mary Falls section of Main Range National Park.

QUEEN MARY FALLS CIRCUIT
Distance: 2kms, allow 1 hour. Easy grade.

The start of the walking track is on the right, at the rear of the picnic area. Follow the paved track for 400m to a track junction, turn right and walk 100m to the Falls Lookout for good views back towards the 40m falls, down onto the track at the base of the Falls and out across the valley. From the Lookout, follow the track downhill, passing a clump of tree ferns before reaching a footbridge near the base of the falls.
The track then climbs back uphill through a small patch of rainforest. Several sets of steps are encountered as you climb up the escarpment. Guard rails have been placed at vantage points to allow safe viewing of the Falls. The track ends at the southern end of the picnic area.

Last reviewed: 21 August 1997

MAP REFERENCE
Sunmap - WILSONS PEAK 1:25 000
A walking track map is issued by QNPWS and is available from the kiosk opposite the picnic grounds.

FACILITIES
The picnic grounds contain tables, shelter sheds, fireplaces with wood provided, toilets with wheelchair access, and water. Camping is prohibited in the picnic area but a private caravan park and camp ground with good facilities is located adjacent to the picnic ground. Their phone number is (07) 4664 7151.

RANGER CONTACT - (07) 4666 1133 - Cunningham's Gap section.
(07) 4661 3710 - Queen Mary Falls section.

MOOGERAH PEAKS NATIONAL PARK

HISTORY
The volcanic plugs of Moogerah peaks surround Moogerah Dam and dominate the skyline of the Fassifern Valley farmlands. Four separate peaks make up this 927ha park that forms part of the Great Dividing Range.
Mt Greville, 770m, is easily identified as it takes on the shape of a *'grazing kangaroo'* or *'baby elephant'*, depending on the angle of the view and your imagination. The Aboriginal name for the Mountain is *Mebatboogan*. In 1828, Allan Cunningham gave the Mountain its European name, after a Scottish botanist. The National Park was gazetted in 1948.
Mt French, 579m, is internationally recognised as one of Queensland's best rock climbing areas. There are over 150 established ascent routes on the cliff known as Frog Buttress. Aborigines called the Mountain *Punchagin*. The original European

name was Mt Dumeresq, named by Captain Logan in honour of Governor Darling's son-in-law. Unbeknown to Captain Logan, Allan Cunningham had also named a mountain on the Darling Downs *'Dumeresq'* on the same day. Captain Logan later changed the name to French, the son-in-law's nationality. The first national park on Mt French was gazetted in 1967 for scenic and historical reasons. It wasn't until 1987 that the famous rock climbing cliffs on the northern peak were added to Mt French National Park and a further parcel of land was bought in 1991 that connects the two areas.

Mt Moon, 784m, has scree slopes and steep cliffs that appeal only to the most eager bushwalker. Derived from the Aboriginal term *'Moorm'* meaning *'old walkabout mountain'*, part of Mt Moon was proclaimed a national park in 1953.

Mt Edwards, 632m, is the conical shaped peak rising from the land alongside the Cunningham Highway. Originally named Mt Bannister by Oxley in 1824, it was renamed Mt Edwards by Allan Cunningham in 1828, in honour of Lieutenant George Edwards who was stationed at Moreton Bay. The National Park was gazetted in 1966 and takes in Mt Edwards, Little Mt Edwards and part of Reynolds Creek and Gorge.

FEATURES

The following description of Mt Greville was made in 1910 by teachers from the Summer School of Geology. It is still relevant today. (Conversions from imperial measurement to metric have been added.)

"The main rocks met on the ascent were similar to those met in the Glass House Mountains and at Mt Macedon in Victoria. From a tourists point of view the feature of the mountain is a magnificent fissure on the eastern slope, abounding in palm trees and huge tree-ferns. This cleft in the mountain side is about a mile long (approx 1.6kms). *It narrows to only a few yards in some places and the greatest width is not more than 10 or 12 yards* (approx 10m). *There are precipitous - almost perpendicular - rocks on each side, the height of which must be well over 200 feet* (approx 60m). *One palm tree that had been cut down measured 99 feet* (approx 30m) *from the root to the first leaf. These palm trees grow in great profusion in the rocky cleft, but are to be seen nowhere else on the mountain. The excursionists were in raptures about its picturesqueness and beauty, and it is certainly worth going a long way to see."*

The oldest rocks in the Mt French area have been dated back to the Jurassic era. Fossil leaves and dinosaur footprints have been recorded from roof shales of some coal seams.

Mt Moon has two peaks that are bisected by deep gorges. The many rock piles in the area are home for rock wallaby colonies.

A wild and beautiful gorge formed by the meandering Reynolds Creek separates Mt Edwards and Little Mt Edwards. The creek flows through a series of pools and rapids creating excellent swimming and canoeing spots.

Open eucalypt forest with montane heath dominates the exposed peaks of Moogerah Peaks National Park.

Remarkable displays of wildflowers in late winter and spring reward those who have troubled to climb through the palm filled gorge of Mt Greville.

A small section of dry rainforest scrub, a remnant of that which once covered the Fassifern Valley is protected on Mt French. Timber getters axed the scrub from the 1880s taking out most of the hoop pines by the early 1900s.

Orchids and flannel flowers grow amongst small areas of scrub and eucalypt forest on Mt Moon, and the gorge at Mt Edwards National Park boasts lovely old trees such as river oaks and river tea trees.

Many varieties of wrens, pigeons and finches have been recorded around the peaks. Eagles are seen soaring in the thermals, and as usual the scrub turkey also makes the area its home. Dingoes, wallabies, echidnas and koalas inhabit the Mountains and patient visitors are likely to see platypus in the pools of Reynolds Creek, along with Jew fish, eels and tortoises.

ACCESS - MT GREVILLE
From Brisbane, follow the Cunningham Highway to Aratula.

0.0kms	Aratula Hotel
4.2kms	Turn left on Moogerah Dam Road - sign posted *Lake Moogerah 22kms*.
8.2kms	Gravel road.
10.0kms	Pass Spicer's Gap turn off.
11.1kms	Cross Coulsen Creek.
15.5kms	Turn right into Mt Greville Road.
16.6kms	*Mt Greville National Park* sign and car park.

MT GREVILLE
Distance: 12kms return, allow 4 hours. Moderate grade.

There are several ways to climb this mountain, however, the route described uses Palm Gorge for the ascent, and South-East Ridge for the descent. The walk starts from the car park and immediately ascends a grassy ridge, following a fence-line to a track junction. Follow the sign left towards Palm Gorge, passing the track to South-East Ridge. Before reaching the Gorge, the heavily eroded track crosses a scree covered slope and passes through a section of lantana. The track is usually well cleared and there is no need to scrub bash. After walking uphill for about 20-30 minutes you reach the start of the Gorge and immediately realise why this is called Palm Gorge. The rocks in the base of the Gorge soon get larger and care is needed when walking on fallen palm fronds. Orchids cling to the cliff on the left side of the Gorge and the tentacle like roots of strangler figs snake down from the rim. The Gorge walls become closer and you pass to the right of a large boulder that appears to cover the floor. As the Gorge opens out again, the easiest path is on the left, but you soon reach an obvious track leading across to the right. The cliff on the right is covered with staghorns, elkhorns, crows nest ferns, basket ferns, mosses and lichens. It is interesting to compare the vegetation on the two sides of the Gorge. When you emerge at the head of the Gorge, you immediately reach a track junction. (The right track leads to the decent route via South East Ridge.) Turn left and begin the climb to the summit along a grass covered ridge, through open eucalypt forest. The grass trees are more plentiful as you approach the top. A large rock cairn has been built at the summit but trees obscure most of the views. Continue left of the cairn to a rocky outcrop for good views towards Cunningham's Gap and the Ramparts along the eastern escarpment of Main Range National Park, including Boars Head, Mt Castle and (if you know where to look) Hole-in-the-Wall. To the right is the conical shape of Mt Edwards, and Moogerah Dam.

To descend, retrace your steps to the track junction at the head of Palm Gorge. Walk past the junction and turn right along a rocky slab. Turn right again at the next track junction. (The left track leads towards Waterfall Gorge.) Continue through the undergrowth until you reach a small cairn at the top of the next rocky slab. The view to the left is Moogerah Dam. The rugged finger of rock on the ridge to the right of the dam is Glennies Pulpit. Directly in front if you is the gorge on Mt Moon. Mt Maroon is behind it to the left. Mts Barney and Ballow are to the right and the Main Range Ridge leads all the way around to the pyramid shaped face of Spicer's Peak on the extreme right.

Walk down the rock face towards Glennies Pulpit, then swing right again towards Mt Moon to locate an obvious track at the bottom right of the slab. The track continues through the scrub before emerging on another rock slab. A clump of grass trees to the right mark the restart of the track. After another scrubby section, the track swings around to the right. There are good views into Waterfall Gorge to the left and into Palm Gorge to the right. Continue to descend, crossing two more rocky slabs and a steep scree covered slope, before reaching a grass covered ridge. Continue through a clump of casuarinas, ignoring a faint track off to the left. When you reach Palm Gorge track, turn left and walk back to the car park.

Last reviewed: 6 August 1997

MAP REFERENCE
Sunmap - CUNNINGHAMS GAP 1:25 000
             MOUNT ALFORD 1:25 000
Track marked on Visitor Information Sheet supplied by QNPWS.

FACILITIES
There are no facilities at all at Mt Greville. Walkers must carry their own water.
Late winter and spring are the best times to see wildflower displays.

ACCESS - MT EDWARDS
Pass through the town of Aratula and turn left from the Cunningham Highway, into Charlwood Road, 100m before the Aratula Hotel.

0.0kms	Charlwood Road.
4.0kms	Turn right into Lake Moogerah Road.
6.7kms	Turn right towards Haigh Park and Lake Moogerah.
8.0kms	Entrance to Haigh Park picnic area.

MT EDWARDS
Distance: 6.5kms return, allow 3 hours. Moderate grade.

Walk across the dam wall and locate the start of the walking track. The well worn track leads away from the dam and then zigzags steeply uphill. After about 15 minutes climb some rocky steps before reaching a track leading off to the left. (This track could be used to descend, via a rocky gorge and a walk around the base of the Lake to the spillway. The track crosses private property and landowner permission is required.) Continue upwards, crossing a rocky slab and some steps leading to a rocky outcrop before reaching the Gorge Lookout. The view is across Reynolds Gorge to Little Mt Edwards. You can see the scars produced by water running down the rocky sides of Little Mt Edwards into Reynolds Creek. The Mt Edwards summit is on the left and the vegetation on the ridge between the summit and the creek is dominated by hoop pine. Note the change of vegetation on the other side of the creek. From the Lookout, the heavily eroded track continues steeply uphill via several sets of stone steps. Robins and finches constantly flit through the trees as you pass an open grassy section before entering an area previously damaged by bushfire. The eucalypt sapling regrowth ranges from one to three metres in height. The track almost levels out as it passes through casuarina regrowth and grass trees, then one final climb to the summit. From the summit, the view to the right is down to Reynolds Creek and across to the steep cliffs of Frog Buttress and the distinctive flat top of Mt French. An irrigation channel to the left of Reynolds Creek provides water
to a chequerboard mosaic of farming land. The trees at the summit still bear the scars of the earlier bushfire. To descend the Mountain, retrace your steps via the same track to the car park.

Last reviewed: 6 August 1997

MAP REFERENCE
Sunmap - MOUNT ALFORD 1:25 000
Track marked on Visitor Information Sheet supplied by QNPWS.

FACILITIES
Picnic facilities with tables, shelter sheds, barbecues, water and toilets (including those for disabled people) are available at Haigh Park on the eastern shores of Lake Moogerah. There are no facilities at all in the National Park area. Carry your own water.
Private camping facilities near Mt Greville and Mt Edwards areas are available at Yarramalong, the western side of Lake Moogerah, Aratula and Boonah. All areas have caravan access.

ACCESS - MT FRENCH
Travel south-west from Brisbane to the town of Boonah. Follow the Boonah-Rathdowney Road to the Dugandan Hotel, approximately 1km south of Boonah.
    0.0kms   Turn right at the Dugandan Hotel.

67

0.3kms	Turn left into the road sign posted *Mt French National Park*.
2.9kms	'T' intersection. Turn left towards Mt French.
3.7kms	Turn right at a sign post marked *Mt French National Park*.
9.2kms	Mt French National Park, car park and picnic grounds.

MT FRENCH CLIFF CIRCUITS
Distance: 4kms return, allow 1.5 hours. Easy grade.

The walking tracks start in the picnic area, near the camp ground. A sign post points towards *North Cliff Lookout*, 360m from the start of the track. This short section of track is paved and suitable for wheel chair access. The western views from the Lookout are spectacular, especially at sunset. Walk back along the paved track and locate a track leading west towards the cliffs.

Follow the track until it swings left and starts to descend towards a gully. At the head of the gully, turn right and continue down the steps to the base of the cliffs. A short track leads to the right where you can explore the cliffs at the northern end of the Buttress. Return to the track junction and continue to descend south along the cliff-line. The vertical fissures along the entire length of the cliff face provide excellent photographic opportunities. As you reach the end of the cliffs, the track starts to ascend. Keep close to the cliff and scramble up some loose rocks to the top of the Buttress. Turn left and follow a faint track north along the escarpment. Be extremely careful not to dislodge rocks onto the climbers below. A track leads off to the right as you approach the gully near the original descent. Follow this track towards the paved North Cliff path. Turn right and walk to the picnic area to the start of the short East Cliffs circuit.

Take the left branch of the track through dry eucalypt forest scattered with grass trees towards the Eastern Cliffs Lookout. The view to the left of a large hoop pine is towards Boonah. The return track crosses rocky slabs and passes through scrubby heath vegetation. It is not uncommon to sight the normally shy echidna along this section of the track. Continue over a small wooden bridge and back to the picnic area.

Last reviewed: 6 August 1997

MAP REFERENCE
Sunmap - MOUNT ALFORD 1:25 000
            FASSIFERN 1:25 000

FACILITIES
There is a picnic and bush camping area at Mt French National Park. Tables, fireplaces, water and toilets are situated in the picnic area. The camping area is popular with rock climbers.

RANGER CONTACT - (07) 5463 5041

GOLD COAST AND HINTERLAND

BURLEIGH HEAD NATIONAL PARK

HISTORY

The Kombumerri Aboriginal people lived around Jellurgal (Burleigh Head) for hundreds of years. Shell middens, bora rings and artefacts found in the area indicate habitation long before European settlement. Many Kombumerri people were relocated onto reserves in the early 1900s but they have still maintained strong family links with the area.

In 1876, a forward thinking journalist with the Brisbane Courier, advocated withdrawing from sale, all land allotments in the region. While checking out the area he avoided, "*...dense thickets of rich green foliage and impenetrable stems.*", by scrambling down the rocks. He was impressed with the black hexagonal basalt columns, "*...lengths of which must weigh hundreds of tons.*". The Kombumerri people called these basalt columns Jabreen's fingers. To these people, Jabreen was the creator of Jellurgal. The journalist continued upstream along Tallebudgera Creek sighting hundreds of fish, then back to his starting point via an old timber getters track. He reported that, "*...the exposed nature of its beach renders it useless as a boating, and dangerous as a bathing, station.*".

Ten years later, in 1886, an 18.4ha oasis in the heart of the Gold Coast was proclaimed as a '*Reserve for Public Purposes*'.

Decades of uncertainty followed – developers attempted to subdivide the region in 1916, vandals left their mark, trees were cut down for firewood, banana growers wanted to clear the slopes for cultivation and fire damage was succeeded by heavy lantana growth. The small colony of koalas was in danger. Following various submissions and reports, Burleigh Head was given national park status in 1947, protecting its rainforest, open forest, koala habitat, basaltic columns and scenery.

In 1949, just two years after proclamation, the area showed signs of regeneration!

In 1950 Burleigh Head National Park was once again under threat. The newly formed local council attempted to procure boulders from the Park. Angry residents petitioned against the council, who were eventually refused permission to remove the boulders and were reminded of the benefits of tourism to the local area.

A gift of land from the estate of Samuel S Pegg was incorporated in the Park in 1959. The current area of Burleigh Head National Park is 27.6ha.

In January 1997, an agreement was reached providing the opportunity for the Kombumerri people to conduct cultural activities at Burleigh Head National Park. They are currently utilising the Burleigh Heads Information Centre as a base for their tourism activities and are working to preserve their culture and language.

Following heavy rain in May 1997, several large rocks broke loose and crashed down to the lower walking track, forcing its closure. The track was finally reopened, only to have more boulders fall onto the track in November 1997 and again in February 1998. Geotechnical surveys have indicated that sections of the track should remain closed. A new track is under construction.

FEATURES
When Mt Warning erupted, molten lava flowed to the current Burleigh Heads coastline. The lava cooled slowly, and as it shrunk and cracked, six-sided basalt columns were formed. Softer sedimentary rock below the basalt was eroded, and the basalt rocks fell into the sea. These basalt rocks now assist in preventing further erosion of Burleigh Headland.
The rich volcanic soil supports littoral rainforest, a rare dry form of rainforest that only grows by the sea. Poorer sedimentary soils support eucalypt forest. Trees found in the Park include; ironbark, forest red gum, bloodwood, brush box, crows ash, red bean, hoya vine and Moreton Bay fig. Pandanus survive on the exposed coastal slopes and small clumps of coastal heath grow around Sandy Cove.
The headland was an important refuge for migratory birds, but much of the surrounding bushland once used by these birds has been lost to *'progress'*. However, honeyeaters, lorikeets, pigeons, kingfishers, and kookaburras are commonly seen in the Park. Brahminy kites, whistling kites, ospreys and white bellied sea eagles hunt fish along the creek.
Many of the animals that originally lived in the Park have been decimated by domestic animals, but possums are often sighted and koalas are still occasionally seen in the north-western section of the Park.

ACCESS
Heading south from Brisbane, take the Burleigh Heads exit, from the Pacific Highway.

0.0kms	*Burleigh Heads* and *Tallebudgera Valley* sign, just past the off-ramp.
0.4kms	Turn left on Tallebudgera Creek Road.
1.8kms	Veer right at the lights on West Burleigh Road.
3.3kms	Turn right towards Coolangatta, on Gold Coast Highway.
4.6kms	Turn left at the Ikkina Road lights, into the Information Centre.

Alternatively, drive south from Surfers Paradise on Gold Coast Highway.

OCEAN VIEW CIRCUIT
Distance: 2.8kms, allow 1 hour. Easy grade.

The Ocean View Circuit starts at the northern end of the Tallebudgera Creek Bridge. The track is completely paved and there are three seats placed at strategic places on the upper track, for tired walkers. Additional seats are likely to be added in future. Ignore the left track junction shortly after the start and continue following the creek bank past Echo Beach. There is a wheel chair ramp leading down to a fishing platform. When you reach the mouth of Tallebudgera Creek the track swings around to the left. The foreshore is covered with large basalt boulders and pandanus grow on both sides of the track. Jabreen's fingers are seen high up on the headland. When you reach Goodwin Terrace entrance, 1.2km from the start, turn left and walk up the steep hill past Jabreen's fingers. You then pass a large pile of hexagonal rock columns as you zigzag up through the forest to a track junction. Turn left and walk to a lookout with views over the mouth of the creek, down the beach and out to sea. This is a popular location to sight humpback whales as they migrate in winter and spring. After taking in the views, follow the track back downhill to the starting point.

Last reviewed: 7 June 1997
At the time of publication, sections of this track were closed until further notice.

MAP REFERENCE
UBD Brisbane Street Directory - Gold Coast section, Map 60
A walking trail map is available at the Information Centre.

FACILITIES
Picnic area, shelter sheds, barbecues and toilets are located at the northern entrance.
The Interpretive Centre and toilets at the southern end have wheelchair access. The walking tracks are also suitable for wheelchairs. No camping is allowed in the Park. If you enjoy watching the migration of the humpback whales, winter and spring are the best time to visit the Park, otherwise any time of the year is suitable.

RANGER CONTACT -   (07) 5576 0271
BURLEIGH INFORMATION CENTRE - (07) 5535 3032

LAMINGTON NATIONAL PARK

HISTORY
The local indigenous *'Murri'* people have lived in the area around Lamington for thousands of years, but the first recorded European visit was by F.E. Roberts in 1864. Roberts was responsible for surveying the Queensland - New South Wales border and naming many of the peaks in the area.
In 1878, Robert Collins, a successful grazier from the Beaudesert area visited the USA at a time when the Americans were establishing the world's first national parks. Collins was impressed with the concept of national parks and after being elected a Member of Parliament in 1896, he began campaigning for the creation of a national park in the McPherson Ranges.
In 1911, Romeo Lahey, a timber miller from Canungra joined the struggle and continued lobbying for the creation of the Park. Lamington National Park, containing an initial area of 18 800ha, was eventually proclaimed in July 1915, two years after Collins' death. It was the fifth national park to be gazetted in Queensland, and was named after an early Governor of Queensland who only visited the Park once, supposedly shooting a koala to mark the event!

Also in 1911, eight members of the O'Reilly family took up occupancy of several blocks of land for dairy farming. The O'Reilly's needed a road into the rainforest covered ranges to ensure the success of their dairies, but when the National Park was proclaimed, this seemed unlikely. Faced with this uncertainty, the concept of a guesthouse evolved. The name *'Green Mountains'* was suggested by Henry Tyron, a member of a naturalist's expedition in 1918.

In 1937, a Stinson airliner with seven people on board, crashed on a mountain to the north of Lamington Plateau, while on route from Brisbane to Sydney, via Lismore. Several days after the crash, Bernard O'Reilly set out on horseback to mount his own search for the lost plane. The tale of his courage and superior bushcraft during the search and ultimate rescue of two survivors is now part of Australian folklore. *Bernard O'Reilly has recounted the heroic story in his book titled Green Mountains, a reading must if you intend walking to the wreck site via Westray's Grave or the Stretcher Track.*

Binna Burra Lodge, situated on Mt Roberts was the brain child of Arthur Groom and a group of like minded people who wanted to provide a facility for people to come and enjoy the wilderness area. Early visitors stayed in tents, after scrambling two kilometres from the end of the road to the present lodge site. Even after the construction of the first buildings, a flying fox powered by a draft horse turning a wheel-winch, pulled the guest's luggage to the lodge. Remains of the wheel-winch can still be seen today. The name *'Binna Burra'* was chosen by Arthur Groom and Romeo Lahey. The most likely explanation is that it comes from the local Wangerriburra dialect and means *'people of the cliffs'.*

During the depression, the Government employed groups of 40 to 50 men at a time to build the graded track network using picks and shovels. This work continued until the war effort took precedence over manpower and finance reserves. Today there are more than 160kms of graded tracks in the 20 600ha Lamington National Park, making it one of the most comprehensive collections of walking tracks in the country.

Lamington National Park was declared part of the Central Eastern Australian Rainforest Reserves World Heritage Area in December 1994.

A new orientation centre, staffed by volunteer members of the Green Mountains Natural History Association, opened in the Green Mountains section of the Park in 1997. A magnificent sculpture to commemorate Bernard O'Reilly's role in the rescue of the Stinson survivors was also unveiled and stands as a memorial outside the Green Mountains kiosk.

FEATURES

Much of Lamington consists of high plateaus covered in subtropical rainforest. It is a high rainfall area and several large river systems with a host of tributaries have carved deep gorges throughout the Park. Lamington is part of the Scenic Rim, a chain of mountains curving around Brisbane in a 100km radius, stretching from the Gold Coast Hinterland to Mt Mistake. Part of the Scenic Rim forms the border between Queensland and New South Wales. Some of the ranges exceed 1 100m.

The rock formations of the Lamington area were produced 22 million years ago by the eruption of Mt Warning, the largest shield volcano in Australia.

The predominant rocks within the Park are basalt and rhyolite. A broad band of tuff (volcanic ash and fine rock) up to 60m thick in places, can be found below the upper layers of rhyolite and basalt in the Binna Burra region.

Rainforest growing on basalt soil covers two thirds of the Park and represents the largest area of undisturbed subtropical rainforest in South-East Queensland. The remaining third is covered with open forest, woodland and heath. Huge buttressed trees, strangler figs, woody vines, orchids, staghorns and birds nest ferns are a feature of the subtropical rainforest that grows at altitudes up to 800m. The rainforest on the drier slopes is dominated by hoop pines, while cool temperate rainforest on the higher slopes support ancient Antarctic beech forests. The age of some of these trees has been estimated at more than 5 000 years.

New England blackbutt, Sydney blue gum and ironbarks grow in the poorer soil of the open forest and woodland. On the upper slopes, rhyolitic soils support low shrubby heath communities that produce good displays of flowers in spring.

Lamington is a haven for bird life. The black and yellow regent bowerbird, (symbol of O'Reilly's guesthouse) is often spotted around the Green Mountains area. Satin bowerbirds, eastern spinebills, crimson rosellas, king parrots and pied currawongs are seen frequently. The wompoo pigeon and the catbird can both be heard as you walk through the Park and you will probably see yellow robins and a variety of wrens flitting through the forest. Log-runners look for food amongst the leaf litter and you will certainly encounter brush turkeys around the picnic areas. During late afternoon or early morning, red-necked pademelons graze on the grassy areas around the camp sites. There is also a small population of dingoes in the area. A night walk into the forest with a torch will often uncover brushtail possums, ringtail possums, gliders, bandicoots and bush rats. The shiny black land mullet (skink family) and a variety of skinks, lizards and goannas are often seen from the tracks during the day, and you need to be on the lookout for green tree snakes and carpet pythons, as well as the more venomous black and brown snakes. The unique blue Lamington spiny crayfish is often seen after summer rains as it moves from pool to pool along the waterfall tracks. A variety of frogs also frequent the pools and glow worms line the banks at night.

A description of all the walks in the Lamington area would fill (and has filled) a whole book. The walks described here are designed to introduce visitors to several different areas of the Park and encourage further individual exploration of the walking trails. There are several old tracks that have been closed due to landslides or lack of maintenance funding, as well as a great number of off track routes, which require considerable experience and navigational ability. **These routes should only be undertaken by fit, experienced bushwalkers.**

ACCESS - GREEN MOUNTAINS
Drive to Canungra, approximately 115kms from Brisbane, or 70kms from the Gold Coast, via Nerang.

0.0kms	Canungra. Turn into Kidston Street, also sign posted *Green Mountains*. Follow the road past the Canungra Hotel.
30.0kms	National Park boundary.
35.1kms	Road to QNPWS camp ground on the right.
35.2kms	Car park.

NB. The road to Green Mountains is sealed all the way to the lodge, but the narrow, steep and winding road is unsuitable for caravans.

TOOLONA CREEK CIRCUIT
Distance: 17.2kms, allow 6-7 hours. Moderate grade.

This circuit leads off the main Border Track that starts from the top end of the car park. The first 700m of the border track has been paved to prevent erosion caused by heavy usage. Follow the border track for 1.7kms to reach the start of the Toolona Creek Circuit. Take the left branch and start heading downhill. After walking for about five minutes, look for a giant brush box on the left of the track with two trunks and a massive exposed root system. The track zigzags downhill past moss-covered banks on the left and a tree fern filled gully on the right. Just past the gully, the canopy thickens preventing any light reaching the ground. The forest floor is covered with leaf litter and devoid of vegetation and after rain has the unmistakable pleasant *'smell'* of the rainforest.

After walking for 2.7kms, continue past the Box Forest Circuit track and keep walking downhill to the right. You soon hear the rushing waters of Canungra Creek deep in the valley below. Five minutes later you reach Picnic Rock and your first creek crossing. The track continues downhill to the Box Forest circuit track junction. The much photographed Elabana Falls is only 70m from this junction and is well worth a visit. A further five minutes walking and you reach the second creek crossing at Triple Falls. The rocks here are covered with moss and are very slippery when wet. From Triple Falls, the track starts to wind slowly uphill past Burraboomba Falls, to the third creek crossing. There are several places where water flows over the track, especially after rain. At the fourth crossing, you reach another spectacular waterfall and the track zigzags uphill to the fifth crossing, past Yalgahn Falls, visible from the track. Cross the creek for the sixth time and continue climbing along the edge of Toolona Gorge. The sides of the Gorge are covered with ferns, mosses and lilies and present many photo opportunities. Continue on to Toolona Falls. The forest canopy opens when you reach a clearing at the top of the Gorge. Cross another small creek and keep walking uphill to Moonwoolba Cascades. The track soon levels out as you walk along the edge of the creek to another small waterfall about 5m high. It then climbs uphill again to another creek crossing and waterfall.

One more creek crossing, one more waterfall, and the track keeps zigzagging uphill. Continue walking through the Antarctic beech forest before arriving again at the main Border Track. Turn left at the Border Track and walk about 50m to Wanungara Lookout. This makes an ideal lunch spot.

Follow the **Border Track** notes from this point, 7.7kms back to Green Mountains.

Last reviewed: 10 May 1997

ALBERT RIVER CIRCUIT
Distance: 20.6kms, allow 6-7 hours. Moderate grade.

The Albert River Circuit leads off the main Border Track, 4.5kms from the trail head. Do not take the Pensioner Track. After walking steadily for about an hour, you reach several large Antarctic beech trees and the start of the Albert River Circuit, at the top of a ridge. Turn right and follow the track as it leads downhill past more beech trees and gullies filled with palms and helmholtzia lilies. After descending for about 30 minutes, you hear the sound of rushing water before reaching Jimbolongerri Falls, an attractive cascade on Lightning Creek. The track does not cross the creek, but swings back to the right and follows the creek downhill, passing several gullies filled with palms, tree ferns and moss-covered trees. This section of the track is particularly attractive following rain. The track zigzags past several small waterfalls before crossing Lightning Creek, just upstream from Lightning Falls. It is not uncommon to hear the cry of the Albert's lyrebird

along this section of the walk. Look for an old sign pointing to the Albert River.
Below you can see the start of Black Canyon. The short side track to Echo Falls
provides ideal photo opportunities. The trail now heads up towards Echo Point,
passing Gurrgunngulli Falls and an old sign marked *'X231'* near the side track to
Mirror Falls. Pass Joolbahla Falls and Gwahlahla Falls before crossing the creek
again below Bithongabel Falls. Continue uphill past a moss-covered bank, to the
final waterfall on Alcheringa Creek.

From here, the track climbs through an area where there has been significant storm
damage before reaching a bush camp-site on the right. (A well worn footpad at the
rear of this camp site leads uphill towards Mt Worendo, Mt Wupawn, the old Rat-A
Tat Hut site, Mt Durigan and on to Point Lookout and the Stinson Wreck. This
rough track is relatively easy to follow, but should not be attempted by
inexperienced walkers.)

Follow the track for a few hundred metres to Echo Point Lookout for good views
towards Mt Warning and the Tweed Valley. From Echo Point, the trail passes
Cominan Lookout before starting downhill past more moss-covered banks. These
banks are home to thousands of glow worms that sprinkle the walls with light at
night. About 500m from Cominan Lookout, look for an old sign reading *'X77'* and
then another reading *'WATER'*. A side track leads left to good reliable water, but
the track is often overgrown and care is needed to avoid getting lost.

You soon reach the top of the ridge near a beautiful old Antarctic beech and start
heading downhill to rejoin the main Border Track, 5kms from Green Mountains.
Another 50m and you reach the Pensioner Track junction. After a long day, the
Pensioner Track makes for a slightly easier trip home and allows you to view a
different section of the forest. Follow the **Border Track** notes from this point to
Green Mountains.

Last reviewed: 25 August 1997

BLUE POOL, STAIRWAY FALLS AND BULL ANT SPUR
Distance: 13.5kms, allow 5-6 hours. Moderate grade.

This walk provides an interesting combination of graded tracks and blazed trails,
but presents no real navigational difficulties. The moderate grade has been
assigned because of the steepness of Bull Ant Spur.

Follow the main Border Track for 250m to the start of the Blue Pool track. The
track turns left and immediately heads downhill past several large strangler figs.
Some of these trees have fallen, leaving a hollow tunnel inside the trunk where the
original host tree has rotted away. You soon enter a storm damaged area
dominated by vine forest and tall stinging trees. Several clumps of cunjevoi are
growing in the gully to the side of the track. It is widely believed that rubbing sap
from the cunjevoi on the skin will soothe the burning itch caused by leaves of the
stinging tree. But don't count on instant relief!

The track soon crosses Darraboola Creek. It continues to descend, passing between
two large red cedars and crosses the creek twice more before reaching a concrete

ford at the fourth crossing. Pass Darraboola Falls and continue to descend past a rocky bank covered in mosses and ferns. The forest canopy gets much thinner as you enter an area where there are several hoop pines and brush boxes and you can see the valley floor way below. Look for an old hollow hoop pine that has fallen on the right of the track. The bark is coming away in distinctive hoops that give the tree its name.

About one hour from the start, you reach the base of Bundoomba Falls and cross Bundoomba Creek. The track climbs along the left bank of Bundoomba Creek and crosses another small creek. A few minutes from this creek you can hear the sound of rushing water below and you pass an area where the trees are covered in mosses as you descend past the circuit junction to Blue Pool. The water in Blue Pool is usually very cold but it is a good spot to cool off on a hot day. Large eels in this pool are attracted by splashing, so be careful if dangling your feet in the water.

The track to Stairway Falls crosses Canungra Creek six times and should not be attempted if the water is above knee height. The rocks become very slippery when wet. Follow the track around the edge of the Pool and rock hop across the creek. An arrow marks the track on the opposite side. Follow the base of a rocky cliff and cross Purragulli Creek. You can see where flooding waters have exposed the roots of trees on the edge of this small creek. (A few minutes past Purragulli Creek, a faint footpad leads uphill to the right. This is the Middle Ridge Traverse trail via Fountain Falls, but it is very steep and should only be attempted by people with sound navigational skills.) The track emerges on a rocky bank and veers left as it follows the creek, crossing it at the base of a rocky slab. The creek crossings are often obscured by weed following extended dry periods, but most crossings still have faint red markers painted on rocks to identify the trail. Beware of stinging nettle as you push your way through weed at the crossings. About 30 minutes (1.8kms) from Blue Pool, you reach the head of Stairway Falls. The track continues to an area beside a pool at the base of the Falls. To return, retrace your steps to Blue Pool.

To locate the Bull Ant Spur trail, follow the graded track back uphill past the rocky slabs to the first right hand bend. The trail leads steeply uphill to the right, just past the buttress roots of a large tree. This trail swings right, across the head of the small rocky slabs before turning left uphill past a brush box on the left and a fig tree on the right. It is very eroded at this point but is relatively easy to follow as it swings to the right of a large buttressed tree and heads straight up the ridge. The trail soon becomes feint, but if you loose sight of it, keep following the top of the ridge-line. This trail was originally a shortcut from the guest house to the pool, but the graded track is now an easier ascent route. About an hour from the pool, after leaving the rainforest, the ridge-line flattens out before climbing steeply again for a further 30 minutes and flattens out again about 20m before reaching the road. Turn left and walk towards the guest house. Follow the road for five minutes and look for a faint trail off to the left, just before a 'Steep Ascent' sign. This is the start of the old Packhorse Track that also leads back to the guest house and avoids the final steep ascent of the road. There has been a great deal of storm damage in this area but it is still relatively easy to locate the old trail. The trail emerges from the forest at a point opposite the start of the Python Rock Trail. Turn left and follow the road 1km back to the guest house.

Last reviewed: 26 August 1997

FOUNTAIN FALLS VIA BULL ANT SPUR
Distance: 18kms return, allow 10 hours. Hard grade.

This *'off track'* route leads to Fountain Falls via the Middle Ridge Traverse. The route is very steep and should only be attempted by people with sound navigational skills. Start walking at the point where the Bull Ant Spur track joins the road to O'Reilly's Guest House. (See the notes for the previous walk.) Vehicles can be left near the start of the walk.

The Bull Ant Spur trail is more difficult to locate in descent than ascent. If you do encounter difficulties, the route to Fountain Falls may be too difficult for you to follow. When you reach Blue Pool, follow the notes for the previous walk to the start of the Middle Ridge Traverse, a few minutes along the graded track, past Purragulli Creek.

A well worn footpad leads straight uphill past the hollow trunk of large fig tree. The original host tree has long since decayed. Continue through a section of vine forest in an east-north-easterly direction, past a giant stinging tree with stag horn ferns high in the canopy. The trail soon levels out and veers right, then left before starting to climb again. There is very little ground cover other than bracken fern interspersed amongst the leaf litter. You pass several false summits before finally reaching the distinct top of the ridge, about 40-50 minutes from the graded track. The route was well marked with tape in November 1997, but if the tape has been removed, the large brush box with the stag horn fern on its trunk is a good marker for the return journey.

Turn right and follow the distinct ridge-line in a south-easterly direction. After about 10 minutes, the trail descends gradually at a point where the ridge widens and the trail becomes partially obscured. Continues along the ridge, ascending again to a massive brush box, covered with lattice like roots of a strangler fig. From here, continue uphill for about 10 minutes to a small rock cairn. (It takes 30-45 minutes from the beginning of the ridge to the cairn.)

The trail now swings left, past a clump of walking stick palm and starts to descend in a north-easterly direction around the side of the ridge. Fallen trees may make navigation more difficult in this area, but the trail is well marked. After descending for about 30 minutes, climb over the fallen trunk of a large hoop pine. Beware of stinging trees and lawyer vines in this area. Fifteen minutes from the fallen tree, listen for the sound of the falls. The track soon turns sharp left, just before a gully and follows the creek downstream for five minutes to a cliff made of basalt columns. Skirt around the cliff to the right, and descend into a gully. Follow the gully beside moss-covered cliffs to a pool at the base of Fountain Falls. This makes an ideal place to cool off and have lunch.

After lunch, locate the old disused graded track on the northern side of the pool. This track climbs downstream for 20m before turning right, zigzagging back upstream, past the top of the Falls. Look for a track marker reading '*AN 157 BIN 8 7/8 MILES*'. The track left is part of an original graded track leading to Binna Burra. It has now been closed by landslides and is overgrown with scunge.

Turn right and walk towards a pool at the base of Toombinya Falls. Cross the creek below these falls and locate an eroded track heading straight up the bank and joining the trail that led to the basalt columns. Turn left here and retrace your steps past Blue Pool and back up Bull Ant Spur to your vehicle.

Last reviewed: 29 November 1997 - NPAQ outing. Leader: John Daly.

NB.   When attempting any off track walk, ensure that you have a predetermined '*turn-around time*'. If you haven't reached your destination before this time, abandon the attempt and try again another day.

MORAN'S FALLS, CASTLE CRAG, LYREBIRD LOOKOUT
Distance: Approximately 12kms, allow 4 hours. Moderate grade.

Whilst not on a complete graded track, parts of this walk follow well worn footpads. It is ideal for those people wishing to practice '*picking out*' a trail by observing where others walkers have been. If you become disorientated, return to where you lost sight of the trail and look for signs of the route before heading off again.

Start walking on the Red Road, 60m before the entrance to the QNPWS camp ground. Walk down Red Road for five minutes and you reach a sweeping right hand bend and a grassy clearing. From here you get good views of the western section of the Scenic Rim. The road leads down to a gate at the site of the old slaughterhouse. One hundred metres through the gate, the 4WD track sign posted '*Moran's Falls*' and '*Balancing Rock*', leads right. It crosses a shallow creek and contours around the side of a grassy hill to another track junction. From here, you can look back up the hill towards the cleared section below O'Reilly's guesthouse. Head to the right and locate a small track at the end of the car park and walk to the lookout. The view from this lookout is down Moran's Creek Gorge. To view the Falls, turn right and walk up the Moran's Falls track, along the bank of Moran's Creek to a concrete bridge, and continue through the rainforest to Moran's Falls Lookout. Retrace your steps back to the road junction and the 4WD track marked *Balancing Rock*. This track climbs steeply uphill under the power lines and veers right as it levels out again and heads back into the forest. You soon reach a well used 4WD track leading right towards a car park used by buses transporting resort guests to Balancing Rock. Continue walking 50m to a second car park and follow a well-worn track to Balancing Rock. From here you can look to the right towards Moran's Falls and Moran's Gorge. To the left you have the Albert River Gorge, deep below the steep cliffs of the Lost World, with Mts Worendo and Throakban at the head of the valley.

To the left of Balancing Rock, there is a well worn but precipitous track towards Castle Crag. The track passes to the left of some large rocks before descending steeply into a saddle. Cross a narrow rocky ledge and continue following the ridge-line, descending to another saddle before reaching the end of Castle Crag. From this point the views are spectacular. Richmond Range is seen to the right of Lost World, then the prominent *'wedding cake'* shaped Mt Lindesay, Mt Ernest, Mts Barney and Ballow, then the Main Range escarpment in the background. Further on are the double peaks of Mt Maroon and then Mt Greville in the distance. Below you see the Albert River as it snakes its way through the valley.

Retrace your steps past Balancing Rock to where the Moonlight Crag track climbs steeply uphill. Follow the ridge-line, ignoring the 4WD track as you reach a cleared section. A sign points the way to *Moonlight Crag* where you get good views back down to Castle Crag. A further five minutes walking up the steep ridge takes you to the next junction and a sign pointing to *O'Reilly's via Lyrebird Lookout*. Another 20 minutes walking along the side of the escarpment as the track winds uphill and you reach Orchid Grotto. There are several large rounded boulders here with orchids and large crows nest ferns clinging to the rocks. From Orchid Grotto, continue uphill. There are a few places where the trail appears to be blocked by large buttress roots as they span out across the track. Skirt to the right and rejoin the ridge-line to find the track. The canopy closes in before entering rainforest again. About 30 minutes from Orchid Grotto you reach Lyrebird Lookout. The view from here is directly across to the Lost World saddle with the steep cliffs of Mt Widgee directly behind. The track soon swings away from the escarpment and heads downhill, across Moran's Creek and uphill again to another junction. (The right fork leads to the Border Track.) Take the track left towards O'Reilly's.

This track is historically significant. Robert Collins originally opened it in 1905 to show visitors the beauty of the area, in an attempt to enlist their support for the preservation of the region as a national park. The O'Reilly brothers reopened the track in 1912 to gain access to the beech forests and lookouts around Mt Bithongabel. The track is steep and was used up until 1947 to cart supplies by packhorses to families living at the old forestry camp. It climbs steadily through an area that suffered severe storm damage in September 1983. Thirty minutes later, you reach a clearing and rejoin the Border Track, only 700m from the guest house. Turn left and make your way back to the start.

Last reviewed: 11 May 1997

ACCESS - BINNA BURRA
Drive to Canungra, approximately 115kms from Brisbane.

0.0kms	Set odometer to zero at Kidston Street, Canungra and continue ahead.
1.5kms	Turn right towards Beechmont and Binna Burra.
4.1kms	Veer left.
17.1kms	Turn right at roundabout.

25.9kms	Visitor Information Centre and car park.
27.4kms	Turn right to the lodge or straight ahead to the car park.
27.7kms	Binna Burra car park.

NB. The bitumen road is winding and very narrow in places. Small caravans and camper vans can access the private camping area.

BORDER TRACK
Distance: 22kms, allow 6-7 hours. Moderate grade.

The Border Track is considered the backbone of the Lamington National Park walking track system because many tracks from Binna Burra and Green Mountains lead off from some point on the Border Track. Where this applies, the walk notes refer you to the appropriate section of the **Border Track** notes to avoid repetition. The appropriate track junction names are listed in **Bold Print.** The track crosses the Queensland-New South Wales border several times along the escarpment from Biby Lookout to Bithongabel Lookout and passes some of the oldest Antarctic beech trees and some of the best lookouts in the Park. There is no public transport between Binna Burra and Green Mountains so it is necessary to arrange a car shuffle. It has been graded 'medium', only because of its length. Although these walk notes describe the track from Binna Burra to Green Mountains, the walk can be completed in either direction.

The Border Track starts at the top end of the car park, past the kiosk. The first section of this is paved to prevent erosion caused by frequent use. A few minutes from the start you pass the Lamington National Park portals and an original survey peg marked *'A1'*. These survey pegs are still in place along many of the walking tracks in the Park. The *'A'* is for the Border Track and the *'1'* is the first peg of the survey. The Rainforest Circuit leads off to the right after 500m.

Continue on for about 250m and look for a large strangler fig on the right of the track. An aerial root from this tree has dropped to the ground on the left side of the track and now looks like the trunk of a separate tree, until you look up. The track heads gently uphill towards the Coomera seat. The Border Track heads off to the left, the **Coomera Circuit** is the middle fork while the **Tullawallal Circuit** turns right. As you walk through the forest, look for vines snaking their way around the trunks of the trees. In the Southern Hemisphere, vines will always follow the direction of water dripping down the tree trunk in a clockwise direction. It is the opposite in the Northern Hemisphere.

The Border Track now heads slowly downhill. About 30 minutes from the start you reach the **Dave's Creek** track junction. Stay on the right hand track as it heads slowly uphill to Joalah Lookout. This is a good spot to rest after the steady climb, but be aware that this sunny break in the trees is also home to families of yellow-faced whip snakes and keelbacks. You will often see them sunning themselves in the branches of the low bushes to the side of the track. The view from Joalah is directly across the Woggunba Valley to the Springbrook Plateau. Follow the track as it descends gradually for about 1km to the Araucaria and Mt Hobwee track junctions. The Border Track continues to the right and soon begins another gradual climb, towards Dragoon Bird Creek that leads into the Coomera River. You may see the distinctive Lamington spiny cray around this point, especially following rain. Another 100m and you reach the **Coomera Circuit** track leading off to the right. About 1km from this junction the Mt Hobwee Circuit heads off to the left and the Border Track continues uphill for another few hundred metres to Biby Lookout where you get good views of Mt Warning and the Tweed Valley. From this point, the Border Track continues to climb past the turn off to **Mt Merino** on the left, to Chakoonya Lookout where you get the only northern views from the Border Track. On a clear day, the view extends from the Gold Coast to the Glass House Mountains north of Brisbane. The Coomera River Valley is directly below and the Dave's Creek heath country can be identified just to the right of Tullawallal with the cliffs of Springbrook further around to the right. The track continues to climb for a while before levelling out and then starting to descend. Look for an old survey peg marked *'OR7 Bb7'*. This is the half way point. Just past here is the point where the old Mt Merino circuit joins the Border Track. You now descend for about 1km passing several *'borrow pits'* (excavations made by the original track workers to get top soil for the track) on the left of the track, to a saddle. From here, you begin to ascend, past Nyamulli Lookout and some storm damaged sections on the way to Wanungara Lookout. Continue uphill past several large moss-covered rocks, through thinning vegetation affording glimpses east towards the coast, before arriving at **Wanungara Lookout**.

This makes an ideal lunch spot. From here on a fine day, you can look over the mountains to the left towards Stradbroke Island, straight ahead past the Limpinwood Valley to Murwillumbah, to Mt Warning on the right and as far as Byron Bay on the far right. There is a large Queensland waratah on the edge of the cliff that flowers in summer. After lunch, follow The Border Track back towards Green Mountains. The forest canopy closes in on the track for several hundred metres before opening up again prior to Toolona Lookout. Ten minutes past Toolona Lookout you reach one of the most photographed stands of Antarctic beech in the Park, with giant exposed roots estimated to be around 5 000 years old. The track meanders through the forest for another 400m to Bithongabel Lookout. It was near this location that Bernard O'Reilly turned his horse loose and headed out on foot to search for the Stinson airliner that crashed in 1937.

Approximately one kilometre from the lookout there is a small sign, *'WATER 20m'*. Follow the track for another 200m, past the turn off to the **Albert River** circuit.

A few minutes past this junction, the track divides. The main Border Track is on the left and the **Pensioner Track** on the right. The Pensioner Track is 100m longer, but follows a slightly easier grade. It descends gradually for 2.5kms before again rejoining the main Border Track. A further 10 minutes walking takes you to the start of the **Toolona Creek** track and from here it is only 1.7kms to Green Mountains.

Last reviewed: 18 September 1997

MT MERINO
Distance: 22kms return, allow 8 hours. Moderate grade.

Mt Merino is approximately half way between Binna Burra and Green Mountains and can be visited on a day walk from either location. It can also be visited as a side trip when walking the **Border Track**. From Binna Burra, follow the Border Track notes for 10kms to the Mt Merino track junction.

The track turns sharply to the left and continues gradually uphill. About five minutes from the track junction, you reach the exposed roots of a giant Antarctic beech tree near Beereenbano Lookout. Continue uphill past beautiful moss-covered trees to another track junction. The track straight ahead leads uphill to a lookout and the main track turns sharply to the right. It is only about five minutes from here to the summit where you get good views of the Tweed Valley, Mt Warning and the Tweed Pinnacle and back around towards Mt Durrigan. Several Queensland waratahs grow around the ridge below the summit, making a show during the spring and summer months. After lunch, return to Binna Burra via the same route.

Last reviewed: 10 January 1998 - NPAQ outing. Leader: Elizabeth Arden.

TULLAWALLAL CIRCUIT
Distance: 5kms, allow 2 hours. Easy grade.

This short walk through the rainforest leads to the 942m summit of Tullawallal, the northernmost habitat of the Antarctic beech (*Nothofagus moorei*). It is also the closest stand of Antarctic beech trees to Binna Burra. The Antarctic beech is a relic from a period when Australia was much cooler, and some trees are up to 5 000 years old. The trees grow from suckers and many new branches ultimately become trunks. It is not uncommon for one gnarled, exposed root system to support four or five trunks.

Follow the **Border Track** notes, 1.9kms uphill to the Coomera Seat and turn right on the Tullawallal track. Climb the steps and walk about 40m to a track junction. Turn right and head uphill through cool temperate rainforest. The track curves around to the right near the summit and climbs several stone steps to a mass of large boulders. There are no views at the summit of Tullawallal, but the ancient beech trees are all around. This area provides some interesting photographic opportunities. Dappled light at sunrise illuminates the ghostly moss-covered trunks. After appreciating the tranquillity of Tullawallal, return to the track junction and turn right. The descent towards Binna Burra leads through cool and warm, subtropical rainforest. Many of the trees support large crows nest ferns, staghorns, elkhorns and orchids high in the canopy. Ignore the Rainforest Circuit junction leading to the right and continue straight ahead to the car park.

Last reviewed: 15 August 1997

DAVE'S CREEK CIRCUIT
Distance: 12kms, allow 4 hours. Moderate grade.

This circuit is the most botanically diverse walk in the Park. It passes through rainforest, eucalypt forest and open heathlands and pass panoramic lookouts. Wildflowers are superb in spring, but something is usually flowering at all times.
Walk 2.2kms along the **Border Track**, past the Coomera seat to the turn-off towards Dave's Creek, Upper Ballunjui Falls and Ship's Stern, and continue downhill to the left. (Use the Border Track notes to this point) You soon pass between two large trees whose buttress roots converge across the track from both sides. It is not uncommon to hear the melodious call of the lyrebird as you descend through the rainforest. The forest begins to thin out and you cross Nixon Creek, before reaching the next track junction. The Ship's Stern and Upper Ballunjui Falls tracks head off to the left. Turn right, to complete the circuit in an anticlockwise direction. The track now climbs uphill past tall tree ferns and New England black butt. As you near the top of the ridge, you pass the upturned roots of a massive tree that has fallen on the left of the track, then through a small section of rainforest, before descending through mallee scrub to open heathlands. The track swings along the edge of the escarpment and reaches a lookout with good views across the Woggunba Valley. A few minutes from the lookout, take the right hand track to Molongolee Cave. Ferns and lilies grow along the walls of the cave and rely on a constant trickle of water for their survival. A narrow, partially overgrown track leads from the cave down towards Molongolee Lookout. Caution is required on the rocky slab, especially if it is wet. The small area around this lookout was the only part of Daves Creek left untouched by fire in 1991.
Scramble straight uphill from the lookout and turn right on the track. You continue through heath country, cross Picnic Creek, and zigzag down hill before starting the climb towards Numinbah Lookout. As you leave the Lookout, you pass an area where much of the ground cover was destroyed by fire. Keep climbing through an avenue of gnarled paperbarks, past an old disused track about 1km from Numinbah Lookout, to a track leading left to Surprise Rock. Climb the stone steps to the top of Surprise Rock for good views of Mts Merino and Hobwee, the Springbrook Plateau, down the Numinbah Valley and across to the Gold Coast. Multi coloured heath covers the slopes below the rock. From the rock you may see wedge tailed eagles soaring on the wind currents. Return to the main track and continue along the side of the rock, past another track leading back towards the rock. After about 10 minutes you pass Neubani Rock, an outcrop of the Surprise Rock dyke, before reaching the Ship's Stern and Upper Ballunjui track junction on the right. A few metres from here you meet the track where you started the circuit. Cross Nixon Creek again and head towards the **Border Track**. When you reach the Border Track, it is 2.3kms back to Binna Burra.

Last reviewed: 1 August 1997

COOMERA CIRCUIT
Distance: 17.9kms, allow 6-8 hours. Moderate grade.

The Coomera Circuit has long been recognised as one of the prettiest walks in the
Binna Burra section of the Park. Following rain, the waterfalls are at their best and
the foliage along the river banks takes on a glossy sheen. However, the track does
cross the Coomera River six times and minor creeks four times, so the circuit
should not be attempted if the water is above knee height. If the rocks at the
crossings are wet and slippery, it is often safer to wade through the water.
Follow the **Border Track** notes, 1.9kms uphill to the Coomera Seat. The track
now divides. The Border Track veers left, the Coomera Circuit goes straight ahead
and the Tullawallal Track branches off to the right. Just past the Coomera Seat, the
track gradually descends through rainforest into an area dominated by tall
eucalypts. After a little more than 5kms, you reach the steps leading down to the
Coomera Lookout. Unfortunately, engineering reports have established doubts
about the safety of the Lookout platform and the structure was closed at the time of
writing. Views of the 64m Coomera Falls and the 150m Yarrabilgong Falls to its
right are obtained from further along the track. The track now winds along the
edge of the Gorge, crosses a small creek and starts a gradual ascent along the steep
edge of the Coomera Crevice. Several waterfalls drop into the river below and the
walls of the Crevice are covered with lilies and ferns. After a few minutes you
reach the first river crossing. Continue straight across and up the steps to the right,
about 70m to the second crossing. A further 70m takes you to the third crossing.
The track now zigzags uphill with the rocky river bed below to the left. After about
15 minutes, the base of Bahnamboola Falls is reached. A few hundred metres from
here a side track leads left to a point mid way up the falls. There is another track
leading left to the top of the falls, 50m further uphill. From the head of the falls,
the track crosses Barrajum Creek and zigzags uphill to a short side track to
Kagoonya Falls. The main track soon crosses Gwongarragong Creek, passes
Gwongarragong Falls, then continues on to the fourth river crossing. Continue
uphill and cross a wide rocky slab before reaching Moolgoolong Cascades. The
track winds uphill, passing Chigigunya Falls, a crossing at Bower Bird Creek and
another small waterfall off to the right before reaching a lily filled gully at Dragoon
Bird Creek. This is a favourite haunt of the Lamington spiny cray. The track soon
crosses the river for the fifth time and keeps heading uphill. A side track, 100m
from the river leads left down to the waters edge. The main track turns sharply
right and heads uphill past Goorawa Falls, the last waterfall on the circuit and
crosses the river for the last time. It is only a few minutes from this river crossing
to the Border Track. Turn left and follow the **Border Track** notes for the 7.6km
trip back to Binna Burra.

Last reviewed: 5 August 1997

LOWER BALLUNJUI FALLS
Distance: 11kms return, allow 4 hours. Easy grade.

Start this walk at the base of the grassy saddle, below the Natural History Associations' bunk house. After about 150m, you enter the National Park and soon reach a massive old tallow wood (*Eucalyptus microcorys*) with a gnarled, bulbous root system on the right of the track. This tree is known as *'big foot'* and the kids love to peer into the hole in the side of the tree. Ten minutes later there is a track junction. The left track goes to Bellbird Lookout. Turn right and continue downhill, past a steep drop on the left of the track before crossing Rifle Bird Creek. There are dozens of crows nest ferns growing along the edge of the track. Head downhill, crossing Chiminya Creek before reaching a side track to Koolanbilba Lookout for views of Egg Rock, Turtle Rock, the Kurraragin Valley and across to Ship's Stern. The track zigzags downhill, crossing Chiminya Creek twice more and passes some high cliffs on the right before reaching Yangahla (Picnic Rock) Lookout.
There are large caves in the cliff below Yangahla. Back on the track, walk 25m downhill from the lookout and locate a faint footpad leading steeply off to the left. This track leads around the base of Yangahla to the caves. Yellow lichen coats many of the rocks along the wall of the caves. Return via the same footpad to the graded track. As you continue to zigzag downhill, you cross a small rocky creek bed, pass between the two halves of Kong Gong Rock, and cross the creek again before reaching a track junction. The left branch is the Lower Bellbird Circuit. Take the right branch and continue downhill, passing between two large brush box before reaching a dense grove of piccabeen palms. Look for a large red cedar on the left of the track. The old sign gives you the height at *165 feet* (50.7m) and the girth of *22 feet* (6.7m). Continue alongside a wide rocky gully to the next track junction. (The Ship's Stern track swings left. It is 14.1kms back to Binna Burra via the Ship's Stern Circuit.) Take the right hand track, continuing 600m uphill, along the banks of Nixon Creek to the base of the 150m Ballunjui Falls. The falls are particularly impressive following heavy rain and make an ideal lunch stop. Return to Binna Burra via the same track. Alternatively, you can extend the walk and return via the Ship's Stern Circuit.

Last reviewed: 3 August 1997

SHIP'S STERN CIRCUIT
Distance: 19kms, allow 5-6 hours. Moderate grade.

Follow the directions for Lower Ballunjui Falls to the track junction, 4.8kms from Binna Burra. The track then descends through a grove of piccabeen palms, along the banks of Nixon Creek, crosses a small rocky creek bed and climbs high along the left bank of Nixon Creek. Large moss-covered boulders are strewn in this attractive section of the creek. The track crosses Chiminya Creek and swings right to cross Nixon Creek before heading gradually uphill, passing Hidden Valley, filled with more piccabeen palms and tall brush box. Continue climbing past a series of cliffs fenced with an avenue of palms. According to Aboriginal legend this area is known as *'skeleton caves'*. Note the loose rocks that have fallen from the cliff face. These are said to have been thrown by the spirits defending the caves.

At the next track junction it is well worth taking a 330m side trip to the top of Charraboomba Rock. You need to climb 85 steps to reach a track leading to the end of the rock. From the left, the view is to Ballunjui Falls, across to Mt Roberts and Binna Burra, the ridge leading to Beechmont, and right towards Egg Rock and the Kurraragin Valley. After returning to the track junction, it is only 100m to the rocky outcrop of Moonjooroora Lookout. The track soon levels out and follows the edge of the Ship's Stern escarpment before reaching another track junction, just past the half way point. Turn left and walk 100m to the end of Kooloobano Point. The views from this point are superb and it makes a great lunch spot.

After lunch, return to the track junction, turn left and head uphill. The track levels out as it reaches Milleribah Lookout, and then Nyoongai Lookout. From here the view is across to the Springbrook Plateau and right to Mt Warning. A few minutes from here, the track forks. The better views are on the right hand track. From the western lookouts, you can look down onto Charraboomba Rock. The trail to the top of the rock is clearly visible. Continue past where the two tracks join again. You now meander in and out of rainforest and eucalypt forest before reaching the Upper Ballunjui Falls Track. (The return trip is only 2.4kms, so if you are still feeling fit, it is worth visiting the head of the falls - this walk is described below.)

Back on the Ship's Stern track, climb uphill out of the rainforest, past a short side track to Ballunjui Cascades and along the bank of Nixon Creek before reaching Nagarigoon Falls. The gully along Nixon Creek is filled with tree ferns. Soon after the Falls, you reach a track leading to a camp site at Nagarigoon Hut. Originally built as a shelter for track workers during the 1950s, it was destroyed by fire several years ago. There is a toilet at the camp site. A few minutes from the here you reach the Dave's Creek Circuit. Turn right and walk for 15-20 minutes towards the Border Track.

As you walk uphill, you will notice the original graded track flagstones, in the middle of the current track. The track has been widened over successive years by people walking to the side of the track to avoid the mud, or to pass other walkers. To avoid damage to the tracks, please keep to the track system and don't take short cuts. When you reach the Border Track, it is only 2.3kms back to Binna Burra.

Last reviewed: 3 August 1997

UPPER BALLUNJUI FALLS
Distance: 12kms return, allow 4 hours. Easy grade.

This walk can be completed as a 2.4km side trip from the Ship's Stern Circuit. (Alternatively, follow the directions for the Dave's Creek Circuit to the start of the Upper Ballunjui Track.) From the Ship's Stern track, the trail leads downhill to the base of Ballunjui Cascades. After leaving the Cascades, it is worth taking a 300m detour on the side track, uphill to Guraigumai Rock, especially if you have not completed the Ship's Stern Circuit. The views from the Rock extend from Beechmont on the left, down the Kurraragin Valley to Egg Rock and right to Charraboomba Rock and the cliffs of Ship's Stern. Return 300m to the track and head downhill, past a side track to the head of Booboora Falls and continue to the track leading to the base of the Falls. These Falls are very attractive after rain and the view from the base is much better than from the top. As you descend, you reach a wide rocky slab where the track crosses Nixon Creek. Algae causes the orange stain on the rock. Be careful crossing the slippery slab and zigzag down hill, crossing Nixon Creek twice more before climbing down some steep steps to the head of the falls. The rock slab at the head of the falls is also very slippery when wet and extreme caution is required. After enjoying the views, return to Binna Burra via the same track.

Last reviewed: 3 August 1997

GWONGOOROOL POOL
Distance: 5.8kms return, allow 2 hours. Moderate grade.

This track starts just below the Information Centre car park and immediately descends. After a few minutes you pass a large moss-covered cleft in the rock, gouged out by water over a period of hundreds of years. You soon reach the first of around 180 steps, then continue on to the Illinbah Circuit track junction. Turn left and walk downhill past cliffs eroded from the same tuff layer as the caves along the Caves Circuit, and after about 20-30 minutes, you reach Barrabareen Falls. A wispy spray feeds mosses and ferns clinging to the side of the cliff. As you zigzag downhill, you pass a dense grove of piccabeen palms and some tall brush box before reaching the return Illinbah Circuit junction. After another 150m, note an old track leading off to the left beside a large brush box, opposite a sign pointing to the pool. (This is the start of the Coomera Gorge trail.) Continue straight ahead a few hundred metres to the Pool. This is an excellent place to cool off on a hot day, however, eels in the pool may frighten small children. Retrace your steps along the same track to the car park.

Last reviewed: 2 August 1997

ILLINBAH CIRCUIT
Distance: 17kms, allow 5-6 hours. Moderate grade.

The Illinbah Circuit provides an interesting look at the lower section of the Coomera River. There are 12 river crossings and after heavy rain it is impassable. Even at other times it is difficult to avoid wet feet. The river can change dramatically after floods and the track may be re-routed in places to avoid log-jams and eroded banks. Like the Coomera Circuit, if the water is above knee height, it is best to abandon the trip. The notes provided follow an anticlockwise route to avoid the 8km climb uphill at the end of the walk.

This track, like the Gwongoorool Pool track starts just below the Information Centre and immediately starts to descend. About 10 minutes from the start you reach a track junction. (The left track leads to Gwongoorool Pool. It is also the Illinbah return track.) The anticlockwise route leads past a small cliff where care is needed following rain. The track soon leaves the rainforest and crosses several small rocky gullies. Whip birds are common here and the melodious call of the lyrebird is often heard. There are several large hoop pines in this area and many pine saplings have sprouted along the sides of the track. After about 4.5kms, the track passes to the right of a piccabeen filled gully and crosses a single wooden plank. Contour around the side of the hill, cross Piccabeen Creek and climb uphill following a rocky gully below a track to the left. As the track levels out, dappled light reaching the forest floor allows ferns to grow around the base of the eucalypts. You can hear the Coomera River as you near the end of the 8km descent. Look for an old track marker on the left reading '*Ill 0.3M Bn 6M*'. You soon reach a track junction 8.2kms from the start. The Illinbah Circuit continues left and follows the old Cedar Road, 8.4kms to Binna Burra.

Prior to 1915 when Lamington was declared a national park, cedar getters from Canungra worked their way up the Coomera River harvesting huge red cedars. The logs were then carted off to the mills by bullock drays. The cedar still standing would have been much too small to fell, 90 years ago. The trees decaying on the side of the track are from natural tree falls. They have not been felled and left by the timber getters, as is often thought.

The track now passes through an area where lantana has taken over and reaches the first river crossing. Orange triangular markers have been attached to trees on both sides of the creek crossings and help to locate the track. The distinct call of bellbirds is in sharp contrast to the raucous screech of cockatoos as they fly through the tree tops. The track at the second crossing is diagonally to the right. After crossing the creek, pass through an old tree that has fallen across the track and a clump of piccabeen palms before reaching the third crossing. The fourth crossing is fairly deep, but a fallen log to the left gives access to a small island and a shallow stony crossing. The track is sometimes obscured at this point but is easily found by walking about 20m to the right. Turn left and walk about 100m to the fifth crossing. Scramble down a 2m mud bank and head diagonally off to the left. This is a good opportunity to get your feet wet. From here, continue past a clump of lantana, through dozens of piccabeens and tall grey gums, across a stony gully and then parallel to the gully before reaching a large pool to the right of the sixth crossing. At the seventh crossing, a tree has fallen across the creek and partially obscured the track markers. Walk downstream for 15-20m to a small grassy island and a shallow crossing. The track then passes the upturned roots of a large tree and a large grey gum. A tall stinging tree behind the gum hosts large staghorns high in the canopy. The track passes through the decaying trunk of another fallen tree and on the left is a tree with buttress roots over two metres tall. A few minutes from here, look for a large strangler fig with yellow lichen growing on its lower trunk, about 10m to the right of the track. The host tree has long been dead and you can hop inside the hollow trunk of the fig and look all the way up to its crown.

The track now crosses several gullies and winds through the forest about 1.5kms to the shallow and narrow eighth crossing. Continue on, through another old fallen tree to the ninth crossing. The haunting cry of the wompoo pigeons is often heard in this area.

Climb down a one metre mud bank and walk straight across the creek and swing right. The track now passes through the fallen trunk of a hollow fig tree. You can see where the host tree has totally rotted away, leaving the weakened hollow trunk. Ford the tenth crossing diagonally to the right and then swing left to regain the track. As you pass through the trunk of another large tree that has fallen, note the damage caused to the canopy as the vines entwined through the canopy pulled other trees down with them.

Follow the track over a small ridge before reaching the next crossing. Climb up a one metre mud bank and continue on to the next crossing. At this crossing there are short angular rocky columns beside a pool on the right. The track now crosses the exposed roots of trees, leads down a gully and runs parallel to the river before turning right, up and around a large boulder to the last crossing. This is an ideal spot to cool off on a hot day. After the final crossing, the track zigzags uphill for 400m to the track junction leading to Gwongoorool Pool. If you haven't been to the pool and you still have the energy, it is well worth the 400m detour each way. From the junction, the track winds 2.5kms uphill, past Barrabareen Falls and the 180 steps leading back to the car park.

Last reviewed: 16 August 1997

COOMERA GORGE
Distance: 15kms return, allow 10 hours. Hard grade.

This walk to the base of Coomera Falls is particularly difficult and should not be attempted by anyone who is not used to scrambling, rock hopping and scrub bashing. To reach the Falls, you follow the Coomera River up the gorge. Consequently, there are few navigational difficulties, but there are no tracks. However, the view from the base of the 64m Falls makes the long walk worthwhile. Follow the walk notes for Gwongoorool Pool, 150m past the return Illinbah Circuit track junction, where you leave the graded track. Continue along the remains of a disused track, to the left of a shallow gully.. When the track fades out, continue through the gully in a south-easterly direction, parallel to the river. After about 15 minutes you pass a massive old strangler fig that can be used as a landmark for the return journey. Contour high up on the bank to avoid the scunge down near the river. Infrequent use allows the growth of lawyer vine and other scunge, so you may need to alter your course several times to avoid the undergrowth. Garden gloves are extremely handy on this walk. You cross a dry rocky gully before reaching a steep mud bank leading down towards the Coomera River, about 40 minutes after leaving the Gwongoorool Pool track. Follow the River on the left bank for about five minutes, then cross to the other side. You soon see the sides of the Gorge, high on the left bank. From here, there is no *'best'* way to follow the Gorge. Successive dry years allow the growth of weed along the creek banks and would totally alter any given set of instructions. Similarly, good flooding rains would flush out the weed and make travel much easier. There are however, several obvious landmarks on the way to the base of the falls. Allowing 3.5 hours to reach the falls from the first river crossing, (about one hour from the start of the walk) the following landmarks will be passed at the approximate times given.

1 hour.   A large landslip on the left, opposite a wide rocky slab.

1.5 hours. A small waterfall on the left. This is a good spot for morning tea.

3 hours.   A narrow section of the gorge with basalt columns on the right hand side.

You arrive at a left hand bend in the river 10 minutes later, with a wispy waterfall dropping over the high cliffs on the right. Five minutes later you come to a 3m waterfall that needs to be bypassed by scrambling up a narrow ledge on the right. The base of the falls is finally reached about 15-20 minutes from this point, or about 3.5 hours after the first river crossing.

Stay a while and enjoy the view before starting the long trek back down the river.

Last reviewed: 2 August 1997 - NPAQ outing. Leaders: John deHorne, John Daly.

MAP REFERENCE
Sunmap - HILLVIEW 1:25 000
                BEECHMONT 1:25 000
                TYALGUM 1:25 000
                LAMINGTON 1:25 000
Hema -   LAMINGTON NATIONAL PARK by ADVENTURE MAPS.   This
             shows most of the walking tracks for Green Mountains and Binna Burra.
Track maps are available from the Information Centres at both locations.

FACILITIES
Lamington National Park can be enjoyed all year round. The waterfall circuits are
at their best following rainfalls in summer. Although the days can be very hot, it is
generally much cooler than lowland areas and many people visit Lamington to
escape the heat. Storms and torrential downpours can occur at any time, but the
storm season is usually between November and March. Spring is a good time for
wildflowers and winter days can be clear and crisp but the nights are cold. Some
tracks (eg. Dave's Creek, Ship's Stern, Illinbah, The Caves and Lower Bellbird)
may be closed during periods of very high fire danger.
Always carry your own water even though some creeks do have good supplies.
The QNPWS camp ground at Green Mountains and the privately run camp ground
at Binna Burra provide all facilities, including hot showers.
Binna Burra camp ground has cooking shelters, a washing up room and laundry
facilities.
Limited bush camping is permitted in restricted areas. No bush camping is allowed
anywhere in the Park between December and January, but seasonal conditions such
as extreme drought, fire or over use may extend these periods. Check with the
Ranger for current information. Bookings are essential.

RANGER CONTACT - (07) 5544 0634 - Green Mountain
                                   (07) 5533 3584 - Binna Burra

SPRINGBROOK NATIONAL PARK

HISTORY
Springbrook National Park consists of three areas totaling 2 954ha. Springbrook
Plateau; an area of scenic beauty and graded walking tracks, Mt Cougal; a
wilderness area, and Natural Bridge; a geological phenomena taking its name from
a bridge of rock, forming an arch where a waterfall on Cave Creek tumbles into the
cave below.
Warrie National Park on the Springbrook Plateau was gazetted in 1937. A short
extract in the Government Gazette stated, *"One thousand and sixty acres (429ha)
of scenic grandeur and tropical growth in the canyon were set aside for all time for
the benefit of Queenslander's and visitors from the south."*

Shortly after, construction of graded walking tracks began, using the natural surroundings wherever possible and cement when necessary. A complete circuit track penetrating deep into the Warrie Canyon was planned. Construction was temporarily halted during the war, but recommenced shortly after 1945, resulting in an impressive walking track system. During this time, road access to the area was for one-way traffic only. Timetables were published notifying motorists of times to go *'up'* and *'down'* Main Springbrook Mountain Road.

The Cougal's area was set aside in 1938 to protect the rainforested areas at the head of Tallebudgera and Currumbin Creeks. Local banana growers established a sawmill in the Cougal's Cascades region in 1943 to produce packing crate timber because most of the country's other timber supplies were being used for the war effort. The sawmill closed in 1955 following an unusually wet winter. Remnants of the old sawmill can be seen when you walk the track from Cougal's Cascades. The park was amalgamated with Springbrook in 1990.

According to Yagambeh Aboriginal legend, the twin peaks of Mt Cougal were called *Barrajanda* and *Ningeroongun* in memory of two hunting dogs belonging to a famed hunter. Legend has it that the dogs were buried beneath the peaks after they had been killed while hunting.

The Natural Bridge section of Springbrook National Park occupies over 200ha of the Numinbah Valley. The Kalibah Aborigines lived in the area for hundreds of years before timber getters arrived around 1893, and cleared large stands of trees. By 1920, dairy farms were expanding throughout the Numinbah Valley. Natural Bridge was declared a Recreation and Scenic Reserve in 1922 and upgraded to a National Park in 1959, before also being amalgamated with Springbrook.

Springbrook National Park was incorporated in the World Heritage Listing as part of the Central Eastern Rainforest Reserves of Australia in late 1994.

FEATURES

The Springbrook Plateau at the eastern end of the Scenic Rim, is a remnant of volcanic activity produced around 22 million years ago by the eruption of Mt Warning shield volcano. The Springbrook cliffs join those of Lamington as they curve into New South Wales forming the rim of the ancient volcano. With a geology similar to that of Lamington, the major rock formations are basalt and rhyolite. The area is the wettest place in Southern Queensland. Numerous creeks have eroded a series of spectacular waterfalls, deep gorges and sheer cliff-lines throughout the Park. Views obtained at the many lookouts around the rim are second to none and display spectacular panoramas to the Gold Coast in the east and Mt Warning to the south. Best of All Lookout, the highest in the area, was reconstructed in 1997 to provide safe, extensive views, close to the cliff face. Rainforest wallabies, or pademelons, are easily spotted along the roadside on the way to the Lookout.

Headwaters of many creeks and rivers flowing to the Gold Coast, including Tallebudgera and Currumbin Creeks and Nerang River, begin on the plateau.

Most of the Park is covered with dense subtropical rainforest with some open eucalypt forest. Under the canopy of the rainforest, huge epiphytes, ferns and vines thrive in the moist atmosphere. The existence of Antarctic beech forests more than 2 000 years old, is evidence of a previous cooler climate. Fine specimens of red cedar, Queensland waratah, flame, brush box, New England blackbutt, coachwood, rosewood and Sydney black wattle trees cover the regions. Less fertile soils support stands of Blue Mountains ash.

The Albert's lyrebird can sometimes be heard in the winter months. Brush turkeys, Rufous scrub birds, bower birds, Richmond Range lyrebirds and rosellas are joined in the forest by noisy pittas, eastern yellow robins and eastern whipbirds. The higher branches of the forest reverberate with the sounds of green catbirds, common koels and wompoo fruit-doves. Lorikeets feed on the flowering black bean trees and noisy yellow-tailed black cockatoos feed on banksias, casuarinas and wattle seeds. Other fruit-eating birds inhabit the Park during springtime. You may hear the boobook owl at night.

Koalas live on the drier northern ridges. Spotlighters may be lucky enough to sight the shy sugar glider and long-tailed greater glider, along with the grey brushtail possum and reddish ringtail possum. Harmless goannas, land mullets and carpet pythons may startle visitors on the tracks. Several species of frogs, eels (the adults breed in the ocean waters, then the young elvers return to the freshwaters to recommence the cycle), and crayfish inhabit the waterways.

Natural Bridge is renown for its colony of glow worms. At night their blue lights illuminate the roof of the cave as they attract insects into their sticky webs.

ACCESS - SPRINGBROOK PLATEAU

All the walking tracks in the Springbrook Plateau section are accessed from Mudgeeraba, south of Nerang.

0.0kms	Wallaby Hotel, Mudgeeraba. Turn into Railway Street, towards Springbrook.
18.6kms	Go straight ahead. Natural Bridge turn off is to the right.
23.8kms	The road to the left leads to Purlingbrook Falls.
26.2kms	The Information Centre and boardwalk are to the left.
26.7kms	The road to the right leads 4kms to Best of All Lookout.
27.5kms	The left hand road leads to Canyon Lookout.
29.5kms	Sign reading 'Bilbrough Lookout 3kms return', on the right.
29.6kms	Goomoolahra picnic area.

TWIN FALLS CIRCUIT

Distance: 4kms, allow 1.5 to 2 hours. Easy grade.

The Twin Falls Circuit is an interpretive walk with signs describing various features of the rainforest. Start from the Canyon car park, 200m from the **27.5kms** turn off. Take in the views from the Lookout before turning right to start the walk in an anticlockwise direction. The track to Twin Falls is heavily used and partly paved to prevent erosion. In the first 500m you pass another two lookouts (views of Twin

Falls can be had from the second lookout), and a track leading to Tallanbana picnic area. Head downhill and over the creek at the top of Twin Falls. About 800m from the start, the track zigzags down a concrete path to a junction. Ignore the sign *'Twin Falls Pool 300m'* to the left and turn right to pass through a cleft in a rock. Pass beside a cliff-line and down some steps for about 50m before reaching another sign posted track junction. Follow the sign left towards Twin Falls. (The track right is for the Warrie Circuit and Pinnacle - see next walk.)

Zigzag downhill for a couple of minutes, passing a track on the left that leads back up to the earlier sign *'Twin Falls Pool 300m'*. Just past here is another sign giving you the option of going to Twin Falls, via the Cave or Cascades. If you take the latter option you may still visit the Cave, by crossing the concrete bridge at the Pool and turning left behind the Waterfall towards the Cave.

From the base of Twin Falls, head right towards Blackfellow Falls, a further 1km. Pass beside impressive cliffs covered in mosses and lichens. Take the time to rest on a seat below the overhanging cliff and enjoy the sounds, sights and smells of the forest. A little further on there is an unmarked track junction. The left track ends at another cave, after a short distance. Continue on the right track to Blackfellow Falls. Once again, pass behind the Waterfall and appreciate views of the Gold Coast from behind a curtain of water.

Climb the final 1km through open forest to the car park. From this part of the track you get good views of the rainforested ridge leading to the rocky outcrop of the Pinnacle, and the deep valley traversed by the Warrie Circuit.

Last reviewed: 3 June 1997

WARRIE CIRCUIT AND THE PINNACLE
Distance: 17kms, allow 5-6 hours, excluding the Pinnacle. Moderate grade.
20kms, allow 6.5-8 hours, including the Pinnacle. Moderate grade.

Follow the directions for Twin Falls Circuit to the sign reading *'Warrie Circuit 16k'*. Turn right at this junction. Walk for about 15 minutes towards Rainbow Falls. Mist from the Falls provides a cool change on a hot day as the track leads behind the Waterfall past a large clump of spear lilies. Three kilometres from Canyon Lookout you reach Goomoolahra Falls before heading further downhill past a small unnamed waterfall. The track opens out for about five minutes before rejoining rainforest. After a further five minutes, look for a large brush box on the left of the track with a hollow base. The large strangler fig to the right has germinated high in the canopy of the brush box and will eventually strangle the host tree. Follow the track along the top of the ridge-line and at a point where the track turns sharply back to the left, look for a stand of brush box trees and a well worn footpad that continues along the ridge-line towards the Pinnacle.

The optional ungraded track to the Pinnacle will add an additional 1.5 to 2 hours return (approximately 3kms) to the total walk distance. From the graded track, follow the footpad downhill and along the ridge for five minutes. Then climb gradually for about 10 minutes, crossing a large tree that has fallen across the track.

Ensure you stick to the top of the ridge passing through open eucalypt forest with lots of brush box and dense fern. You need to be aware of your surroundings as you reach an open cleared section of the track. The trail veers to the right. (A false trail leading downhill to the left is not obvious on ascent but may cause some confusion on descent.) You soon reach a knoll covered in low-lying woody tea tree shrubs. Make your way through the trees and you get your first clear view of your destination, the Pinnacle. Descend into a little gully and head up the left side of a rocky outcrop. Scramble up the precipitous (don't take kids) track to the top of the Pinnacle where you will be rewarded with 360° views of the surrounding countryside. Look back towards Canyon Lookout and across to the Gold Coast and south to the twin peaks of Mt Cougal.

Return via the same route to the graded track, taking care not to follow the false trail mentioned above. (A wrong turn here will lead you steeply down into a gully.) From the start of the Pinnacle trail, the Warrie Circuit leads downhill past another stand of giant brush box close to the track. Six kilometres from the start you cross a creek at Ngarri-dhum Falls. You have passed through open eucalypt forest with more brush box standing like sentinels along the track. Another 50m and you reach a track to Kadjagooma Falls. This track has been closed for some time and should be ignored unless it has been reopened.

The main track winds downhill, crosses a creek and follows the side of the creek bank before reaching another creek crossing. This crossing requires extreme caution following rain. A short distance from the crossing you arrive at a junction, 11kms from the start. A short track leads down to some rocky slabs at the Meeting of the Waters where Little Nerang Creek meets Mundora Creek. This makes an ideal lunch spot.

From the Meeting of the Waters, the track climbs steadily uphill for five minutes to Gooroolba Falls. Continue uphill through the rainforest for about one hour to a short side track leading to Poonyahra Falls. One kilometre from the car park you meet the Twin Falls Circuit track junction. Follow the track behind Blackfellow Falls to return to the car park.

Last reviewed: 15 February 1998 - NPAQ outing. Leader: John Daly.

PURLINGBROOK FALLS CIRCUIT AND WARINGA POOL
Distance: 6kms, allow 2-3 hours. Easy grade.

Start from the Gwongorella picnic area, 300m from the **23.8kms** turn off mentioned in the access notes. Walk down the paved track to a junction. You will return via the track on the right, so make your way left through open eucalypt forest to a lookout with good views of Purlingbrook Falls. Here the paved track ends. The track now leads around the top of the escarpment, crossing a wooden bridge over a small rocky creek at the head of Tanninaba Falls. Descend into the valley via a series of concrete steps and notice the vegetation changing to thick rainforest. Twenty minutes from the creek and wooden bridge, you arrive at the base of Tanninaba Falls. Pass the cliffs, heading downhill to a track junction near the foot

of spectacular Purlingbrook Falls that plunge more than 100m into the valley.
Turn left to reach Waringa Pool, passing an attractive stand of piccabeen palms
along the way. Many people cool off in Waringa Pool during summer. The view
up the creek is impressive and a short rock hop will lead to the base of
Purlingbrook Falls. After retracing your steps back to the Purlingbrook Falls track
junction, you pass behind the Waterfall.   The cliffs around the Waterfall are
covered in spear lilies. Their pink flowers make a colourful display when in bloom.
The two kilometres back to the car park is all uphill, leaving the rainforest and
entering a section of forest previously damaged by fire. Healthy regrowth borders
the track. Upon reaching Purling Brook, take the short detour to the Lookout.
Enjoy the views over the valley and the track behind the waterfall that you have just
traversed, before heading back to the car park.

Last reviewed: 3 June 1997

BILBROUGH LOOKOUT
Distance: 3kms return, allow 2 hours. Moderate grade.

Walk 100m back along the road from the Goomoolahra car park, across Mundora
Creek. Locate the sign showing the way to Bilbrough Lookout. Pass the paling
fence of a residential property on your right and follow the path uphill. You will
soon come to a small creek crossing before entering rainforest. The track becomes
quite steep as you climb the rocky stairway, and is slippery after rain. As you near
the Lookout the terrain opens up onto a grassy slope before reaching a trig point at
the summit. Regrowth has obscured some of the views, but you can see across the
valley towards Byron Bay. Return via the same track.

Last reviewed: 3 June 1997

BEST OF ALL LOOKOUT
Distance: 600m return, allow 30 minutes. Easy grade.

While hardly qualifying as a *'bush walk'*, the short stroll to the highest lookout on
Springbrook Plateau does pass through some very attractive rainforest. A good
sample of Antarctic beech trees is passed along the way. If you don't like to
venture too far from the car park, this may be the only chance you get to view these
magnificent old trees. Pause at the viewing platform and imagine the scene 22
million years ago as Mt Warning erupted, creating the lava flow responsible for the
whole Scenic Rim.

Last reviewed: 3 June 1997

MAP REFERENCE
Sunmap - SPRINGBROOK 1:25 000
Various maps available from the Information Centre.

FACILITIES

There are well maintained facilities at Gwongorella, Tallanbana and Goomoolahra picnic areas. All sites have shelter sheds and barbecue areas with firewood supplied. Toilets with wheelchair access are located at Gwongorella and Goomoolahra. Camping is permitted at Gwongorella. Private accommodation, meals, some supplies and petrol are available on the Plateau.

Visit the Park at any time of the year. Nights may even be cool during summer. The waterfalls are at their best following summer rains.

RANGER CONTACT - (07) 5533 5147

ACCESS - MT COUGAL

Access Mt Cougal section of the Park from the Pacific Highway, south of Nerang.

0.0kms	Turn right at the Currumbin turn off, into Stewart Road, sign posted *Mt Cougal National Park 19kms*. (It may take years for the signs to be updated.)
1.0kms	Turn left at Currumbin Creek Road. A sign post points to *Mt Cougal National Park 18kms.*
6.1kms	Ignore road to right. Go straight ahead. Sign post shows *Mt Cougal National Park 13kms.*
8.6kms	Turn left at Tomewin Road. (Continue straight ahead 10.2kms to reach Cougal's Cascades.)
17.6kms	Tomewin border gate.
18.8kms	Turn right into the narrow, gravel Garden of Eden Road.
21.2kms	Park near the fence. Leave driveways clear.

THE COUGAL'S

Distance: East Peak only - 8.5kms return, allow 4 hours. Moderate grade.
Including West Peak - 10kms return, allow 5.5 hours. Hard grade.

Climb over the gate and head immediately left uphill, alongside the border fence. Local residents have erected a *'Mt. Cougal walking track'* sign, just inside the fence. The track leads steeply uphill for about 10-15 minutes before reaching a gate. There is a section of sugar cane growing on private property to the left and severe lantana infestation on the right. As you continue uphill, you get good views across to Mt Warning, down the Tweed Valley and east to the coast. A little further on, as the track veers left and down along the border fence, the long ridge-line leading to the twin peaks of Mt Cougal comes into view. To the right you can see the rocky finger of Boyd's Butte with the sheer cliffs of Mt Tallabudgera further to the right.

About 30 minutes from the start the track descends steeply, before heading uphill again, reaching a large tree at a cleared section of the track. The tree has a surveyor's blaze on the trunk. The Government arrow, the letter *'E'* and the number *'8'* are still clearly visible. This section of the Queensland-New South

Wales border was originally surveyed by F E Roberts in 1864. There are a few sections where the track leaves the fence-line to skirt around fallen trees. About one hour from the start, near some obvious storm damage, the trail leads very steeply uphill and the fence stops at the base of a small cliff.

Skirt right around the cliff-line, over the gnarled exposed roots of several old trees. After a few minutes, look for a lesser track heading straight uphill to a cave. The main track continues to the right. The entrance to the cave is hidden from view but is easily located. It is possible to walk into the cave with a torch, climb through a very narrow section at ground level, and look through a hole on the south face of the Mountain. Forget the cave if you suffer from claustrophobia or a wide girth.

From the cave, follow the cliff-line a short distance to the right to meet the main track, then scramble up a steep rocky section through a clump of spear lilies. There are plenty of exposed roots for hand and foot holds. You soon reach a track junction at the top of the ridge. Remember this spot for your descent.

(Experienced walkers with good navigational skills can use the track to the right, to scrub bash their way across to Boyd's Butte. There is a rough track leading past Boyd's Butte, to a ridge going down to the old sawmill at Cougal's Cascades.)

Turn left and walk through some large grass trees a short distance to the summit of East Peak. From here, there are good views of Mt Warning and the Tweed Valley, Springbrook Plateau and West Peak of Mt Cougal.

(The optional climb to West Peak is graded 'Hard' and will add another 1-1.5 hours return to the time allowed for this walk. Do not attempt it unless you are a confident, experienced scrambler.)

To climb West Peak, locate an obvious track from East Peak summit, heading steeply downhill through the spear lilies. Descend to the right of a 3m rocky slab and then to the left around a large tree before reaching a saddle. You soon reach a narrow ridge covered in grass trees. Locate a track off to the right. The track straight ahead ends at a steep bluff. As you start to climb, look for a track heading steeply back uphill to the left. Make sure you remember this point for the descent. This track leads up and then right to the Peak. There is a small clearing at the top. You need to push your way through clumps of spear lilies and grass trees to reach the summit. Extreme caution is required. There are many small tracks at the top of the Peak, obviously made by people looking for that *'better view'* and they can cause confusion on descent.

Return to East Peak, and then back down the border fence to your vehicle.

Last reviewed: 7 June 1997

COUGAL'S CASCADES
Distance: 1.6kms return, allow 30 minutes. Easy grade.

The sealed track from the car park leads uphill gradually along the banks of Currumbin Creek. After 250m, you reach a viewing platform at Cougal's Cascades. The southern bank is overgrown with lantana, but on the opposite side of the creek, there is an attractive stand of piccabeen palms amongst the rainforest.

It is only 150m up the track to Mountain Pool and another viewing platform. From here, walk a further 400m to the site of the old sawmill. There are several small picnic spots along the creek banks.

Just past the sawmill, a track leads uphill. After 25m, another track leads down to where a small creek joins Currumbin Creek. (The rough track to Boyd's Butte -see the Cougal's walk - is on the left, about 30m up this small creek. The walk to Boyd's Butte is steep and should only be attempted by walkers with good navigational skills.)

Last reviewed: 7 June 1997

MAP REFERENCE
Sunmap - SPRINGBROOK 1:25 000
             MURWILLUMBAH 9541-11-N
Walking track maps are included in the Visitor Information pamphlet prepared by QNPWS.

FACILITIES
There are no facilities available at Mt Cougal. Visitors should be self sufficient and carry ample water.
A picnic area with tables and toilets is situated at the Cascades parking area. The Mountain Pool is an ideal swimming spot on hot days. Wheelchairs are catered for along the bitumen track that leads to the Cascades.

RANGER CONTACT - (07) 5576 0271

ACCESS - NATURAL BRIDGE
Natural Bridge can be accessed via Beechmont Road, 4kms west of Nerang.

0.0kms	Sign along Beechmont Road shows *Natural Bridge 35kms.*
2.9kms	Be sure to continue straight ahead.
32.9kms	Turn left into the Natural Bridge section of Springbrook National Park.
33.3kms	Leave your vehicle in the car park.

NATURAL BRIDGE
Distance: 1km, allow 30 minutes. Easy grade.

This short paved track starts from the end of the bitumen road, just past the tourist information stand. The track zigzags down some steps towards the banks of Cave Creek. Follow the track across a concrete footbridge, turn right on the far side of the creek and walk uphill. Within a few minutes you reach a side track leading down to a pool. The track leads past the pool and descends to a wooden boardwalk at the cave entrance. The cave is big enough for many people to enter under the near perfect arch. It comes alive with thousands of glow worms at night. Smoking in this area can kill the sensitive glow worms, so please refrain. Torchlight, candles and insect repellent also harms these delicate creatures. Keep in mind future generations of people who will also wonder at the little glow worms.

The walking track leaves the cave and heads up to a viewing platform at the top of the cave. From here, it crosses the creek again and leads back to the road past an avenue of hoop pines and the large buttress roots of a yellow carabeen. As you make your way back around the track, look for two old strangler figs beside the track that have totally destroyed their host plant, leaving a hollow pretzel-like trunk supporting the canopy above.

Swimming in the pool is discouraged and diving into shallow creeks has caused serious injury, and even death. Please restrain small children around the water's edge. Jumping through the cave roof is illegal and the Ranger's do issue $180 on-the-spot fines to people who disobey this regulation.

Last reviewed: 26 August 1997

MAP REFERENCE
Sunmap - SPRINGBROOK 1:25 000

FACILITIES
The picnic grounds at Natural Bridge have electric coin operated barbecues, toilets and water. There is no camping in the Park but private accommodation is available nearby.

RANGER CONTACT - (07) 5533 5147

TAMBORINE NATIONAL PARK

HISTORY
The Wangeriburra Aboriginal tribe once hunted in the eucalypt forests and gathered yams and other edible plants from the rainforested areas of the Mountain. Many stone axes and flints have been discovered in sections of the Park.

When European settlers arrived, much of the land was cleared for farming. In 1896 Robert Collins was elected a Member of Parliament and began a campaign for the creation of a national park in the McPherson Ranges. Many years before, he had visited the USA at a time when the Americans were creating the world's first national parks. Although he was impressed with the concept, very few people felt the need to preserve parcels of land because Australia had so much undeveloped land. His perseverance finally paid off when in 1908, Queensland's first national park was proclaimed at Witches Falls on Mt Tamborine. Forestry officials at the time claimed the land was "*...unfit for any other purpose*".

It wasn't until 1925 and 1927 that Palm Grove National Park and Joalah National Park were declared as Queensland's 10th and 11th national parks.

Today, Tamborine National Park is made up of what used to be eight small national parks and two environmental parks, with a total area of around 1 160ha. Heavy residential development and cleared farmland has isolated many of these smaller parcels of land but the Parks provide excellent views, great family picnic spots and an ideal opportunity for many people to experience their first *'bush walk'*.

FEATURES

Tamborine Mountain was formed as a result of the eruption of Mt Warning, 22 million years ago. This massive shield volcano was responsible for the creation of the Tweed Valley caldera and the surrounding arc of ranges, of which Mt Tamborine is a part. Over millions of years, erosion has created a series of plummeting waterfalls, sheer cliff-lines, broad valleys and rocky gorges. From the western escarpment, the prominent features of Mt Barney, Main Range and Lamington National Parks dominate the skyline.

The different sections of Tamborine protect remnants of the eucalypt and subtropical rainforest that once covered most of the area. More than 300 tree species have been identified in the Park. The Palm Grove section contains a magnificent stand of piccabeen palms as well as yellow carabeen trees with large buttress root systems. The Macrozamia Grove section at the southern end, preserves a grove of ancient cycad plants. The species probably dates back more than 300 million years. Other sections of the Park contain massive strangler figs, dry vine scrub, orchids, creepers, ferns and giant eucalypts.

Almost 200 species of birds live in the Park, from the common brush-turkey that incubates its eggs in great mounds of dirt, to the rare Albert's lyrebird. The lyrebird is often heard at dawn and dusk but is rarely seen.

Koalas live in the eucalypts of Tamborine Mountain and platypus can be seen around the creeks at dawn and dusk. Nocturnal echidnas also live in the Park. Shiny black land mullets, the largest skinks in the world, can regularly be seen along the walking tracks and more than 20 species of snakes have been identified.

ACCESS

Tamborine Mountain can be reached from Brisbane via Beenleigh and Tamborine, or from Oxenford on the Pacific Highway. The following road directions to the various sections of the Park start from the Information Centre at Doughty Park.

ACCESS - WITCHES FALLS

0.0kms   Drive west from Doughty Park on Main Western Road.
1.4kms   Shelter shed at Witches Falls.

WITCHES FALLS CIRCUIT

Distance: 3.4kms, allow 1 hour. Easy grade.

Walk left from the shelter shed and follow the track as it zigzags down the side of the Mountain through open, exposed grassy slopes and eucalypt forest. After about 10 minutes you reach a rocky gully, a large stand of piccabeen palms and moss-covered boulders. Notice the lack of ground cover on the forest floor due to the dense canopy overhead. Walk beneath a massive tree that has fallen and is now supported by a large fig on the opposite side of the track. The forest floor is littered with palm fronds that continue to fall. Pass two seasonal lagoons fed by a femoral, or seasonal creek. It the wet season, these perched lagoons overflow and the track could be covered with 15-30cm of water. Continue past a large strangler fig whose buttress roots encroach on the track, and a stand of macrozamia palms before reaching a track junction. Walk 200m to Witches Falls viewing platform.

The Falls are the result of a small creek dropping over the edge of a precipitous shelf that runs along the side of the Mountain, about 100m below the plateau. These falls make an impressive display following rain, but often stop flowing totally during dry periods.

Return to the junction and follow the track left through a dense palm forest before it zigzags to the top of the escarpment. The track leads along the edge of the Park boundary, behind the cemetery and back to the starting point.

Last reviewed: 17 March 1997

ACCESS - PALM GROVE
0.0kms	Drive north from Doughty Park on Geissmann Drive.
0.5kms	Turn right into Curtis Road past Tamborine Mountain State School.
1.3kms	Curtis Road car park.

PALM GROVE AND JENYN'S FALLS CIRCUIT
Distance: 5.4kms, allow 2 hours. Easy grade.

The Palm Grove Circuit is an excellent introduction to a lush palm forest. The track zigzags slowly down through a large grove of piccabeen palms before reaching a junction at a giant leaning fig tree, 10 minutes from the start. The left track leads to Palm Grove Avenue picnic area. Turn right and walk for a further five minutes to another track junction. Take the left track past two massive yellow carabeen trees with large buttress roots. Continue walking in a clockwise direction through subtropical rainforest, ignoring the Palm Grove Circuit track on the right.

About 30 minutes from the start you reach the track leading to a seat at Burrawang Lookout. From the Lookout you get superb uninterrupted views to the Gold Coast. Return to the main track.

A further 10 minutes walking takes you to a short sign posted track leading down to Jenyn's Falls. The rocks around the top of the Falls would be particularly dangerous after rain. From the Falls, walk back to the track junction and continue walking in a clockwise direction through open forest with large grey gums, tallow woods and ironbarks. Walk past the Palm Grove Circuit track on the right and through more tall piccabeens back to your starting point

Last reviewed: 17 March 1997

NB. The Rangers have placed additional signs along the track in October 1997, making this walk much easier to follow.

ACCESS - JOALAH

0.0kms	Drive east from Doughty Park on Geissmann Drive.
0.9kms	Turn right into Eagle Heights Road.
1.3kms	Turn left into Dapsang Street. Follow signs to parking area.

CURTIS FALLS TRACK AND JOALAH CIRCUIT

Distance: Curtis Falls: 1.5kms return, allow 45minutes. Easy grade.
Curtis Falls/Joalah Circuit: 3.3kms return, allow 1.5 hours. Easy grade.

Purist bushwalkers may argue this easy stroll should not be included in a list of bushwalks. The Park is surrounded by heavily used roads and is a long way from providing a wilderness experience. However, the area gives hundreds of visitors their first example of subtropical rainforest and closed eucalypt forest. Hopefully, the experience will encourage many visitors to pursue walking for enjoyment and become interested and concerned about preservation of our national parks.
The walk starts at the car park and after a 10 minute stroll past some giant gums and a large strangler fig you reach a lookout platform. From here you look down to the forest floor through a grove of piccabeens striving for light through the canopy. This canopy protects the forest floor from the sun's rays and provides a moist environment for numerous ferns and vines. Continue on the track until you reach a junction. Turn left and walk towards Curtis Falls. The original circuit track was closed by a rock fall and will not be reopened, so retrace your steps to the car park.
Alternatively, extend this walk to include Joalah Circuit by turning right at the track junction and following the Creek's palm lined banks down to a small pool. Excellent examples of epiphytes growing on tree trunks and in the canopy make this a delightful nature walk. Staghorns, elkhorns, birdsnest ferns, hairsfoot and muletail ferns and many orchids can be found along the track. A small footbridge leads across Cedar Creek and the track follows its northern bank to the main track, crossing the Creek again before returning to the car park. The track on the northern bank was also closed by a rock fall, but extensive repair work to reopen this loop circuit was completed by QNPWS staff around September 1997.

Last reviewed: 17 March 1997

MAP REFERENCE

Sunmap - TAMBORINE 1:50 000
Walking maps are available from the Tamborine Mountain Information Centre.

FACILITIES

There are no camping facilities in any part of Tamborine National Park. Picnic facilities with shelter sheds, barbecues, water and toilets are available at most sections of the Park. Electric barbecues have been provided at Witches Falls. Any time of the year is suitable to visit Tamborine National Park. In summer you can escape the heat under the rainforest canopy. It is usually about 10°C cooler than the township. Swimming at Cedar Creek Falls is also a great way to cool off, but to prevent erosion, it is actively discouraged in other areas of the Park.

RANGER CONTACT - (07) 5545 1171

SUNSHINE COAST

MT COOLUM NATIONAL PARK

HISTORY
Mt Coolum, a prominent Sunshine Coast landmark between Maroochydore and Noosa, was gazetted as a national park in 1990. This followed a conservation battle lasting approximately 10 years, with residents, environmentalists, scientists and politicians all calling for the area's protection. The Park contains an area of 69ha and is part of an important green belt of natural coastal environments along the Sunshine Coast.
There is evidence of early Aboriginal habitation around the Park and almost every Aboriginal legend of the area involves Mt Coolum in some way.

FEATURES
Mt Coolum belongs to the same landform category as the prominent peaks of the Glasshouse Mountains and has similar columnar structures on its cliffs. It is 208m high and around 25-26 million years old.
The Mountain has major botanical significance with more than 700 plant species recorded. This includes 590 flowering plants, 49 ferns and more than 100 species of lesser plants such as liverworts, mosses and lichens. More than 50% of the vascular plant species recorded in the Sunshine Coast area are found within this small park. Thirty four percent of the Park is made up of heathland communities found only on one other peak in the area. Until recently, it was thought that several species were unique to Mt Coolum, however, all except the *Allocasuarina thallasoscopica* have now been recorded in other locations.
Several factors have contributed to the evolution of the Mountain's flora, including topography, proximity to coastal salt spray and wind shearing.
The most significant birds found on the Mountain are a resident pair of vulnerable Peregrine falcons.

ACCESS
Take the Bli Bli turn-off from the Bruce Highway and follow the David Low Way to Coolum township.

0.0kms	Turn left at Tanah Street West.
0.3kms	Car park at Mt Coolum National Park.

MT COOLUM
Distance: 2.5kms return, allow 2 hours. Moderate grade.

This track starts heading uphill almost immediately through sandy terrain with long grasses and bracken ferns growing amongst the paperbark trees. After about 10 minutes climbing you reach a *National Park* sign near the edge of an old quarry. Exposed vertical cliffs along the side of this track present a potential danger at this point and walkers should keep to the track. From here, the terrain changes. The track is rocky and steep and there are more grass trees amongst the eucalypts and an absence of paperbarks. You soon reach a section where the track consists of steep, rocky steps. Continue climbing to a cliff-face made up of hexagonal columnar shapes. Look across to the left and you can see the south-east face of the Mountain. Half way up the cliff-face there is a ledge where the hexagonal columns are clearly visible. As you continue towards the summit, these rocky columns make a natural stairway to an exposed outcrop. The track continues steeply uphill and the vegetation changes again to low windswept heaths and grasses. As you reach the summit the vegetation is taller and more profuse.

From the summit, 360° views extend along the coastline from Double Island Point to Moreton Island, and around to the cane fields and wetland areas of the Maroochy River Valley. After enjoying the views and the wildflowers follow the same track back to your starting point.

Last reviewed: 6 July 1997

MAP REFERENCE
UBD Brisbane Street Directory - Sunshine Coast, Map 49

FACILITIES
There are no facilities in this park. Camping is not permitted. Carry your own water. Although the springtime displays of wildflowers are spectacular, you can almost be guaranteed some species will be in bloom any time you visit.

RANGER CONTACT - (07) 5447 3243

MOOLOOLAH RIVER NATIONAL PARK

HISTORY
There are two chains of thought on the derivation of the word *'Mooloolah'*. The most commonly accepted is that it comes from the Aboriginal word *'mullu'*, meaning red bellied black snake. Another early source states that Mooloolah means schnapper. There have been problems with the spelling of Mooloolah over the years. A map published in 1842 spelt the word as *'Moboolah'*. Whatever meaning or spelling you like to adopt, there is no getting away from the scenic beauty of the Mooloolah River area.

Aboriginal middens containing stone implements have been found along the River. Discussions following the discovery of a *'scarred tree'* in the north-west section of the Park, indicated the bark from the tree was used by Aborigines to build canoes.

Gazetted in April 1960, Mooloolah River National Park protects a diversity of wallum vegetation types and the habitat of the rare ground parrot. Six hundred and seventy six hectares in size and one of the few mainland coastal parks in Southern

Queensland, the area is less than 5km upstream from the mouth of the River and the seaside town of Mooloolaba.

FEATURES
Vegetation types found in the area are disappearing from the coastal areas of South Queensland. The river system and lakes host several mangrove swamps. Low-lying sand flats inland from melaleuca swamps support wallum banksias, heath shrubs and low scrub. Clay and sandstone ridges to the north are covered with eucalypt forests featuring scribbly gum, bloodwood and blackbutt.

The ground parrot likes to nest in the melaleuca swamps along the eastern bank of the Mooloolah River. Burning (arson is a major problem in the Park), clearing and drainage has altered the parrot's specialised habitat and there have been no sightings of this rare bird in the Park for some time.

Many other species of birds come to the Park. The azure kingfisher has been sighted and predatory raptors build nests in the area.

ACCESS - WESTERN AND SOUTHERN END
The western and southern sections of the Park are reached by exiting the Bruce Highway just north of the Ettamogah Pub. Take the Sunshine Motorway exit towards Mooloolaba.

0.0kms	Drive under the Bruce Highway.
0.7kms	Take the Buderim exit.
1.0kms	Turn right into Sippy Downs Drive (Sippy means birds) towards the university. (Sippy Downs Drive was previously known as Mountain Creek Road.)
1.4kms	Pass through the roundabout.
3.7kms	Turn right into Claymore Road. The gravel road follows the boundary of the Park.
5.8kms	*National Park Boundary* sign indicating a walking track, on the left.
6.3kms	Locked gate and start of Robur Fire Management Trail on the left.

ROBUR FIRE MANAGEMENT TRAIL
Distance: 4.5kms return, allow 2 hours. Easy grade.

From the Park boundary, follow the old road east along the fence-line. After about 10 minutes the track turns right and then left again, following the Park boundary. After a further 10 minutes, at a point where two steel gate posts have been erected in the fence, the track swings right to skirt around a swamp. Follow the track as it curves around in a semi-circle through a stand of very tall melaleucas with some large cabbage palms competing to reach the light. The track rejoins the fence-line and continues east towards the River. The melaleucas inside the Park still show signs of an earlier fire, while the trees outside the Park do not appear to be damaged at all. The firebreak has obviously done its job. You soon reach another swampy section that is passed by skirting around on the (slightly) higher ground to the left. Rejoin the fence-line and continue for another 10 minutes before reaching another swamp. Skirt around to the left again. The ground on the right is lower and much wetter. One more swampy area is reached just before the banks of the Mooloolah River. Pass this section on the right, and continue to the River bank. Cross the Park boundary fence and follow the River bank downstream for a few hundred metres to a large clump of mangroves. You soon reach an impassable swampy gully, extending in a westerly direction from a bend in the River. Spend as long as you like admiring the bird life along the River bank before retracing your steps to the starting point.

Last reviewed: 4 July 1997

THE OLD NORTHERN ROAD
Distance: 2kms return, allow 1hour. Easy grade

From the start of the Robur Fire Management Trail, head north on an old road, about 15m inside the Park boundary. You soon reach the remains of another old road leading off to the right. Follow this road and after walking for about five minutes, you leave the forest and walk through low heath and swamp grasses. Look for a 'Y' junction with another track leading off to the right, just before you re-enter the forest. The right branch of this road appears to curve around the swamp but soon reaches a boggy impassable section. The road you can see on the other side of this swamp is that road described below in the **Wallum Heath Walk.**
When walking back to the 'Y' junction, the right branch leads towards the swampy area and veers left. This track continues in a westerly direction before turning south, where your progress may be blocked by another swamp. If the water level is low, continue through the swampy area to reach Claymore Road, passing through attractive, very tall open forest / woodland dominated by *Eucalyptus signata*. Several species of birds congregate around this area. Otherwise return to your vehicle via your original route.
(The last section of this walk can be accessed from Claymore Road at the 5.8km point described in the access notes. A *National Park* sign indicates the start of the short 500m walk to the swamp.)

Last reviewed. 4 July 1997

ACCESS - NORTHERN END
Access the northern end of the Park by continuing along the Sunshine Motorway towards Mooloolaba and taking Mountain Creek exit.

0.0kms	Mountain Creek exit.
0.8kms	Turn right at the traffic lights into Karawatha Drive.
1.1kms	Turn right at roundabout into Bundilla Boulevard, (towards Brisbane).

2.0kms	Turn left just past Woorilla Court into a unmarked dirt road.
3.5kms	Turn right at the top of the hill. This is Military Road.
3.7kms	Where the power lines cross the road, locate the start of a walking track on the left. Park your vehicle here. There is no vehicle access from this point.

WALLUM HEATH TRAIL
Distance: 9kms return, allow 3 hours. Easy grade.

This walk follows several fire management trails that may be sign posted in the future.

Walk south along an old track for 15m and turn right at a 'T' junction. The track runs parallel to Military Road. After about five minutes, turn left at another track junction and pass through low heath interspersed with melaleucas. The trail leads slowly downhill past a very boggy section, then out onto a low plain dominated by wallum heath. A wall of tall melaleucas can be seen off to the left, and coastal heathland spreads out to the right. After a further 10 minutes, the road curves right skirting around a low-lying swampy area filled with melaleucas and crosses a small gully. The gully is filled with ferns and taller shrubs and stretches across the plain to the right. The road now swings around to the left and your progress is blocked by another swamp. This is the swamp that blocks your progress when doing the **Old Northern Road Walk**. Return to the 'T' junction at the beginning of the walk, but to complete this walk, continue along the road, instead of turning left towards your vehicle. Another five minutes walking takes you to a road leading from the Park boundary steeply downhill to the right. Follow this track for 300m through heath, banksias, callistemons (swamp bottlebrush) and melaleucas to a 'T' junction. This area is particularly attractive in spring. Turn left and follow the road as it curves around to the left through riparian vegetation before reaching the Park boundary. Turn left again and walk back along Military Road to your vehicle.

Last reviewed: 4 July 1997

MAP REFERENCE
UBD Brisbane Street Directory – Sunshine Coast, Maps 79 and 89.

FACILITIES
There are no facilities at all and camping is not permitted in the Park. Drinking water is not available, so ensure you carry sufficient, especially if visiting the Park during the summer months.

Wildflowers are at their peak during spring when the visitor is rewarded with a spectacular extravaganza.

If travelling up river, launch canoes or boats at the mouth of the Mooloolah River.

RANGER CONTACT - (07) 5494 3983

NOOSA NATIONAL PARK

HISTORY

Early settlers in the Noosa region recognised the importance of protecting this unique section of Queensland's coastline from urban development. Noosa Town Reserve was set aside in 1879 as a refuge for native plants and animals and as a spot where local townspeople could enjoy the pleasures of the bush. Two small parcels of rainforest were gazetted as national parks in 1930. Further sections were added to the Park in 1939 and again in 1989, preserving a total of 454ha. Thirty five years of debate between developers and conservationists had finally paid off!

A cyclone in February 1954 severely damaged sections of the Park and many of the walking tracks needed repair.

During the Second World War, all the land east of Lake Weyba was used as an artillery range. Following the War it became a timber reserve and in the early sixties the Government leased several sections for pastoral development. It was then found that swampland east of Murdering Creek still contained unexploded ammunition. The lessee quickly handed it back to the Government and received other land in its place!

Also during the sixties, the sand mining industry moved in and prospected for rutile, zircon and other heavy minerals. A successful campaign waged in the early seventies put a halt to the threat of large scale sand mining.

In 1991, after 20 years of lobbying, 1 140ha of land bordering the eastern side and south-western tip of Lake Weyba were added to Noosa National Park. The Noosa Council then gifted a corridor of land that connected the area with the Noosa Headland site. This, combined with areas at Marcus Beach and Coolum, has resulted in protection of a total area of 2 280ha of land encompassed under the banner of Noosa National Park.

Noosa National Park is the most visited park in Queensland, with more than one million visitors each year. The early lobbyists would be very proud of this achievement.

Heavy visitation necessitated a $440 000 project to upgrade facilities at Noosa National Park. This was completed in September 1997. The redevelopment has improved traffic flow and pedestrian access to the Park.

FEATURES

Cliff-lines, open headlands, beaches, sand dunes, swamp lands, a lake and some small creeks are all part of Noosa National Park, one of Queensland's few coastal national parks.

A short diversion from the beaches and visitors can walk through vegetation ranging from dense rainforest containing hoop pines, piccabeen palms and Moreton Bay figs in the northern section of the Park, to coastal wildflowers or heathland country in the southern section. Open eucalypt forests with sand cypress, forest oak, scrub box, banksias and bloodwoods cover other areas within the Park. Orchids, staghorns and elkhorns thrive amongst the rainforest vegetation.

Prop roots anchor pandanus palms to rock platforms along the headlands. The pandanus tolerates salt spray from the ocean, but over the last few years has become infested by an insect that causes dieback. This small insect, the flatid or *'leafhopper'* is threatening the survival of pandanus from Hervey Bay to Northern NSW. The insect is a native of North Queensland where its natural predator, a native wasp, controls its spread. These wasps do not occur naturally in South Queensland but small numbers were released in 1995 and 1996. Constant monitoring of flatid numbers over a period of several years will indicate whether biological control can be used effectively against the spread of this pest A short term solution to the problem has been achieved by stem injection of the infected plants with insecticide and this has controlled the immediate spread of flatids.

The section adjacent to Lake Weyba preserves high dunes as well as scribbly gum and heath forests. The lake itself is a fish habitat reserve and is not contained within the National Park. The Park boundary extends to the high water mark.

Hundreds of birds make their home in the Park. Sea eagles, kites, ospreys, goshawks and falcons can be seen soaring on the wind currents around the Headland. Cormorants, herons, egrets, storks, spoonbills and ibis are relatively common around the waters edge and a variety of rosellas, parrots, lorikeets and galahs feed on the rainforest trees.

Koalas, rarely seen, were released into the Park by the Noosa Parks Association in the mid sixties, restoring one species of fauna originally living there. Other fauna includes grey kangaroos and swamp wallabies, possums and gliders. Several snakes, including the tiger, the red bellied black and the eastern brown are worth watching for and large goannas are common.

ACCESS
Noosa Heads is about 24kms from the Bruce Highway, via Cooroy and Tewantin. Follow the signs to the business centre.

0.0kms	Roundabout at eastern end of Hastings St.
0.1kms	Turn left into Park Road.
1.2kms	National Park entrance and car park.

NOOSA HEADLAND CIRCUIT
Distance: 7.3kms, allow 2 hours. Easy grade.

There are several short walks starting near the QNPWS Information Centre at the rear of the new car park. The walk described here provides a comprehensive look at the various terrain and vegetation types contained within the Noosa Headland section of the Park and includes the **Tanglewood** track and the **Coastal** track.

Locate the start of the Tanglewood Track near the Information Centre. The track climbs uphill through rainforest where many of the trees have been labelled by QNPWS staff. Ignore a rough footpad leading off to the right towards Pandanus Street and continue on to a track junction, 1km from the starting point. (The track to the left goes to Noosa Hill.) Continue straight ahead on the Tanglewood Track, ignoring several service roads that cross the trail. The terrain changes at this point. Grass trees dominate the understorey and banksias, melaleucas and old gnarled gums compete for the sunlight. You reach a second track junction 1.7kms from the Park headquarters.

Turn right and walk 1.2kms to Alexandria Bay. The vegetation changes again as you walk downhill to the beach. The forest opens out and grass trees crowd the sides of the track. After a further 400m you reach a track junction. Take the left track towards Alexandria Bay, ignoring the right hand track leading to Sunshine Beach. Continue steeply downhill to reach Alexandria Bay.

If you have the time, it is worth exploring the beach off to the right towards Oyster Rocks before heading north along Alexandria Bay. (Alexandria Bay is used by nude sun bathers, so if nudity offends, then it may be best to avoid this section.)

When you reach the northern headland, you can't help but notice bare patches along the cliff-line that used to be covered with pandanus prior to flatid infestation. Climb the steps past a large healthy clump of banksias to a track junction. An emergency phone is located a few metres off to the right.

Turn right, 100m from the top of the steps and head towards Hells Gates. The vegetation opens out along the top of the ridge and you get good views up and down the coast. From Hells Gates, a short walk around the Headland takes you past the Fairy Pools, Picnic Cove and Winch Bay, before reaching Granite Bay. This appropriately named bay is well worth exploring.

From Granite Bay, continue along to Dolphin Point. The track is heavily used and paved from this point. It re-enters the forest and heads down towards the beach at Tea tree Bay, another appropriately named bay and then climbs through a large stand of gnarled, weather beaten tea trees before reaching a lookout at The Boiling Pot. A further five minutes walking and you are back at the car park.

Last reviewed: 5 July 1997

NOOSA HILL TRACK
Distance: 3.4kms return, allow 1.5 hours. Easy grade.

The track starts near the end of the Noosa Headland Circuit. This track, part of the Murri Cultural Trail, immediately climbs uphill through scrubland and open eucalypt forest. There are some views through the trees on the way to the summit. After climbing for 1.2kms, you reach a junction, with a short trail leading 120m to the top. The views from the summit are partly obscured.

From the summit, the trail winds gradually down to meet the Tanglewood Track. Turn right and head back to the car park.

To complete your exploration of the different vegetation types in the Park, take the 1km Palm Grove Circuit. This flat track winds through attractive rainforest and interpretive signs have been strategically placed along the way. Many of the trees have been labelled.

Last reviewed: 5 July 1997

MAP REFERENCE
UBD Brisbane Street Directory – Sunshine Coast, Map 9.
Walking track maps can be obtained from the Information Centre.

FACILITIES
Picnic areas in the Park are equipped with electric barbecues, tables, toilets, cold showers and drinking water. Toilet facilities and water are also situated at Tea tree Bay. No camping is allowed in the Park. Private accommodation is available at Noosa and nearby towns.
Any time of the year is pleasant to visit the Park, but carry drinking water when walking.

RANGER CONTACT - (07) 5447 3243

GREAT SANDY NATIONAL PARK
COOLOOLA SECTION

HISTORY
Great Sandy National Park is the largest park in South-East Queensland. The northern section of the Park was originally gazetted in 1971 to protect Fraser Island and some surrounding areas. With the introduction of the Nature Conservation (Protected Areas) Regulation in 1994, several other parks were amalgamated under its banner. These included Woody and Little Woody Island National Parks, declared in 1960, Noosa River National Park, declared in 1968, two Environmental Parks on the north shore of the Noosa River, declared in 1983 and Cooloola National Park, declared in 1975. Additions to the Cooloola section have increased it to 54 700ha, and Great Sandy National Park now encompasses a total of 140 000ha.
The Cooloola section described in this edition stretches from the mangrove-lined bays of Tin Can Bay in the north, to the shores of Noosa River in the south. For ease of management it is divided into three main areas; the northern section, the southern section and the waterways. It protects the largest tract of natural coastline in Southern Queensland, the heathlands and rainforests of the surrounding area and the catchment area and waterways of the Upper Noosa River.
Many Murri creation stories and significant historical events have been centred around Cooloola Coast. The story surrounding the Coloured Sands along Cooloola Beach gives another perspective to the formation of these magnificent sand cliffs. The Murri people relate the tale of a beautiful young maiden who lived on the banks of Noosa River. She fell in love with the rainbow who came to visit her, but she was captured by a cruel man from a distant tribe. When trying to flee from her captor, she turned back to see a terrible killing boomerang, full of evil spirits coming to kill her. She fell to the ground, as Rainbow who was coming to save her was attacked by Boomerang. The loud roar as they met killed Boomerang and shattered Rainbow into many pieces. These pieces form the hills and cliffs of the Coloured Sands.

Captain James Cook was the first European to record a sighting of Double Island Point Headland. He sighted and named the Headland during his discovery voyage in 1770. Construction of Double Island Point Lighthouse was completed in 1884.

Eliza Fraser was one of the survivors of a ship wrecked on Swain Reefs in 1863. Along with her husband, who was Captain of the ship, and some crew members, she escaped in a long boat to Fraser Island where they were captured by Aborigines. Subjected to slavery and torture, she witnessed the death of her husband and other crew members. Three months later, some surviving crew members were discovered on Bribie Island. A party was sent north to rescue any remaining survivors. Eliza, who had suffered terribly from her ordeal, was discovered at Lake Cootharaba, just before she was to be claimed by a vicious tribal elder.

Cootharaba sawmill operated at Mill Point on the shores of Lake Cootharaba between 1869 and 1892. It helped mill the vast amounts of timber being harvested from the area. Red cedar, beech and kauri pine were felled and transported to Brisbane via paddle steamers. In 1872 Governor Normanby described the sawmill operation as follows (metric conversions have been added): *"...covered by a shed 120 feet (37m) long by 33 feet (10m) wide, containing circular saws and travelling benches of the latest make and largest capacity, weighing over 20 tons (20.3tonnes). The machinery was driven by a 25 horsepower (18.6kw) engine supplied by two boilers - 20 feet (6m) and 13 feet 6 inches (4m) in diameter."* About 60 families resided at Mill Point and the town boasted a school, hotel, post office and blacksmith's and butcher's shops. Floods in 1893 and competition with other sawmills in the area were the main reasons for the demise of Mill Point sawmill and the settlement soon disappeared. Relics of the mill and some dwellings serve to remind us of this important era.

The area around Harry's Hut on the banks of Noosa River was a logging camp. Huge kauri and hoop pines, cypress and beech were floated down Noosa River to be loaded onto bullock and horse drays at the camp. The original hut is believed to have been a shelter for the winch operator. It now belongs to Harry Springs and is contained within a leased area at Harry's Hut camp ground. The lease will exist for the lifetime of the owner.

The rusting remains of the *'Cherry Venture'*, an empty cargo vessel that ran aground in huge storms in 1973, provides a prominent landmark on Teewah Beach, just south of Double Island Point. Numerous attempts to refloat and salvage her failed and she remains firmly wedged in the sands of Teewah Beach.

FEATURES

The extremely diverse northern section of the Park contains mangrove-lined beaches and waterways, coloured sands and white beaches, lakes, open heathlands, banksia, blackbutt and eucalypt forests and coastal rainforests.

The mangrove swamps are an essential component of the food chain and breeding habitat for many crustaceans, molluscs, invertebrates and fish. It has been determined that each square metre of mangrove forest yields around 1kg of organic matter every year. The plants are supported and oxygenated by prop and aerial roots. Mangroves have adapted to life in salt water by expelling the salt through sacrificial leaves, or by restricting the ingress of salt by chemical action. At low tide the mud flats become a feeding ground for many water birds. Flying foxes and honeyeaters also frequent the mangrove swamps.

Once thought only to be a haven for mosquitoes, many hectares of mangroves have been lost to canal estate developments and sporting fields.

Many of the eucalypt forests are dominated by scribbly gums, the patterns on their trunks being the result of burrowing moth larvae.

The southern section of the Park contains the Noosa River and many of its tributaries and protects the wet heathlands. Water drains into Noosa River from wallum heathlands on the western shores of the River. *'Wallum'* is a Murri term for one of the sweet honey banksias found in the area. It has been said the wildflowers of the Park rival those of Western Australia. Boronias, wild may, banksias, parrot pea, wedding bush, waxflowers, heath dogwood, vanilla lily, devil's rice, milkmaids, bottlebrushes and leptospermums are alive with blooms during late winter and early spring. During an NPAQ outing in the spring of 1995, one member identified at least 71 different species of flowers!

As you travel further south and east, a different range of flowers is found under the eucalypt canopy. The southern banks of Noosa River, downstream from Lake Cootharaba, preserve undeveloped areas of forest and swamp communities.

Lake Cootharaba forms the entrance to the waterways section of the Park. The Lake and its tributaries, Kin Kin Creek and Noosa River, are ideal spots to be explored by row boat or canoe. Kinaba Island, at the mouth of Kin Kin Creek was formed by silt deposits washed down from the rivers and creeks. The water is brackish till about 3kms upstream. Giant mangrove ferns, native hibiscus, paper barks and swamp oaks line the banks of the tributaries and flourish on Kinaba Island. Remnant rainforest covers an area about 4.5kms upstream from the mouth of Kin Kin Creek.

Figtree Lake at the entrance of Noosa River supports a large population of waterbirds and aquatic plant life in its shallow waters. Tea trees are prominent in an area thought to be an ancient Murri corroboree site.

Sedges, a plant variety whose spongy air filled cavities keep them upright, line the banks at the entrance of Lake Como. They also grow with melaleucas around Lakes Como and Cooloola. It is not uncommon to see kites and ospreys at Lake Como.

Lake Cooloola, a freshwater lake, is not accessible by boat as the only time it has any outflow is after heavy rains.

The brownish coloured waters of some of the Lakes and the Noosa River is a result of decaying vegetation. Mirrored reflections in the waters make this a photographer's dream with shutter bugs from all over coming just to capture these reflections.

Australian bass live in a relatively undisturbed habitat in the upper reaches of Noosa River. This is one of the reasons motorised boats are not permitted in these areas.

Yellow faced whip snakes, carpet snakes, cicadas, sugar gliders, swamp wallabies, dingoes and bandicoots have a safe habitat in the Park.

Literally hundreds of Eastern grey kangaroos feed around the cleared camp site area of Elanda Point, making this a great place to take overseas visitors to ensure they see kangaroos in the wild.

Large lace monitors are a common sight around the Lakes and camp grounds. Due to '*kind*' people feeding these creatures, they have become a real pest to campers and picnickers. Please refrain from feeding all wildlife in the Park.

ACCESS - ELANDA POINT

Travel north from Brisbane on the Bruce Highway and take the Cooroy exit, following the signs to *Pomona, Kin Kin* and *Boreen Point.* Upon entering Pomona continue along Summit Road, turn right into Boreen Road and follow the signs to *Boreen Point.*

0.0kms	Turn left at a sign to *Elanda Point 5kms*, just before the township of Boreen Point.
1.7kms	Gravel road.
2.0kms	Veer right at signs *Elanda Point 1.8kms* and *Cooloola National Park.*
3.5kms	Ranger's station and self-registration booth for those camping in the National Park.
3.9kms	Elanda Point camp ground, kiosk and start of the Cooloola Wilderness Trail. (Although in national park grounds, this camp ground is privately run.)

THE KINABA TRACK

Distance: 11.4kms return, allow 4 hours. Easy grade.

The walking trails from Elanda Point start from the northern end of the private camp ground. The first section of track runs parallel to Lake Cootharaba and may become waterlogged after rain. A few minutes from the start, the track passes through clumps of dune cypress, cabbage palms and tall melaleucas (paperbarks). The ground cover is mainly grasses and ferns. You soon pass a patch of casuarinas (swamp she-oaks) before reaching a clearing and a sign pointing to *Mill Point 600m.*

The built up track to Mill Point follows the original rail mound. Continue through a beautiful avenue of tall melaleucas towards the Lake. After exploring the ruins on the Lake's shore, return to the track junction and examine the chimney and remains of a tank stand, then follow the sign towards *Kinaba Information Centre.*

Walk along the old road to the next junction and turn right. Continue for one more kilometre, turning right again at the next track junction. (The **Cooloola Wilderness Trail** leads left towards Kin Kin Creek, Fig Tree Point and Harry's Hut.)

The vegetation changes from open forest to areas dominated by melaleucas and swamp banksias. About 20 minutes from the junction, the track becomes boggy and swings left through a clump of cabbage palms towards the banks of Kin Kin Creek. As you enter a section of casuarinas with ground cover of mangrove ferns, look to the left for a surveyor's blaze on a dead tree. The Government arrow and the numbers '*239*' are still clearly visible. Five minutes from the blazed tree you reach the boardwalk leading to Kinaba Visitor Information Centre. Interpretive signs at the Centre and along the short Mangrove Circuit Walk provide an insight into the fragile nature of the Lake's ecosystems. Take the time to look for local wildlife before retracing your steps to Elanda Point.

Last reviewed: 11 December 1997

ELANDA TO FIG TREE POINT
Distance: 20.4kms return, allow 6 hours. Moderate grade.

Follow the notes for the previous walk for 2kms to the point where the **Cooloola Wilderness Trail** turns left towards Kin Kin Creek. This track also follows an old road and is very exposed. After about 15 minutes you reach a small creek where a few strategically placed log seats offer a shady rest spot.

A few minutes from here, the track turns left and a sign post points to *Fig Tree Point 6.5kms*. Cross a wooden bridge over Kin Kin Creek and follow the track as it runs parallel to the Creek. The rainforest provides a welcome change to the exposed open forest at the start of the walk.

Further on, cross two small wooden footbridges near a clump of cabbage palms. The forest floor is littered with palm fronds. As you walk along the Creek bank you can hear startled frilled lizards diving into the water. One more bridge is crossed before reaching the Boronia Trail junction about half way between Elanda and Fig Tree Points. Continue on to the right. After 10 minutes, look for a large hollow fig tree on the left with buttress roots extending across the track. A few minutes later the terrain changes to open forest before reaching a section where cabbage palms form a complete canopy overhead. Cross one more bridge and after another 30 minutes you reach a track junction. The **Cooloola Wilderness Trail** leads left towards Harry's Hut. Turn right and walk 700m to Fig Tree Point camping and day use area.

After lunch and a swim, locate the start of the 500m Melaleuca Circuit. A boardwalk leads you through attractive cabbage palms and melaleuca wetlands before rejoining the track leading down to the camp ground and day use area. Turn right and retrace your steps to Elanda Point. As you approach Mill Point, ignore the track to the left and continue straight ahead, past a locked gate at the northern end of the camp ground. This leads you beside another stand of melaleucas and into the camping area. You will normally find hundreds of Eastern grey kangaroos in this section of the Park.

Last reviewed: 11 December 1997

FACILITIES
There are areas for launching canoes and small motor boats at Boreen and Elanda Points.

Full facilities including cabins, kiosk and a water sports hire centre are available at the privately run camp ground at Elanda Point.

Fig Tree Point can only be accessed on foot or by canoe. Toilets, tables and barbecue facilities with firewood provided make this a very pleasant camp spot. Bookings are essential and permits must be obtained prior to camping.

ACCESS - HARRY'S HUT CAMPING AREA

From the Bruce Highway take the Cooroy exit and follow the signs to *Pomona* and *Kin Kin.* Continue on Kin Kin Road to the start of Cooloola Way. This unsealed road is impassable for conventional cars and coaches during wet weather.

0.0kms	Turn right on Cooloola Way.
0.8kms	Veer right at 'Y' junction.
4.1kms	Turn right into Harry's Hut Road.
8.7kms	*Cooloola National Park* sign.
10.7kms	Fig Tree walking track on right.
13.2kms	Cooloola Wilderness Trail joins road on the right.
13.7kms	Cooloola Wilderness Trail joins road on the left.
15.1kms	Harry's Hut. Continue straight ahead to camp ground and picnic facilities.

HARRY'S HUT TO FIG TREE POINT

Distance: 17.2kms return, allow 5 hours. Moderate grade.

Start walking on the **Cooloola Wilderness Trail**, 200m south of Harry's Hut, near the helipad. The start of the track is very sandy with sparse ground cover and the vegetation is mainly casuarinas and low swamp banksias. Within a few minutes a section of boggy depressions is reached that could be very muddy following heavy rain. After about 10 minutes the track crosses a low gully via two planks as you enter an area with melaleucas and cabbage palms. Continue on until you reach Harry's Hut Road, turn right and walk 500m to the point where the track turns left, away from the road.

The track rises slightly and then descends along the side of a low ridge past masses of cabbage palms and the forest floor is littered with palm fronds. You soon reach a tall melaleuca wetland where the track has been raised and corded. The ground cover is predominantly fern.

Follow the track as it climbs slowly around the side of a low hill before reaching a fire break road. Turn left and walk through open eucalypt forest until you reach a track junction sign posted *Fig Tree Point 700m*. Continue straight ahead.

After lunch and a swim, follow the Melaleuca Circuit described in the previous walk to rejoin the road for the trip back to Harry's Hut.

Turn right where the Melaleuca Circuit joins the road and retrace your steps to the point where the **Cooloola Wilderness Trail** joined the fire break road. Continue uphill on the Fig Tree Walking Track. This short detour takes you through more open eucalypt forest and a section dominated by casuarinas and swamp banksias before reaching Harry's Hut Road. Turn right and follow the road 4.4kms back to Harry's Hut.

Last reviewed: 12 December 1997

HARRY'S HUT TO WANDI WATERHOLE
Distance: 19.4kms return, allow 6 hours. Moderate grade.

Locate the start of the **Cooloola Wilderness Trail** at the northern end of the camp ground. The flat sandy track follows the western bank of Noosa River through sections of casuarinas, melaleucas, callistemons, banksias and beautiful yellow gum trees. The ground cover is mainly grasses, ferns and grass trees.

Cross a low gully where the track has been corded before reaching a service road. Turn left and follow the road. This section of the walk is open and exposed. Tall melaleucas, interspersed with casuarinas and banksias fringe the left of the track while the vegetation on the plain to the right is low wallum heath and grass trees. The track leaves the road after about 10 minutes and heads right, towards a low sandy ridge. The vegetation changes constantly and the area would be covered with wildflowers in spring. Cross another section of corded track and start climbing gradually towards the top of a low sandy hill. Look to the east for good views of Cooloola Sandpatch. Continue down through a boggy area with tall grasses encroaching on the track, before climbing again to a rocky ridge. The track swings right and follows the top of the ridge before descending again. A further 10 minutes and you reach the southern tail of Wandi Waterhole. Cross the boggy section, turn right and walk parallel to the Waterhole towards a track junction. (The **Cooloola Wilderness Trail** heads left towards Cooloola Way.) Turn right and after a few minutes you will see the bush camping area off to the left. Turn right again to reach the Waterhole. This is an ideal

Natural Bridge, Springbrook National Park.

Upper Portals, Mt Barney National Park.

OVERLEAF *Coomera Falls,*
          Lamington National Park.

Antarctic Beech, Lamington National Park.

Curtis Falls, Tamborine National Park.

Grass Trees, Bunya Mountains National Park.

Mt Mitchell, Main Range National Park.

Brigalow Scrub, Bendidee National Park.

Heathlands, Mooloolah River National Park.

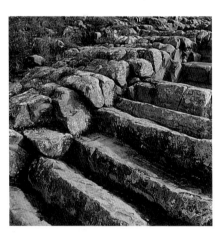

Basalt Columns, Mt Coolum National Park.

Salt Plains, Lake Bindegolly National Park.

OPPOSITE *Red Rock Gorge,*
Sundown National Park.

Lake Wyara, Currawinya National Park.

Mt Greville, Moogerah Peaks National Park.

Mt Coonowrin, Glass House Mountains National Park.

Ascending the Pyramid, Girraween National Park.

Neabul Creek, Thrushton National Park.

Twin Falls, Springbrook National Park.

place for a swim before retracing your steps to Harry's Hut.

Last reviewed: 13 December 1997

HARRY'S HUT TO CAMP SITE 3
Distance: 14kms return, allow 4 hours. Easy grade.

There is no road access to the walking track on the eastern side of Noosa River. If you don't have access to a canoe, swim across the River to a sandy landing opposite Harry's Hut. Wrap empty water bottles (to increase buoyancy) and your pack in a sheet of plastic and float it across the River. Fill the bottles from the River before starting the walk. (It is recommended that all water from the Park be treated prior to drinking.)

The walking track runs parallel to the River through attractive scribbly gum forest sprinkled with casuarinas and banksias and a ground cover of grass trees, grasses and ferns. After walking for about 40 minutes you reach Camp Site 1. Early morning light produces brilliant reflections in the stained waters of the River. Even average photographers can get great photographs from here.

The track passes through clumps of cabbage palms before reaching Camp Site 2. The soft fronds of Prince of Wales feather lean over several sections of the track. This plant is a sedge, not a fern as is often thought.

Continue walking for a few minutes to a small creek. At the time of writing, hundreds of froglets were living around the edges of this creek. The track continues past an area where a low plain, covered with wallum heath interspersed with grass trees, stretches from the edge of the tree line to the western edge of the coastal dunes. Cooloola Sandpatch is easily seen through the melaleucas. This area is alive with wildflowers in spring. Cross another small creek draining water from the plain into Noosa River before arriving at Camp Site 3.

If you are not walking to Cooloola Sandpatch, retrace your steps to the starting point and swim back across the river. Alternatively, a small group could arrange for some of the party to paddle from Harry's Hut, leaving the canoe for you to paddle back, then walking back themselves.

Last reviewed: 19 January 1998

CAMP SITE 3 TO COOLOOLA SANDPATCH
Distance: 12kms return, allow 4 hours. Moderate grade.

Apart from the attraction of the Sandpatch, spring wildflowers make this an extremely attractive walk. Follow the old road east for 500m to a sign post at the start of the walking track. The first section of the soft sandy track is flat and the vegetation is sparse. After about 10 minutes, the track starts to climb and the soft sand gives way to firm ground making for easier walking. You start zigzagging uphill through hundreds of grass trees and the vegetation becomes more dense. Continue climbing for about 30 minutes to the top of a ridge. The track here is very exposed and hot in the middle of the day with the sun reflecting off the white sandy track. Only five minutes from this point the track starts climbing again to a section where tall banksias provide some welcome shade. The Sandpatch comes into view as you continue along the track to the top of another ridge. Follow the track for a further 20 minutes to a set of wooden steps leading uphill to the edge of the Sandpatch.

Hang gliders are often seen soaring in the thermals above the Sandpatch. Mt Cooroora (venue for the annual Man of the Mountain run) is visible to the south-west. Spend as long as you want enjoying the panoramic views before retracing your steps to the starting point.

Last reviewed: 19 January 1998

FACILITIES

Camp sites, barbecues with wood supplied, bush toilets and picnic tables, including some with shelters, are located at Harry's Hut camp ground and day use area. Jetties are provided for commercial and private boats.

Camp sites 1, 2 and 3 have bush toilets. Camp sites 1 to 15 can only be reached by canoe, small motorised boat, or by walking. All these camp sites are for self sufficient visitors only and open fires are not permitted. Bookings are essential and can be made through Kinaba Information Centre.

ACCESS - MT SEAWAH

From the township of Cooroy follow the signs to Tewantin.

0.0kms	Turn left on Moorindil Street towards the Noosa River Ferry.
1.9kms	Noosa River Ferry. A vehicle fee applies.
4.2kms	Turn right into Beach Road. This road becomes gravel just past Sundowner Hotel.
6.3kms	Turn left towards Noosa North Shore Wilderness Camp.
8.7kms.	Camp ground on the right. If you are not camping at the Wilderness Camp you may leave your vehicle on the verge to the left of the road. Walk through the camp ground to the beach and start of the following walk.

MT SEAWAH AND LAKE COOTHARABA

Distance: 21kms return from Wilderness Camp, allow 6 hours. Moderate grade.
8kms return from start of the walking track. Allow 2.5 hours. Easy grade.

Walk through the Wilderness Camp to the beach, turn left and head north for 6kms past Teewah village, then continue along the beach for a further 500m. The walking track is behind the dunes, 200m south of a *Great Sandy National Park* sign. Walk through an obvious depression in the dunes, past several casuarinas to the start of the track. Turn right at the sign post and walk towards Lake Cootharaba. The track is well maintained and passes a swampy section on the right. Melaleucas beside the track still show evidence of an earlier fire. Continue walking for about 15 minutes to a track junction and turn right towards Mt Seawah. The track leads through an area covered with grass trees before entering a banksia forest at the start of the climb. You soon reach a low heath-covered ridge where you get your first views of the coastline and the summit of Mt Seawah. Follow the track as it leads around the eastern side of Mt Seawah to a ridge covered with low wallum banksias and grass trees. The wildflowers here are particularly attractive in September and October. The track soon swings right for the final climb to the summit. This section of the sandy track gets steeper before levelling out for an easy climb to the top. Be sure to stay on the track and not form new tracks through the fragile vegetation. Apart from the sweeping views of the coastline you can see south to Mt Coolum, then arc around to the south-west past Mt Tinbeerwah, Mt Cooroy, Black Mountain, Mt Cooroora, Mt Cooran and then Mt Pinbarren.

From the summit, retrace your steps to the track junction and turn right towards Lake Cootharaba. Within 30 minutes you will reach Teewah Landing. This is an ideal place for a swim before returning to the beach via the same track.

Last reviewed: 17 January 1998

FACILITIES
Private camp ground facilities are available at Noosa North Shore Wilderness Camp and Lake Cooroibah Holiday Park. Beach camping is not permitted in Noosa Shire.

ACCESS - FRESHWATER
This day use picnic area and camp ground can only be accessed by 4WD, or on foot if through-walking in this section of the Park. For access from the southern end follow the road directions for Mt Seawah, continuing along Beach Road a further 200m from the turn off to Noosa North Shore Wilderness Camp.

0.0kms	Enter the beach at the end of Beach Road and turn left.
8.5kms	Pass Teewah village on the left.
9.0kms	Beginning of inland walking track to Mt Seawah and Lake Cootharaba.
22.3kms	*Cooloola National Park* sign and self-registration booth for campers.
36.9kms	Self-registration booth at Little Freshwater Creek.
39.7kms	Turn left into Freshwater picnic and camping areas.

If accessing Freshwater from the north follow the directions to Rainbow Beach. Check current beach conditions and tides at Department of Environment office.

0.0kms	Pass the Shell Service Station and Cypress Street on your left.
0.2kms	Turn left into Rainbow Beach Road.
0.6kms	Turn right into Clarkson Drive.
0.9kms	Pass through Rainbow Beach Car Park and turn right onto the beach.
11.9kms	This area of the beach is impassable at high tide.
12.8kms	Turn right onto the boarded Leisha Track.

13.8kms   Turn right at end of the Leisha Track at Teewah Beach.
14.5kms   Pass Cherry Venture wreck.
19.6kms   Turn right into the entrance of Freshwater picnic and camping
                   areas.

FRESHWATER TO POONA LAKE AND BYMIEN PICNIC AREA
Distance: 19.2kms return, allow 6 hours. Moderate grade.

The start of Lake Freshwater walking track is on the left side of the road, 100m from Freshwater day use picnic area. The track immediately climbs uphill past some gnarled eucalypts before entering an area dominated by banksias, callistemons and prickly broom heath (*Morotoca scoparia*). Midyen (*Astromurtus duclis*) is very obvious in the mid layer and the ground cover consists of grasses, ferns and leaf litter. Continue beneath the overhanging branches of beautiful white scribbly gums to some steps leading downhill to a gully. After 10 minutes, the track crosses the gully and climbs high on the left bank before reaching a track junction. Turn right and walk 200m to Freshwater Lake. After a swim, return to the track junction and head towards Poona Lake. Several trees have been temporarily labelled along the side of the track. Your walks will become more enjoyable if you can memorise the various trees and then look for more of the same as you continue walking. You soon reach a clump of macrozamias and a grove of piccabeen palms on the right, before the vegetation changes to rainforest. A few minutes into the rainforest you pass a large kauri pine, before reaching a sign pointing towards *Bymien and Poona Lake*. Climb a small ridge and pass the tall hollowed trunk of a strangler fig on the right of the track and large vines extending from the canopy to the forest floor. The track follows the gully up and down for about an hour before finally climbing a stony section of track, out of the gully to the top of a ridge. It is only a few minutes from here to a track junction leading towards Poona Lake. Turn left and climb a small ridge before starting the final descent towards the Lake. This makes an ideal place for lunch and a swim.
From the Lake, return to the track junction and head left towards Bymien picnic area. After 600m you pass the track turning right towards Rainbow Beach. Many of the trees in this area are spotted with patches of lichen. Christmas orchids flower along the sides of the track in December and January. Look for a massive brush box on the right, covered with a lattice of strangler fig roots. Turn left for a 260m detour along the Dundathu Circuit, where interpretive signs have been placed near many of the trees. Take note of the giant kauri pine and the large buttress roots of a blue quandong before reaching the picnic area. Return to Freshwater via the same route.

Last reviewed: 17 January 1998

FACILITIES
Freshwater day use area has gas barbecues, picnic tables, toilets and tap water. The camping area is equipped with hot showers and toilets (suitable for disabled people), tap water and a public telephone. Beach camping is permitted from the Cooloola Shire boundary to Little Freshwater Creek. Rubbish collection points have been

placed along the beach and at the picnic area and camp ground. The whole area, including Freshwater camping area, is designated a *'fuel stove only'* zone.

Bymien picnic area has toilets with wheelchair access, water, picnic tables and barbecues with firewood provided.

ACCESS - DOUBLE ISLAND POINT LIGHTHOUSE

0.0kms	Entrance to Freshwater camp ground.
5.1kms	Cherry Venture wreck.
5.8kms	Leisha Track to Rainbow Beach is to the left.
8.4kms	Start of the Lighthouse Walk.

DOUBLE ISLAND POINT LIGHTHOUSE

Distance: 2.2kms return, allow 1 hour. Easy grade.

To reach the Lighthouse, walk up the road at Double Island Point, past clumps of banksias and pandanus. At the time of writing, the pandanus showed no sign of die-back that has affected most of the pandanus in the Noosa area. The road climbs very steeply past several casuarinas to the top of the hill before reaching a sign pointing 500m to the *Lighthouse Walking Track*. Turn right at the next track junction and walk up the paved driveway to the Lighthouse. The left track leads down towards Rainbow Beach that is only accessible at low tide.

The views from the Lighthouse are spectacular and provide great photographic opportunities at dawn and dusk. To the north-east, waves crash over Wolf Rock at low tide. Fraser Island lies across Wide Bay, north of the huge arc of Rainbow Beach. Noosa Headland is 50kms to the south. During migration, humpback whales may be seen quite close to the shore. Sea birds fish in the waters around the Point. Take note of the stunted salt tolerant vegetation along the edge of the cliffs. Wind sheer has shaped much of this vegetation. After enjoying the view, return to the beach via the same route.

Last reviewed: 18 January 1998

ACCESS - RAINBOW BEACH

From Brisbane follow the Bruce Highway to Gympie and take the bitumen road to the township of Rainbow Beach. (Four kilometres before Rainbow Beach township a sand road suitable for conventional vehicles leads to Bymien picnic area. The road from Bymien picnic area to Freshwater picnic area and camp ground is only accessible by 4WD vehicles.)

To reach the starting point for the following walk continue on from the Department of Environment office and turn right into Double Island Drive.

0.0kms	Double Island Drive.
0.2kms	Left into Cooloola Drive.
0.5kms	Cooloola Drive veers right.
1.2kms	Roundabout at Rainbow Heights. The car park and access to Carlo Sandblow is to the left, from the roundabout.

CARLO SANDBLOW TO BYMIEN PICNIC AREA
Distance: 14.5kms return, allow 5 hours. Moderate grade.

The walking track starts from the car park and immediately enters the National Park. Vegetation consists mainly of banksias, casuarinas and scribbly gum with a ground cover of bracken fern and leaf litter. It is only 600m from the start of the car park to a boarded section of track leading to a platform at the edge of Carlo Sandblow. After enjoying the views and watching the hang gliders, make your way to a high point on the other side of the Sandblow, directly opposite the platform. Locate a feint trail leading steeply down to the walking track below the southern end of the Sandblow. Be careful not to make additional trails as you head down to the track. Turn left towards Bymien. You will notice how the sand is encroaching on the track as you walk through the scribbly gum forest. After about 20 minutes of ups and downs you reach a track junction. Turn left and walk 50m to Murrawa Lookout for views over the coloured sand cliffs and along the coastline to Fraser Island. The cliffs near the Lookout are likely to become unstable so keep well back from the edge.
Rejoin the track and follow it as it winds up and down for a further 30 minutes towards the next track junction. (The track straight ahead leads towards Double Island Point). Turn right towards Bymien. The track soon starts to descend and after about five minutes the scribbly gum forest gives way to rainforest. Look for the hollow base of a massive fallen tree on the right of the track. The hollow is home to a colony of moths. The brush box in this area are a popular host for germinating strangler figs. The track continues to descend through more palms to a large grove of macrozamias. A few minutes from here, track marker signs have been erected to guide the way through a carpet of fallen palm fronds.
The rainforest opens out in an area where buttress roots from a large tree extend almost 10m towards the track, a few minutes before reaching Freshwater Road. Cross the road and continue towards Bymien Picnic Area. After a few minutes, you reach a wooden platform in front of a massive kauri pine. Continue walking to the next track junction. From this point, turn right and follow the notes for the Freshwater to Bymien walk for the final 600m into the picnic ground. (Alternatively, turn left and walk a further 1.6kms to Poona Lake for a swim, before retracing your steps to the start of the walk.)

Last reviewed: 18 January 1998

RAINBOW BEACH COLOURED SANDS
Distance: 15kms return, allow 5 hours. Easy grade.

Appreciate the grandeur of the coloured sand cliffs by walking south along the beach from Rainbow Beach. Carlo Sandblow is passed after about 30 minutes of walking. Continue along the beach past some rocks that may be covered at high tide, then cross several freshwater creeks before reaching the towering sand cliffs. With blue sea and white waves to your left, the cliffs provide a beautiful contrast on your right. Pinks, mauves, yellows, greys, oranges, whites and browns form a natural mosaic of colour that can best be appreciated on foot. Sunlight adds different hues at various times of the day and the changing forces of nature create something different to see on each visit. Note the deep canyons and pinnacle-like structures that have been eroded over the years.

After enjoying these magnificent cliffs and appreciating that our national parks protect such formations, walk back to Rainbow Beach.

Please remember it is dangerous to attempt to climb these unstable cliffs. What appears to be solid rock is actually sand.

Because of the large number of 4WD vehicles using the beach, walkers should be constantly alert. It is often difficult to hear vehicles approaching above the noise of the surf.

Last reviewed: 20 January 1998

FACILITIES
Private accommodation and all facilities are available in Rainbow Beach township. Commercially run day tours and safaris leave frequently from the town. Hang gliding is permitted from Carlo Sandblow and the platform just north of Teewah village.

Graded bushwalking tracks of varying difficulty, lead past spectacular wildflower displays that are at their peak during spring. Carry ample water if walking during the summer months. There are plenty of opportunities to cool off on hot summer days in the river and lakes in the Cooloola section of Great Sandy National Park. Surf swimming is only encouraged at the patrolled area on Rainbow Beach.

Please keep off the sand cliffs. They may become very unstable and accidents do result from climbing over the cliffs. It is an offence to climb over or remove sand from any section of the coloured sand cliffs.

MAP REFERENCE
Sunmap - TOURIST MAP - COOLOOLA REGION

COOLOOLA COAST MAP - for Boating, Off Road Driving, Bushwalking and Fishing. (This can be purchased locally from many outlets.)

Walking track maps for the Cooloola section of Great Sandy National Park are available from QNPWS.

RANGER CONTACT -   (07) 5486 3160 - Rainbow Beach.
(07) 5485 3245 - Elanda Point.
(07) 5449 7364 - Kinaba Information Centre.

SUNSHINE COAST HINTERLAND

GLASS HOUSE MOUNTAINS NATIONAL PARK

HISTORY
The different sections of Glass House Mountains National Park cover an area of about 883ha and protect the eroded remnants of volcanic plugs. Four of the distinct peaks; Tibrogargan, Ngungun, Coonowrin (Crookneck) and Beerwah, were national parks in their own right until their amalgamation into Glass House Mountains National Park in 1994. Road signs in the area and some locally produced tourist information brochures, still refer to the Mountains as individual national parks. The first parks were originally proclaimed in 1954, with minor additions being made in 1955 and 1960. In 1994 Mt Elimbah (Saddleback), Mt Mikeeteebumulgrai and Blue Gum Creek Environmental Parks were added to the National Park. Coochin Hills, the last section to be included under the banner, was added in 1995.

Mt Tibrogargan is an example of the size of early national parks. A boundary encompassing '1 square mile' (259ha) was often drawn around an area to be protected. This may have been a distinct mountain like Tibrogargan or Beerwah, or a particular waterfall, or some other scenic location.

Aboriginal legend has it that the Mountains Tibrogargan and Beerwah were the parents of the other mountains making up the Glass House Group. Tibrogargan noticed the seas rising and hurried to gather his children. He asked Coonowrin, the eldest child, to help his mother who was again pregnant but Coonowrin ignored his father. Tibrogargan became very angry and hit Coonowrin, dislocating his neck. Mt Tibrogargan has turned his back on him and Mt Beerwah remains pregnant.

Evidence of early Aboriginal settlement can be observed in scattered remains of bora rings and stone tools.

The peaks were sighted and named 'Glass House' by Captain Cook during his epic voyage in 1770. Perhaps the unusual formations reminded him of ancient Celtic burial mounds near his home in Yorkshire, England. The Celtic word for burial mounds is 'Glashous'.

Europeans cleared the surrounding land in the late 1800s and pineapple plantations now cover much of the land around the Glass House peaks. Conservationists and local action groups have raged many battles with successive State Governments over the proposed expansion of quarrying activities in the area. During recent years, fires in the Park and the surrounding region causing loss of life, as well as destruction of large parcels of land, have posed problems for management staff. Vast areas of commercial pine forests surround the farming land.

FEATURES
Formed by volcanic activity more than 20 million years ago and subsequent weathering over the years, the 13 distinct domed and lopsided peaks of the Glass House Mountains provide a spectacular sight, rising behind the flat lands of the

Sunshine Coast. Views of the Mountains are particularly impressive from the Bruce Highway as you drive north from Brisbane; from Mary Cairncross Park near Maleny, and across the Pumicestone Passage on Bribie Island.

Newspaper reports in March 1997, claiming that large sections of Coonowrin were in danger of collapsing, have since been discredited. Nothing has been produced to support the original claim despite several *'examinations'* by *'experts'*.

The complex variety of plant life growing around the peaks supports a wide range of bird and animal life. There are 19 rare and endemic plant species found amongst the summit vegetation. Open eucalypt forests of bloodwood, blackbutt, ironbark and tallow wood thrive on the ridges. Heath plants grow in the shallow soils of rocky areas and ground orchids are a common sight. The summit of Mt Ngungun cradles a profuse community of tea trees that produce spectacular flowers indicative of those found on the rest of the peaks.

Peregrine falcons are often seen soaring above the cliffs and honeyeaters and many different types of parrots swarm around the Mountains.

Koalas, lizards, echidnas and wallabies also make the Mountains their home.

ACCESS

Follow the Bruce Highway north from Brisbane. Take the Glass House Mountains Tourist Route towards Landsborough. Continue past Coonowrin Creek and turn left into Glass House Mountains township. Turn left again, following the signs to Coonowrin Road. Follow Coonowrin Road to a 'T' intersection at the junction of Old Gympie Road. Directions for all peaks described commence at this point.

ACCESS - MT NGUNGUN

0.0kms   Turn right into Old Gympie Road.

0.9kms   Turn right into Fullertons Road. This is a gravel road.

2.1kms   Ngungun car park.

MT NGUNGUN TRACK
Distance: 1.5kms return, allow 2 hours. Easy grade.

This is the only peak in the Glass House group with a maintained graded track to the summit. It is also the best place for *'beginner'* bushwalkers to obtain spectacular views of the area surrounding the Glass House Mountains, without tackling the steep routes of Beerwah and Tibrogargan. The popular track is heavily eroded with many exposed tree roots along the way. After about 10 minutes of walking uphill you start climbing steeply on a rocky track through a gully, passing a cave on the right. Be careful not to dislodge loose rocks in this area. Fifteen minutes from the start you reach an open cleared section with views up towards the basalt columns on the face of the Mountain. A further 10 to 15 minutes uphill past some bushfire damage, you reach a ridge leading left to the summit.

From the summit you are rewarded with good views of all the major Glass House peaks. The latest QNPWS management plan for Ngungun classes the rocky pavement below the summit on the north-western side of the Mountain, as a *'non-visitation area'*. Monitoring points are due to be established in 1998 to assist with preservation of the fragile, unique vegetation.

After enjoying the view, retrace your steps to the starting point.

Last reviewed: 9 June 1997

ACCESS - MT BEERWAH

0.0kms	Turn left into Old Gympie Road.
0.4kms	Turn right into Mt Beerwah Road.
2.5kms	Start of gravel road.
5.4kms	Veer left into Beerwah section of the Park.
5.6kms	Car park.

MT BEERWAH CLIMB

Distance: 2kms return, allow 2-3 hours. Hard grade.

The climb to the 556m summit of Mt Beerwah involves scrambling over steep, smooth rocky slabs and should only be attempted by confident, experienced scramblers. Do not attempt the climb if the rocks are wet or if rain threatens. The climb has been rated *'hard'*, because of its precarious nature.

A graded track leads a few hundred metres from the car park to a picnic area and the views of the Mountain face from here are very good. From the picnic area, follow the track uphill, over some steps and past a section of hand railing. The track swings around to the right and ends at the base of a steep rocky slab.

This is the start of the climb to the summit. The QNPWS maintain the track to the base of the Mountain, but no further. A series of yellow markers lead the way up the slab. There are some hand-holds up the slab, but if the climb appears too daunting at this point, it is best to abandon the attempt. An obvious route leads from the slab to a small sandy ledge. From the tree at the end of the ridge turn left and follow a depression in the rock. A rough trail to the left of the next slab makes for easier scrambling. When you reach the tree line, an eroded sandy track leads straight up to the base of the cliffs. The cliffs are honeycombed with hundreds of small caves inhabited by swallows and the top of the cliff hangs above you in layers. Turn right and follow the white powdery trail past some impressive eroded formations to the end of the cliffs. Scramble around the north-western face of the Mountain and follow the markers around to the south-western face, past clumps of flowering heath. An obvious trail then leads up to a small rocky knoll just below the summit. One trail turns right and follows the ridge but the easiest route to the summit contours below the ridge with one small scramble to the top. The 360° views from the summit are stunning. The lake-like areas behind Mt Tibrogargan are actually Pumicestone Passage, which separates Bribie Island from the mainland. After enjoying the views, descend via the same route.

Last reviewed: 18 August 1997

131

BEGINNER TO EXPERIENCED

The concept of K2 Extreme is to make available the opportunity for people to experience the outdoors to their own level of satisfaction. We introduce inexperienced people to new and exciting activities as well as arrange more advanced events for those who have not yet been challenged.

CURRENT ACTIVITIES OPERATING

- *Bushwalking* • *Climbing* • *Canoeing* • *Kayaking* • *Rafting*
- *Mountain Biking* • *Cycling* • *Abseiling*

OTHER EVENTS

This is up to your imagination! Suggest an activity and we will investigate.

K2 EXTREME IS DESIGNED TO ENVIRONMENTALLY EDUCATE PEOPLE WHILST ENJOYING OUTDOOR EXPERIENCES.

Phone for details

MEMBERSHIP: *$25 per year*
Newsletter published every 2 months with a calendar of events

K2 Extreme
140 Wickham Street,
Fortitude Valley, Brisbane 4006

Phone: (07) 3257 3310
Facsimile: (07) 3854 1281
Internet: k2extreme.com.au

ACCESS - MT TIBROGARGAN

0.0kms	Turn left into Old Gympie Road.
1.5kms	Turn left into Marsh Road.
3.3kms	Turn right into Tibrogargan car park.

MT TIBROGARGAN CLIMB

Distance: 2.5kms return, allow 3 hours. Hard grade.

Like the climb to Mt Beerwah, only confident, experienced scramblers should attempt to climb to the 364m summit of Mt Tibrogargon. It is rated *'hard'* because of the precipitous nature of the climb. The track is steep and exposed and loose powdery dirt makes many of the rock slabs slippery. Although the climb is shorter than Beerwah, the track is more exposed and it is not a climb for young children.

The sandy track from the car park zigzags steeply uphill, across an eroded rocky section leading to a short scramble near the base of a small cliff. From here, the climb begins. Scramble up a cleft in the rock and follow the obvious trail left, then around to the right, to the base of a short cliff. This section of the climb is probably the most daunting, as you scramble up the exposed rock. From here, follow the trail as it winds from one side to another, bypassing precarious sections. You soon reach an eroded gully where the dirt is loose underfoot but the track is less exposed. Care is required not to dislodge loose rocks onto climbers below. There is one more steep slab before the summit ridge and care is required here, especially if the fine powdery dust has settled on the rocks. From the summit ridge, follow the track to the second peak and down to a rocky ledge for good views of the coastline. On a clear day the views extend from Noosa in the north, and south to Brisbane. It is much easier to make out Bribie Island beyond Pumicestone Passage, than from the summit of Beerwah. The Sandhills of Moreton Island are clearly visible. Descend carefully via the same route to the car park.

Last reviewed: 18 August 1997

ACCESS - MT ELIMBAH (SADDLEBACK)

0.0kms	Turn left into Old Gympie Road.
4.5kms	Veer left towards Beerburrum.
5.0kms	Turn right into a gravel road.
9.5kms	Cross over a bitumen road.
11.5kms	Pipe gate on the left and entrance to National Park.

MT ELIMBAH TRAIL

Distance: 3kms return, allow 1.5-2 hours. Easy grade.

The scramble to the top of this minor peak provides a different perspective of the area surrounding the Glass House Mountains. Whilst there is no graded track to the peak, there are no navigational difficulties.

Follow the old road for a few minutes to a 'T' junction. Turn right and follow the road uphill to the top of a small crest. As the road flattens out and swings downhill to the right, look for a faint vehicle track leading straight ahead. This track soon turns into a footpad and contours around the side of the Mountain, through open eucalypt forest with grassy ground cover. Follow the footpad for about five minutes to a small, flat, rocky area spotted with patches of yellow lichen. From here, turn left and walk straight up towards the Mountain through clumps of thin, woody tea trees that produce spectacular flowers. Scramble over the large boulders at the base of the cliff and head straight up to the ridge. Turn right at the ridge and follow a faint footpad a short distance to the summit. There are two rare species of plant around the western edge of the summit (*Keraudrenia hillii* and *Dodonaea rupicola*) so please keep clear of this area.

The view is north to Mt Tibrogargan. Mt Coonowrin (Crookneck) is to the left and Mt Beerwah can just be seen between the two peaks of Tunbubudla (The Twins). The conical shaped hill to the west, behind a pineapple plantation is Mt Miketeebumulgrai. Return via the same route. If tall grass obscures the footpad, head north, veering slightly to the left of the ridge to regain the old road.

Last reviewed: 18 August 1997

MAP REFERENCE
Sunmap - GLASS HOUSE MOUNTAINS 1:25000
Ngungun   UBD Brisbane Street Directory – Sunshine Coast, Map 115
Tibrogargan   UBD Brisbane Street Directory – Sunshine Coast, Map 125
Elimbah   UBD Brisbane Street Directory – Map 37
QNPWS Visitor Information Guide shows most peaks.

FACILITIES
Camping facilities are not provided in any section of the National Park. Privately run caravan parks are available outside the Park boundaries. Mts Beerwah and Tibrogargan have picnic tables (shelter shed at Beerwah), toilets and water. Wood barbecues are located at Mt Tibrogargan but please supply your own firewood. Do not collect firewood from within the Park.

Mt Coonowrin and the east face of Mt Tibrogargan are suitable only for experienced rockclimbers. Maintained walking tracks lead to the cliff-lines of Mts Beerwah and Tibrogargan. Summit climbs should only be attempted by those with some bushwalking and climbing experience (refer to the notes for each walk).

Mts Miketeebumulgrai and Coochin Hills areas are accessible to bushwalkers, but no tracks are provided.

Carry plenty of water when climbing any of the peaks, especially during summer. April to September provides the best walking and climbing conditions. The wildflowers are at their peak during late winter and early spring.

Please ensure that barbecue fires are lit only in designated fireplaces and doused thoroughly when cooking is completed.

RANGER CONTACT - (07) 5494 3983

NORTH COAST RAIL GROUP OF NATIONAL PARKS

HISTORY

In 1918, Eudlo National Park was gazetted to preserve an area of scenic beauty for the rail travelling public. It became Queensland's sixth national park. Dularcha National Park, the seventh to be gazetted in Queensland, was proclaimed in 1921. At the time, rail travel was very popular and it was the intention to declare a series of small, scenic parks at intervals all the way along the North Coast rail line. Although the idea was a good one at the time, only four parks were ever gazetted. **Eudlo Creek National Park** consists of two small sections with a total area of only 41.9ha. **Ferntree Creek National Park** at 72.4ha now contains the area originally called **Tuckers Creek National Park**, and **Dularcha National Park** is the largest at 138ha.

Even though it was a national park, Dularcha was surveyed for a rifle range in 1930. This idea was abandoned. Then, local banana growers claimed the area contained some good banana land and a number of ex-servicemen were willing to take up the land to increase local production. There was also pressure to log the area during the 1930s. Despite these pressures, the National Park was kept intact. A cyclone damaged the Park in 1954 and more damage was caused by a bushfire in 1960. Dularcha is the local Aboriginal name for *'blackbutt country'*.

In the early days of national parks, few people considered that national parks deserved protection but despite demands to use them for other purposes, these small parcels of land did survive.

FEATURES

The Parks are extremely small and in some cases contain only a narrow strip 200m wide, along the sides of the railway line. However, they do contain an example of bushland that is rapidly being lost to residential development.

When Dularcha was proclaimed, it was said that, "...*much of the area consists of hardwood jungle and has a permanent watercourse through it*".

Plant species living in the Parks include; flooded gum, grey gum, turpentine, box, red stringy bark and bloodwood, as well as palms and tree ferns.

The bushland is home to many bird species including grey butcher birds, red-browed firetails, little wattle birds, honeyeaters, treecreepers, wrens, eastern whipbirds, golden whistlers, rose robins, cuckoos and whistling kites.

ACCESS

These Parks certainly do not provide extensive opportunities for bushwalking. However, access details have been included for those who are interested in locating the Parks.

ACCESS - FERNTREE CREEK NATIONAL PARK

Ferntree Creek National Park consists of two sections. The southern section was previously known as Tuckers Creek National Park. Nambour Golf Course and the rail line abut either side of this section.

0.0kms	Turn right, off National Park Road into Zealey Road.
0.3kms	Turn right into a dirt road.
0.5kms	National Park Boundary. Still sign posted *Tuckers Creek National Park.*

MAP REFERENCE
UBD Brisbane Street Directory – Sunshine Coast, Map 56

ACCESS - EUDLO CREEK NATIONAL PARK
Travel from Landsborough to the town of Eudlo.

0.0kms	Turn right at Eudlo on Coast Road towards Palmwoods.
1.4kms	*Eudlo National Park* sign on left.
1.6kms	Turn left over a culvert. A maintenance track leads 200m to the railway line.

The northern boundary of the Park is at Bamboo Road, 1.3kms from the southern boundary.

MAP REFERENCE
Sunmap - NAMBOUR 1:50 000
UBD Brisbane Street Directory - Sunshine Coast, Map 76

ACCESS - DULARCHA NATIONAL PARK
Travel to Landsborough and turn right immediately over the railway line and drive to the end of the main street.

0.0kms	Turn left into Cribb Street.
0.1kms	Turn right past the State School.
0.7kms	Turn left into Myla Road.
1.0kms	Turn right, on Myla Road.
1.5kms	Turn right into Beech Road.
2.1kms	National Park boundary.

THE TUNNEL WALK
Distance: 4.6kms return, allow 1.5 hours. Easy grade.

Leave your vehicle at the Park boundary and walk along the 4WD track for 300m. When you reach the railway line the road turns left and runs parallel to the rail tracks. After 1.2kms, another track commonly used as a bridal trail leads off to the left. Continue straight ahead for 200m and veer left alongside the tracks. Ignore a second old trail, 200m from this point and walk a further 200m to a spot where the rail line has been diverted. The 4WD track now follows the original location of the old line for about 600m before reaching the tunnel entrance. Walk through the tunnel for about 100m, then retrace your steps back to your vehicle.

The northern Park boundary is only 800m from the northern end of the tunnel.

This unusual National Park, about 200m wide and 3.5kms long gives an insight into thinking behind the early creation of national parks. Parks like Dularcha have played an important role in the evolutionary process of national park selection.

Last reviewed: 9 June 1997

MAP REFERENCE
Sunmap - LANDSBOROUGH 1:50 000
UBD Brisbane Street Directory – Sunshine Coast, Map 96.

FACILITIES
There are no facilities at any of these Parks but they are all close to villages of the Sunshine Coast Hinterland.

RANGER CONTACT - (07) 5494 3983

KONDALILLA NATIONAL PARK

HISTORY
Kondalilla National Park is situated on the western slopes of the Blackall Ranges, in the Sunshine Coast Hinterland.

A 73ha area around Kondalilla Falls was originally protected and set aside for recreation in 1906. It was given national park status is 1945. Obi Obi National Park was merged with Kondalilla National Park in 1988 taking the total area to 327ha.

The Blackall Ranges, originally called *'Bonyi Bonyi'* after the nut bearing bunya pine, were a gathering place for the Gubbi Gubbi tribe of Aboriginal people. They met for celebrations and ceremonies about every three years during good bunya nut seasons.

The Aboriginal meaning of the word Kondalilla is *'rushing waters'.*

During the 19th century European settlers logged the Blackall Ranges for red cedar, white beech, bunya pine and blackbutt. The area was named the Blackall Ranges during the 1860s, after Samuel Blackall, Governor of Queensland from 1868-1871.

After the land was cleared, dairy farms were established and citrus and pineapple plantations thrived in the rich soils. Today, macadamia and avocado trees are prominent and replace many of the dairy farms. Fresh fruit and vegetables direct from farmer's gardens are sold at roadside stalls.

Baroon Pocket Dam was officially opened in July 1989 to provide water for the rapidly growing Sunshine Coast. More recently, unique villages complete with period style shops have provided a tourist boost to the local area. Quaint coffee shops provide refreshing drinks after walks in the Park, while local arts and crafts are retailed from charming premises.

FEATURES

This section of the Blackall Range is on the western extremity of basalt flows that extend from Maleny to Mapleton. Skene Creek has eroded a series of attractive cascades and rock pools at the head of the 90m Kondalilla Falls.

The area contained within the National Park protects remnants of original subtropical rainforest and tall open forest that once dominated the north coastal highlands, including 10 plant species that are either rare or endangered. Bunya pines, hoop pines, piccabeen palms, red and white cedars and mahogany, grow in heavily timbered subtropical rainforests and open forests of the Park. Some unusual rainforest species include; incense wood, Whitsunday kurrajong, brown cudgeree (mango bark) and native tree of heaven (white bean). Epiphytes such as elkhorns, staghorns and orchids grow amongst these trees.

The forests are inhabited by at least 107 species of birds including red goshawks and Australian Peregrine falcons.

Parrots, pigeons, honeyeaters, whistlers, fern birds and thrushes are often seen and the call of the wompoo pigeons can be heard as you wander along the tracks.

Seventy species of reptiles and 32 species of frogs have been identified. The gastric brooding frog was found at Picnic Creek in 1972 but there have been no further sightings since 1979. This frog is unique in that the tadpoles develop in the female's stomach. The froglets are regurgitated when they are ready to lead their own lives.

The protected Queensland lungfish lives in streams and pools in the Park. The lungfish has gills like normal fish as well as an air bladder, that it uses like a lung. This allows it to breathe either in or out of water. Platypus and freshwater crayfish also depend on the streams for their survival.

ACCESS

Head north from Brisbane for about 54kms and leave the Bruce Highway at the Landsborough, Maleny turn off.

0.0kms	Turn left through the township of Landsborough and follow the signs to Maleny.
10.0kms	Turn right towards Montville.
21.0kms	Pass through Montville.
23.0kms	Turn left on the sign posted road to *Kondalilla Falls National Park*. Head down this road until you reach the car park.

PICNIC CREEK CIRCUIT

Distance: 2.1kms, allow 1 hour. Easy grade.

From the car park, walk down through the picnic area to the start of the walking track. The track heads downhill to a bridge over Picnic Creek. Cross the Creek and climb the steps to the right and follow the track to a junction. Take the right hand track that zigzags downhill and finally reaches a pool at the top of Kondalilla Falls. (The left hand track leads back to the bridge over Picnic Creek.) This is an ideal spot for a swim on a hot day. A helipad has been constructed on the site. Stop for a while and enjoy the sweeping views of the valley below. A cleared section of farming land in a 'V' at the end of the valley marks the spot where Skene Creek flows into Obi Obi Creek. To complete this walk, retrace your steps to the junction. Continue straight ahead for 800m, again crossing the bridge and back to the picnic area.

Last reviewed: 8 February 1997

KONDALILLA FALLS CIRCUIT
Distance: 2.7km from the top of the Falls, allow 1.5hours. Easy grade.

From the pool at the top of the Falls, take the right hand track and continue downhill via another series of steps until you reach a track junction. Turn left and walk 100m to some large boulders at the base of the Falls. Return to the junction and follow the track over a wooden bridge that crosses Skene Creek. The track now winds slowly uphill providing good views north to the ranges around the headwaters of Mary River, then out of the rainforest, finally arriving again at the top of the Falls. Return to the car park via Picnic Creek circuit.

Last reviewed: 8 February 1997

OBI OBI GORGE
Distance: 14kms, allow 7-8 hours. Moderate to hard grade.

For the more adventurous, this strenuous walk / rock hop / float / swim provides a different look at this section of the Blackall Range area. You will need to arrange a car shuffle, leaving one vehicle at Baroon Pocket Dam car park (the sign posted road to Baroon Pocket Dam is 200m south of Montville township), and another at Kondalilla Falls car park.

To start the walk, follow the directions for Kondalilla Falls circuit until you reach the wooden bridge over Skene Creek. At this point, leave the graded track and rock hop down the Creek. There are some relatively well worn footpads but for most of this part of the walk you will need to pick your own way amongst the rocks in the Creek. Skene Creek winds through large stands of piccabeen palms and distinctive dome shaped bunya pines. The subtropical rainforest scenery is often spectacular, especially in areas where the Creek bed consists of wide rocky slabs. After about 1.5 hours you will reach a large boulder in the centre of Skene Creek where it meets Obi Obi Creek. Pick your way around to the left and up an embankment where you will find an old footpad. Follow this track along the Creek for about three hours, crossing the Creek several times before you reach the southern end of Obi Obi Gorge. This steep sided Gorge hosts a variety of epiphytic orchids and ferns. Here, wrap your back pack in a large plastic bag, inflate your air bed (if you have one) and swim or float about 200m through the Gorge. Once through the Gorge, continue rock hopping upstream for about 30 minutes

until you reach a wide right hand bend just past a good swimming hole.
The graded track to Baroon Pocket Dam car park is found about 100m on the left, upstream from the swimming hole. The track and steps lead uphill to the car park. If you miss the track entrance you will soon reach the dam wall where you will find another footpad leading to the top car park.
(To view the Gorge without completing the whole walk, rock hop down stream from the dam for 30-45 minutes. This is a pleasant spot for a picnic and a swim.)

Last reviewed: 8 February 1997 with NPAQ – leader John Daly.

NB. This walk should not be attempted by poor swimmers or after heavy rain when water may be released from Baroon Pocket Dam.

MAP REFERENCE
Sunmap - WITTA 1:25 000
Walking track maps are provided on the QNPWS Visitor Information sheet.

FACILITIES
No camping is allowed. Private accommodation is available in the surrounding townships. Picnic areas with tables, barbecues, shelter sheds, toilets, and water are provided. Swimming is popular at the pool above Kondalilla Falls. The Park is at its best in spring or autumn. Motorised boats are not allowed on Baroon Pocket Dam but other water sports including angling and wind surfing are permitted

RANGER CONTACT - (07) 5494 3983

MAPLETON FALLS NATIONAL PARK

HISTORY
Mapleton Falls National Park, a 25.9ha area of scenic beauty around Mapleton Falls was proclaimed a national park in 1973. It had been set aside for recreational purposes since 1935. Like Kondalilla National Park, this relatively small National Park is situated on the western slopes of the Blackall Ranges.
The Gubbi Gubbi tribe of Aboriginal people travelled through this section of the Blackall Ranges about every three years on the way to bunya nut feasts and other tribal celebrations.
The area surrounding the Park was heavily logged during the 19th century prior to the establishment of dairy farms. In recent times, avocado, macadamia, citrus and pineapple plantations have been established on these original dairy farms.
The nature of the area has changed somewhat over the last decade with the adjoining towns of Mapleton, Montville and Maleny attracting many day visitors.

FEATURES
The area surrounding this small National Park is on the western extremity of the basalt flows extending from Maleny to Mapleton.

Cooling and contracting of these lava flows produced basalt columns around the Mapleton Falls escarpment. Pencil Creek tumbles 120m over Mapleton Falls and ultimately flows into the Mary River catchment area.

The Park protects remnant examples of subtropical rainforest and tall open forest that once covered much of the Blackall and Conondale Ranges. The terrain and vegetation are very similar to that found in Kondalilla Falls National Park with both hoop pine and bunya pine spread throughout the Park. Staghorns and elkhorns are also common.

The 107 species of birds, 70 species of reptiles and many of the 32 species of frogs identified in the Blackall Ranges can all be located by keen observers. The Peregrine falcon, that uses abandoned nests of other birds, can often be spotted soaring above Mapleton Falls.

ACCESS
Follow the directions for Kondalilla National Park.

0.0kms	Road to Kondalilla Falls. Continue straight ahead towards Mapleton.
6.1kms	Turn left.
9.0kms	Veer right.
9.8kms	Mapleton Falls car park.

WOMPOO CIRCUIT
Distance: 1.3km, allow 1 hour. Easy grade.

Start walking from the car park, through the picnic area and locate the start of the short walking track. Walk down from the picnic area and then up some steps as the track follows the Creek through rainforest. Turn left at the track junction and walk 50m to Peregrine Lookout. You can't view the Falls from here, but you do get good views down Obi Obi Valley. Look for Peregrine falcons soaring on the thermals above the Valley. Return to the track junction and turn left. You have left the rainforest and are now walking through eucalypt forest. After five minutes, turn right and head downhill past some large grey gums. A small footbridge crosses a swampy gully as you head through a stand of piccabeen palms on the way back to the car park.

Last reviewed: 9 June 1997

NB. The original 160m track to Mapleton Falls Lookout has been closed. There are plans to refurbish the Park and build another lookout in a safe location as soon as Government funds are available. Check with the Ranger for current details.

MAP REFERENCE
Sunmap - GHEERULLA CREEK 1:25 000
Walking track maps are provided on the QNPWS Visitor Information sheet.

FACILITIES
There is no camping allowed.   Private accommodation is available in the surrounding townships.
Toilets with wheelchair access, picnic tables, shelter sheds, and barbecues are located in the picnic area.

RANGER CONTACT - (07) 5494 3983

CONONDALE NATIONAL PARK

HISTORY
Concerned citizens and action groups commenced lobbying as early as the 1960s to gain government approval to protect the mountains, forests, gorges and endangered fauna found in the Conondale Range. Logging began in earnest in the 1950s, after the construction of the Mt Gerald Trail, referred to in the Mt Langley walk.
'Save the Conondale Range Committee' was formed in 1976 and the following year they submitted their first proposal for a 31 000ha area to be set aside as a national park. Subsequently the Queensland Government declared two separate areas, totalling only 2 126ha as national parkland.
Lobbying to have the Park area extended continued and studies were undertaken to ascertain the effects of extensive logging on local fauna. Sadly, by 1984 two of three species of fauna considered endangered and being studied at the time, had disappeared from the Conondales. The gastric brooding frog and southern dayfrog were last seen in 1979.
In 1987, plans were announced to reopen an old gold mine on North Booloumba Creek as an open cut mine. The following year the mining company planned to expand the operation to make it more financially viable. They intended trucking 100 000 tonnes of ore into the Conondales from other mines for processing. When the State Government rejected the plan, the mining company shut down their operations and removed their equipment. They subsequently went into receivership in 1990, leaving an area of devastation, including holding ponds of extremely noxious sodium cyanide. The State Government only held a $20 000 rehabilitation bond from the mining company but they eventually allocated $860 000 to repair the damage. The restoration took three years with the final stage of the rehabilitation process, revegetation, being completed in April 1997.
Hard work and perseverance by many forward thinking people, including those of the Conondale Range Committee over a period of nearly 20 years, finally resulted in more of the Conondale Range being protected for future generations. An additional 4 855ha was added in 1995, taking the total area of Conondale National

Park to 6 980ha. A quote from Napoleon Bonaparte surely applies here, *"...victory belongs to the most persevering"*.

FEATURES
Mountainous ranges of subtropical rainforest and eucalypt forest form the wilderness area of Conondale Range. The forest is almost impenetrable due to dense woody vine intertwined through the trees. The Park houses five of the tallest peaks in the Sunshine Coast Hinterland; Mts Langley, Ramsden, Lofty, Cabinet and Constance and takes in the upper catchment of East and West branches of Kilcoy Creek and some sections of Ramsden, Peters, Bundaroo and South Booloumba Creeks. The latter three flow into the Mary River, one of the State's largest, supplying water needs for a growing population.

The Park includes examples of the six major forest types of the ranges, ie. four types of rainforest, dry sclerophyll (eucalypt) forest and tall scrubby forest. Bunya pine and cedar are significant in the area. The rainforest surrounding Mt Gerald Trail section of the Mt Langley walk is representative of rainforest that covered most of the Blackall Range prior to European settlement. Large areas of diverse forest types have been heavily logged and today hoop pine plantations, incorporated in State Forest, flank several sides of the Park.

The region has many unique fauna species, some found only in the Conondales. More than 180 species of birds, including 22 rare and endangered species, have been recorded. The plumed frogmouth is considered one of the rarest birds in Australia and has been recorded at only a few other sites. Other birds include the powerful owl, sooty owl, double eyed fig parrot, red goshawk, Peregrine falcon, yellow-eyed cuckoo shrike, paradise riflebird and the black-breasted button-quail.

Found only in the Conondales, the gastric brooding or platypus frog is the only vertebrate in the world to raise its young entirely in its stomach. The froglets are regurgitated after six weeks. This is unique, not only for a frog, but for the whole animal kingdom. It is the only truly aquatic frog in Australia and the most primitive amphibian.

The marsupial frog, whose young develop in pouches at the sides of the adult male, is also found in the Park. Other rare and vulnerable species recorded in the Park include the giant spiny lobster, the lungfish, Stephen's banded snake and the yellow-bellied glider.

ACCESS
Take the Bruce Highway and follow the signs to Maleny. From the township of Maleny drive north on Kenilworth Road, 33kms to Booloumba Creek Road. If travelling south via Kenilworth, Booloumba Creek Road is 500m south of Little Yabba Creek.

0.0kms	Turn into Booloumba Creek Road, at the sign post marked *Booloumba Creek 5kms.*
4.0kms	Cross a grid, then ford Booloumba Creek and enter Kenilworth State Forest.

4.4kms	Second ford on Booloumba Creek.
5.0kms	Booloumba Camping Area 1 on the right.
5.3kms	Booloumba Picnic Area 2 on the right.
6.0kms	Cross another ford.
6.5kms	Booloumba Camping Area 3 on the right.
6.6kms	Booloumba Camping Area 4 on the left.
7.1kms	*Conondale National Park* sign.
13.1kms	Locked gate on left at the start of North Goods Fire Management Trail.
14.9kms	*National Park Boundary* sign on the right.
15.4kms	Booloumba Falls car park on the right.
15.6kms	Cross Booloumba Creek
17.3kms	Locked gate on left at the start of South Goods Fire Management Trail.
21.5kms	Turn left into Sunday Creek Road towards Jimna.
28.0kms	*Conondale National Park* sign.
28.6kms	'Y' junction. Sign on left shows *Conondale National Park.* Take left fork on Peters Fire Management Trail. The right hand branch leads 14kms to Jimna.
30.2kms	Locked gate and commencement of Mt Langley walk.

NB. When parking vehicles near any locked gate at the start of fire management trails please ensure they do not block the gateway. These trails are used by authorised vehicles during fires and other emergencies and to maintain the fire break roads.

NORTH GOODS FIRE MANAGEMENT TRAIL
Distance: 12kms return, allow 3 hours. Easy grade

This walk along the fire management trail provides an insight into some vegetation types typical of the Conondale area. The trail starts at the **13.1kms** point in the access details. Follow the trail as it winds up and down through the forest. You will reach an open cleared section on the left of the track about 15 minutes from the start. Piccabeen palms are scattered amongst the tall flooded gums on the left of the track. Continue for a further five minutes to a track junction. (The Walsh Fire Management Trail leads off to the right.) Follow the road downhill for another 20 minutes taking note of the changing vegetation as you leave the National Park and enter heavily logged areas.

Turn back when you reach an area of obvious fire damage and retrace your steps to the starting point. If you have time take a short detour down Walsh Fire Management Trail before returning to your vehicle.

Last reviewed: 8 July 1997

NB. Alternatively, a walk along South Goods Fire Management Trail provides excellent examples of typical riparian vegetation, piccabeen palm forests and rainforests.

MT LANGLEY WALK
Distance: 9kms return, allow 5 hours. Moderate grade.

This is the highest point in the Sunshine Coast Hinterland (868m), but the start of the walk is also high in the Conondale Ranges. The *'moderate'* grade has been assigned because of the final climb from the road to the summit.

Walk along Peters Fire Management Trail about 500m from the gate to a 'T' junction and another locked gate. Continue straight ahead on the Mt Gerald Trail through dense, attractive rainforest. Staghorn and elkhorn ferns, orchids and mosses cling to the tree trunks high in the canopy. The road climbs up and down as it follows the ridge-line through the forest. Lawyer vine and wild raspberry invade the sides of the track. Try to identify the different bird calls as you head through the forest. The most easily identifiable are wompoo fruit-doves, cat birds, whip birds, butcher birds and of course, kookaburras. This is a particularly good area for birdwatching.

After about an hour of ups and downs, you reach a cleared section at the top of the ridge. Short stumps on either side are the remains of trees that have fallen across the track. As you descend again, massive tree ferns hang over the sides of the track. The bank on the right gets steeper as the track winds along the side of the ridge. You soon reach a relatively flat section before descending again. About 10 minutes from the cleared section, the road swings left around the head of a deep gully. A mound has been built up across the road to channel water into the gully. (At the time of writing there was a taped marker on a tree to the right.) Climb up the steep muddy bank and continue straight up the slope through vine forest for a few minutes to the base of a tall buttressed tree. Skirt to the left of this tree, then up again to a tree fall. This tree has been down for years and the branches are beginning to rot, causing a potential safety hazard. Scramble to the right (western) end of the fallen tree, taking care not to dislodge the rotting logs.

Continue climbing diagonally uphill to the right (south-west), skirting around clumps of lawyer vine until you reach the top of a ridge about 20 minutes from the tree fall. Turn left and follow a definite footpad for a few minutes to a cleared grassy section where a mossy rock cairn marks the summit. There are no views from the top.

Return via the same route, taking care not to swing too far to the right (east). If you loose sight of your ascent route, head straight down the side of the Mountain (north) to rejoin the road.

Last reviewed: 5 January 1998

BOOLOUMBA FALLS AND THE BREADKNIFE
Distance: 3.5kms return, allow 1.5 hours. Easy grade to the Lookout.

This walk is in state forest, not national park, but it has been included because it leads to a well known Conondale Range landmark, right at the edge of the National Park boundary. It starts from Booloumba Falls car park at the **15.4kms** point in the access details.

The graded track leads through open eucalypt forest with a ground cover of grasses and bracken ferns. After about 10 minutes, the vegetation changes and tree ferns are scattered amongst the eucalypts. The track starts to descend, parallel to the banks of Bundaroo Creek. About 15 minutes from the start, the track swings left and then right through a stand of piccabeen palms. You soon reach a safety fence and a set of wooden steps leading down to a popular swimming hole at the head of Booloumba Falls. If you do swim, do not dive into the pool. Submerged rocks and logs can cause serious injury. The track continues to a lookout platform with good views towards the Breadknife and Booloumba Gorge. The Breadknife is at the junction of Bundaroo and Peters Creeks.

For competent, experienced scramblers there is a well worn track eroded into the finger of rock leading down to the Breadknife. Follow this track parallel to the watercourse, to a pool on the left at the base of the Breadknife. A rough track leads from the rear of this pool to an eroded footpad up the side of the Breadknife, to the summit. Extreme caution is required on the track to the summit. It is definitely not an area for children. The summit is very exposed. Return via the same route to the graded track and then back to the car park.

Last reviewed: 5 January 1998

MAP REFERENCE
Sunmap - MOUNT LANGLEY 1:25 000
                CONONDALE 1:25 000

FACILITIES
There are no graded walking tracks or facilities within the National Park. However, walking is permitted along the fire management trails. Only experienced bushwalkers with sound navigational skills should attempt any off track walking.

When the Park boundary was extended, it was decided that all existing recreational facilities would remain within the State Forest.   The Department of Natural Resources maintains these recreational areas and the Department of Environment is responsible for conservation issues in the National Park.

Graded walking tracks, picnic and camping facilities are provided in the State Forest. Camp Site 1 has cold showers, toilets, barbecues with wood provided, some picnic tables, water and a public telephone. There are bush camping sites only at Camping Area 3. Access for caravans and large groups is at Camping Area 4 where there are toilets, water and barbecues with firewood provided.   All camping areas have self-registration booths.

Summer temperatures can be quite high in the Conondales, but the nights are cool. There are several spots in the State Forest where swimming is permitted. Spring and autumn are the best times for walking.

RANGER CONTACT - (07) 5494 3983

ISLAND PARKS

ST HELENA ISLAND NATIONAL PARK

HISTORY

Aborigines visited St Helena Island around 2 500 years prior to European habitation. They were attracted to the Island each year during the warmer months, when large colonies of fruit bats congregated. During the winter they hunted dugong in the surrounding waters. Huge middens of bone and shell, one being the oldest man-made relic on the Island, are evidence of their long term use of the area. St Helena was originally described as one of the *'Green Islands'* by Matthew Flinders, in 1799. It was named St Helena in 1828, when a troublesome Aborigine named Napoleon was exiled there from Dunwich penal settlement on North Stradbroke Island, after stealing an axe. Unlike his namesake, he later escaped in a self-made canoe.

During the mid 19th century, the Island was used as a base for dugong fishing operations. In 1866 it was selected as the site for a quarantine station and prison labour was used for construction. However, the isolation of the Island lent itself to the establishment of Queensland's most notorious penal colony in 1867. The harsh treatment dished out to inmates gained it a reputation as the *'Hell Hole of the Pacific'.*

The prison settlement quickly became self-sufficient, and it was soon heralded as one of the finest examples of self-sufficiency and profitability in the world.

The first buildings were constructed from bricks and timber brought from the mainland. Timber growing in the rainforests was considered unsuitable and was only used to construct fences. It wasn't long before the colony boasted two cell blocks as well as a hospital, lime kiln, boathouse, kitchen, Superintendent's cottage, bakehouse and stables, and even a mill to process sugar cane grown on the Island. The workshops housed carpentry, blacksmithing, tinsmithing, boot and shoe making, saddle making, candle making, tailoring, book binding and sail making industries. Queensland's first tramway system was established on the Island. The surviving beach rock walls and causeway are recognised as notable engineering feats.

The original rainforest was cleared for pastures and crops. Introduced plants soon began to grow around the supervisor's cottages. The prison Superintendent encouraged visiting ship's captains to bring native trees from their homelands and many of these were planted around the Island. Olive groves produced fruit that won prizes for their oil quality in Italy, and Ayrshire dairy cattle raised on the Island were common amongst award winners at Brisbane RNA shows.

During 1891, Queensland shearers went on strike for better working conditions. Many of the ring leaders were subsequently charged, convicted and jailed on St Helena Island.

Shark feeding was actively encouraged to deter prisoners with thoughts of escaping by swimming to the mainland.

Changing attitudes to prison reform led to the goal being changed to *'prison farm'* status in 1921. It remained a prison farm until its closure in 1932.

Ownership was handed to the Lands Department in 1939 and areas were subsequently leased to graziers prior to the 75.1ha island being declared Queensland's first Historic Site National Park in October 1979.

School excursions to St Helena are encouraged to teach children about our early history.

FEATURES

This small tadpole shaped island is surrounded by a relic coral reef. Basalt escarpments rise from the south-west corner and form steep ridges on the southern, northern and western sides of the Island. A thin band of forest and mangroves lining the eastern shore are all that is left of St Helena's original vegetation.

There are very few native animals living on the Island but wallabies, introduced in the 1980s, are occasionally seen in the shade of the ruins.

Large numbers of native birds including rainbow bee-eaters, honeyeaters, plovers, kingfishers and quails inhabit the Island, along with many migratory waders and introduced peacocks. Cattle still graze on the Island, in keeping with the theme of this Historic National Park.

The fresh water on St Helena originally fell as rain on the Darling Downs, near Toowoomba. This water drains into the Great Artesian Basin, the largest artesian basin in the world, and flows underground across Moreton Bay to St Helena.

The ruins on St Helena are reminiscent of those found at Port Arthur and on Norfolk Island, yet they are easily visited on a day trip from Brisbane.

The remaining relics are all built of beach rock (cay sandstone) quarried on the Island by prisoners. The surface beach rock initially used proved much too soft for building materials. Harder rock was found following further excavation.

The Rangers have positioned a large beach rock *'block'* near the site of the old quarry for visitors to *'touch'* and feel how easily it erodes.

The Wynnum-Manly Rotary Club has built a train line to carry visitors from the southern end of the Island to the start of the guided walk. The train line follows the site of the original tramway and is run by commercial tour operators.

ACCESS

St Helena is located in Moreton Bay, 8km from the mouth of Brisbane River, and about 7km north-east of Manly. Two tourist launches leave from Breakfast Creek and Manly, according to demand. Look in the Brisbane Yellow Pages for current details.

Private boats can be anchored in the area adjacent to the causeway.

To preserve the fragile ruins, access to the restricted sections of the Island is only permitted with an accredited tour guide, or a National Park Ranger. Rangers guide tours departing daily, at midday, from the shelter shed near the start of the causeway. Check for current details prior to your visit. Fees are levied for the tours.

THE ST HELENA RUINS
Distance: 2-4kms, allow 2 hours. Easy grade.

The guided walk takes in all the major historical sites on the Island, but the route varies, depending upon the number of groups on the Island at the time. As you walk from the boat along the jetty, you pass the old jetty ruins, and one of the first things you notice is the remains of the swimming enclosure. The iron posts were designed to provide protection from sharks. Then, either board the train for a 900m ride, or walk past numerous old water wells to the start of the main ruins. From here, your guide will explain history and construction of the remains of various buildings including the administration block, the blacksmith's shop, the prison cells, solitary confinement cells, kitchens, the Superintendent's garden and the dairy. One of the old buildings has been restored and houses many interesting relics relating to the prison era.

The tour then leads back down to the southern end of the Island to the silos and the sugar mill, past the prisoner's and warden's cemetery and the lime kiln, before ending at the old quarry and an Aboriginal midden.

While waiting for your boat to leave for the mainland enjoy strolling or lazing around the cleared, grassy flats of the unrestricted zone that extends from the quarry and old tramway up to the southern boundary of the first grazing paddock.

Last reviewed: 7 November 1997.

MAP REFERENCE
Sunmap - WYNNUM 1:25 000
A Visitor Information Sheet is available from Naturally Queensland, 160 Ann Street, Brisbane, or by contacting the Park Rangers.

FACILITIES
Picnic tables and shelter areas are located near the causeway. Toilets are situated in the picnic area and the Superintendent's garden. Drinking water is available at these points. Any time is a good time to visit this unique national park but mosquitoes may be a problem during summer.

RANGER CONTACT - (07) 3396 5113

BLUE LAKE NATIONAL PARK

HISTORY
This 501ha national park lies on the eastern side of North Stradbroke Island, the largest of three sand islands extending almost 200kms from Moreton Bay to Maryborough. The chain of islands separates the mainland from the Pacific Ocean, forming Moreton Bay, known as *Quandamooka* to local Aborigines.

North Stradbroke Island, known as *Minjerrib,* has particular cultural significance to these Aborigines and evidence of shell middens can be seen at various locations on the Island. The rich source of seafoods, animals and plants provided an excellent diet for the Aborigines. They even trained dolphins to herd fish close to shore, where they were netted and speared. In keeping with Aboriginal culture, the catch was then shared with the dolphins.

North and South Stradbroke were originally part of one island, but European activity and a severe storm as late as 1896 formed what is now Jumpinpin Passage. It is thought that the southern end of the original island was once connected to The Spit at Southport and the northern end joined Moreton Island. Neither Captain Cook nor Matthew Flinders mentioned the Passage at Southport in their voyages of 1770 and 1799. In 1799, Flinders was the first to record the South Passage Bar that separates North Stradbroke Island from Moreton Island.

Rocky reefs, shifting sand bars, rough seas and bad weather have claimed many shipwrecks around the Island.

Sandmining activity on North Stradbroke Island has continually caused confrontation between mining companies and environmentalists. Protests and blockades continue to bring public attention to conservation issues and increases pressure on mining companies to ensure rehabilitation of the mined areas.

Blue Lake National Park was proclaimed in 1962. It protects significant Aboriginal culture, two freshwater lakes, one being a '*window lake*', the other a '*perched lake*' and part of the complex dune systems of the Island.

FEATURES

The intricate dune system on North Stradbroke Island was formed by sand shifting along fast flowing rivers to the sea, following erosion of highlands in Eastern New South Wales and Southern Queensland. The sands carried by ocean currents were blocked by the volcanic rock of Point Lookout. Several hundred thousand years of changes in sea level, along with wind action have resulted in the sands being redeposited inland, forming the dunes.

Pigface, a succulent plant with a bright pink flower, grows over the dunes, helping stabilise them and curbing sand erosion.

Eucalypt, melaleuca and banksia forests surround the Lakes and swampy areas of the Park. Wattles, banksias and heath communities grow throughout the area and erupt in a colourful display during late winter and early spring.

Blue Lake is an example of a '*window lake*' that occurs when the ground level falls below the water table. With a surface of 7.3ha, it has a maximum depth of only 9.4m.

Tortoise Lagoon is a '*perched lake*', that occurs when water is held by impermeable sandrock depressions between the sand dunes, well above the water table level. It reached a depth of 1.4m when full in 1974. You will note many of the trees around the Lake are dead. This is a result of the 1974 floods.

Both these lakes are protected within the Park. The acidic waters of the Lakes support little animal life. Grebes, ducks, black swans and other waterbirds gather around Blue Lake which is also home to the southern sun fish.

Eighteen Mile Swamp teems with birdlife.   The rainbow lorikeets make a particularly pretty and noisy *'show'* as they feed on flowering native trees.

Grey kangaroos and koalas live on the Island and if you are lucky, you may spot a golden wallaby. This is a distinct variation from the common swamp wallaby of the mainland.

Many tree frogs, lace monitors and goannas can be seen in the trees. The yellow-faced whip snake occasionally startles visitors to the Park as it rustles amongst the leaf litter beside the tracks.

ACCESS

Take the vehicle ferry from Cleveland or Redland Bay on the mainland to Dunwich, an historical township on the western side of the Island.

0.0kms   Disembark from the ferry and drive straight ahead to the second intersection.

0.4kms   Veer right on Mallon Road. This becomes Martin Way.

8.3kms   Turn right into Blue Lake car park.

NB. Alternatively, a water taxi leaves from Cleveland, but if this is used you would need to make your own arrangements to travel to the National Park.

TORTOISE LAGOON AND BLUE LAKE

Distance: 5.5kms return, allow 2 hours. Easy grade.

The walking track to Blue Lake starts from the car park at the entrance to Blue Lake National Park. It is to the left of the 4WD road. Locate the track and turn right at the junction, ignoring the sign pointing left towards Neem-Beeba. Follow the graded track as it runs parallel to the 4WD track. The track passes through an area dominated by acacias, wattles and melaleucas with some heath. After about 700m you reach a lookout above Tortoise Lagoon. From the lookout you can see, or at least hear, several species of bird life.

The track continues along the ridge and eventually joins the sandy road, 700m from Blue Lake car park. It is only another 100m from this car park to the edge of the Lake. The first thing you notice about the Lake is the clarity of the water, however, the Lake is susceptible to pollution that affects the sensitive ecosystem. For this reason and because of the cultural significance of the Lake, swimming is discouraged. The boarding along the edge of the Lake is designed to prevent erosion of the soft bank. Climb the steps and continue to follow the track as it leads past the edge of the Lake for about 400m to a bridge. This small creek drains water from Blue Lake into Eighteen Mile Swamp. Return to the Lake and retrace your steps to the car park.

Alternatively, you could extend the walk and return via Neem-Beeba, as described below.

Last reviewed: 11 August 1997

BLUE LAKE, THE BEACH AND NEEM-BEEBA
Distance: 13.5kms, allow 4 hours. Moderate grade.

This circuit walk provides access to some seldom visited sections of the Park. Follow the directions for the previous walk to the creek at the end of Blue Lake. From the creek crossing, walk 50m to a track junction. Turn left and follow the track steeply uphill along the fire break road to a 'T' junction, near the top of a ridge. Turn left and walk through tall casuarinas to the next 'Y' junction and veer right towards the top of the hill. The track turns left, right and then left again before descending through stands of banksia and melaleuca to a dirt road along the edge of Eighteen Mile Swamp. Continue along this road, across a culvert draining water from the creek into the Swamp. Walk along the edge of the Swamp for about 20 minutes to reach the road to Dunwich. The dirt road to the right crosses Eighteen Mile Swamp and leads 800m to the beach access.

After visiting the beach, retrace your steps to the start of the bitumen. Walk along the sealed road towards Dunwich for about 1.5kms and look for a fire break road leading uphill into the National Park on your left.

Enter the fire break road and continue past some large eucalypts and a clump of tall casuarinas and banksias. Turn right at the top of the ridge, ignoring the track leading left. Low heath covers the ridge-line. The track soon swings to the right and leads towards a cross roads. Turn right underneath the power lines and look for a sign reading, *'No vehicular access to National Park'* on your right. Follow this road for a few minutes to Neem-Beeba Lookout.

The Aboriginal word *'Neem-Beeba'* means *'to see'* and from the Lookout views extend from one end of the Island to the other. A rough track leads away from the front of the Lookout and heads north along the ridge-line passing more banksias, melaleucas, wattles and large scribbly gums. About 20 minutes from the Lookout, the ridge descends towards the road to Dunwich, turns left and runs parallel to the road. Wildflowers along this section of the track are particularly attractive. The older trees bear scars of an earlier bushfire. The track follows the remains of a disused road, finally reaching the car park, about 3kms from the Lookout.

Last reviewed: 11 August 1997

MAP REFERENCE
Sunmap - DUNWICH 1: 25 000
A walking track map is supplied on the Visitor Information Sheet available from QNWPS.

FACILITIES
There are no facilities in this small Park. Those wishing to camp may do so along the beach (permit and fee imposed), or at private camp sites at Dunwich, Amity Point and Point Lookout.

Whale watching has become very popular from Point Lookout and various vantage spots along the eastern beach during migration of the humpbacked whale.

Wildflowers are in bloom in July and August making bushwalking, birdwatching and photography very enjoyable. Walking tracks can become extremely hot during summer so be sure to wear a hat, apply sunscreen and carry plenty of water. The water in Blue Lake is not suitable for drinking.

RANGER CONTACT - (07) 3286 9261

MORETON ISLAND NATIONAL PARK

HISTORY
Aborigines of the Ngugi tribe inhabited Moreton Island 1 500 years ago leaving many large shell middens as testimony to their passing. The Island provided rich nourishment from the land and surrounding sea.

Captain Cook named '*Morton*' Bay and Cape '*Morton*' during his epic voyage of 1770. Named after the Earl of Morton, then president of the Royal Society in Britain, it was misspelt in one account of Cook's voyage. Matthew Flinders used this incorrect spelling when he discovered that the Cape was part of an island and named it Moreton Island.

European settlement began in 1848 when the Amity pilot station on North Stradbroke was shifted to Bulwer. Civil prisoners were used to build Cape Moreton Lighthouse in 1857, following several shipping disasters in the area. The Lighthouse, Queensland's oldest, still operates today. Ownership has recently been transferred from the Commonwealth's Australian Maritime Safety Authority to the State. The Government now includes Cape Moreton Lighthouse, which is surrounded by national park, in its '*Protected Area Estates*'.

During the First and Second World Wars, fortresses were erected at Cowan Cowan and Toompani Beach to protect the Brisbane area from attack. Relics of gun emplacements can still be seen today.

Many prominent points on the Island were named after features around Gallipoli where Australian soldiers fought so valiantly during the First World War. These include '*The Nek*', '*Chanuk Bair*', '*Storm Mountain*' '*Pimple*' and '*Gun Ridge*'. Military cartographers named these locations prior to the Second World War.

Queensland's only whaling station was operational from 1952 to 1962 at Tangalooma.

With exception of the townships, some oyster leases and Tangalooma Resort, the whole of Moreton Island is national park. The Park was known as Mt Tempest National Park until March 1986 when it was expanded to include 81% of the Island and the name was changed to Moreton Island National Park.

Sandmining was introduced in 1947 and continued until 1992 when pressure was bought to bear by conservation groups. The mining land then became part of the 16 800ha National Park.

FEATURES
Made up mostly of pure silica sand deposited by prevailing winds, waves and sea level changes, Moreton Island protects both *'window'* and *'perched'* freshwater lakes. They provide excellent swimming spots, but extreme care should be taken not to pollute these lakes. Cape Moreton, which consists of andesite, rhyolite and basalt, is the only rock formation on the Island.
Forested Mt Tempest, at 285m is the highest stabilised sand dune in the world.
Volcanic plugs of the Glass House Mountains, situated behind the mainland's Sunshine Coast, can be seen from the north-western beaches of the Island.
The Island maintains a delicate balance between many plant communities on its sand-based environment. Spinifex grasses and fragile ground covers such as pigface, strive to bind together the fragile dunes. The sandy soil is of low nutritional value. Protection of the dunes is the responsibility of all visitors.
Hardy plants such as grass trees, pink bloodwoods, banksias, callistemons, black wattles, pandanus and scribbly gums grow in open forests and heathlands. Burrowing moth larvae causes the unusual patterns in the bark of the scribbly gums. Melaleucas (paperbarks) grow around the many swamps that provide homes for frogs and bird life.
Pigs and goats were introduced in 1865 to provide food for shipwrecked sailors. The descendants of these early animals have become feral and along with wild cats on the Island, threaten native bird and animal life.
As well as an abundance of marine life, the foreshores and tidal areas support hundreds of wading birds each year. These birds migrate from the Artic Tundra, Eastern Siberia and other parts of the Northern Hemisphere.
The pied oyster catcher, a common bird on the Island, only hatches two eggs at a time. It is some time before the chicks can fly so they often become a tasty meal for predatory birds on the Island. You may see the female bird trying to spirit her chicks away from danger, while the male feigns a broken wing to distract the predator or inquisitive human.
White-bellied sea-eagles, red-capped plovers, royal spoonbills, brahminy kites, noisy friars, black-necked storks and laughing kookaburras are just some of the birds that make the Island a bird lover's paradise.
Loggerhead and green turtles come ashore to nest between November and February and migrating whales pass close to the eastern beach from August to October.
It is very important to maintain the fragile natural ecology on the Island. Please do not to interfere with any bird or animal life and only drive on existing tracks through the sand dunes.

ACCESS
Travel to Moreton Island by barge, resort boat, plane or private boat. The Moreton Venture barge operates from Whyte Island, near Lytton, and the Combie Trader operates from Scarborough Harbour. The Tangaloomer Flyer takes resort guests and day visitors to the Island daily, leaving from Holt Street, Pinkenba. Island roads are suitable for 4WD's vehicles only. A 4WD taxi operates from Bulwer.

ACCESS - MT TEMPEST

From the western beach, just north of Tangalooma Wild Dolphin Resort and The Wrecks, travel 7kms along the *'one-way'* Eastern Beach Road.

0.0kms	Exit from Eastern Beach Road and turn left along the beach.
1.3kms	Turn left into the *'one-way'* Western Beach Road.
	(Both roads are also referred to as Middle Road.)
1.9kms	Turn right and park here to complete the following circuit track.

MOUNT TEMPEST, TELEGRAPH TRACK, HONEYEATER LAKE AND EASTERN BEACH CIRCUIT

Distance: 22kms, allow 8 hours. Moderate grade.

This circuit walk is graded *'moderate'*, but walking on soft sand can become very tiring, especially along the beach at high tide. The complete circuit provides the walker with a comprehensive look at this section of the Island.

Start walking along the road towards Mt Tempest walking track. After about five minutes the road starts to climb gradually uphill, passing areas dominated by open forest and woodland with a ground cover of common bracken ferns and a sedge known as Prince of Wales feather. The drumming call of the coucal pheasant is often heard around this area. The start of the walking track is reached 2.5kms from the car park. Start climbing uphill past several old banksias towards a track junction. (The Telegraph Track leads off to the right.) Turn left and continue uphill. After about 10 minutes a set of steps lead straight up to a heath covered ridge and the summit comes into view. Follow the track as it ascends more sets of steps to the summit. The eastern view extends north from Cape Moreton to the southern end of the Island and across to Stradbroke Island. The Glass House Mountains are clearly visible to the west. To complete the circuit walk, return via the same path to the start of the Telegraph Track and follow this track as it leads steeply downhill. The terrain is now undulating as the track follows a gully between two ridges. Rusting poles, relics of the original telegraph line, are evident along the sides of the track. The vegetation here is predominantly closed heaths, mallee heaths and tall shrublands and during spring, it is a blanket of flowers. After walking steadily for about 2-2.5 hours you can see Cape Moreton Lighthouse and the coastline from the end of a long ridge. There is only one more descent and about 15 minutes of walking to reach the road to the beach.

Turn right and follow the road for about one hour to reach Blue Lake parking area on the right. (The track to Blue Lake is on the left, just past the car park.) It is only a five minutes walk from here to the edge of Honeyeater Lake which makes a good spot for a swim and a late lunch. After lunch, walk a further 1km along the road to the beach and turn right. It is 5kms to Eagers Creek camp site and 7kms to Middle Road. Walking along the beach gives you the opportunity to admire the bird life. Groups of terns huddle together facing into the wind, sea eagles soar above you, and pied oyster catchers scurry out of your path as you head towards them.

Turn right at Middle Road and walk about 600m to your vehicle.

There are obviously many variations to this walk. If the full circuit appears too daunting, then the 6km return walk to the summit of Mt Tempest from the car park would be one option. Alternatively, arrange for a vehicle to meet you at the point where the Telegraph Track joins the road.

Last reviewed: 23 August 1997 - NPAQ pre-outing. Leader: Ann Hill

ACCESS - SANDHILLS AND MIRAPOOL

0.0kms	Exit from Eastern Beach Road and turn right along the beach.
6.6kms	Note Aboriginal shell middens on right.
7.8kms	Pass White (sometimes called Camel) Rock on the beach. There is a large midden on the sand dunes behind the rock.
11.2kms	Pass the remains of Rous Battery gun emplacements at Toompani Beach.
15.3kms	Turn right from the beach and drive about 1.2kms along a track to a camping area amongst the casuarinas. This is an ideal spot to leave your vehicle to commence the **Sandhills Walk.**
15.5kms	First small clump of casuarinas.
15.7kms	Second small clump of casuarinas. (These two clumps of trees provide a prominent landmark from the Little Sandhills.)
18.8kms	Road to Kooringal turns off to the right.
21.3kms	Mirapool Shorebird Roost Site at southern end of the Island.

LITTLE SANDHILLS TO BIG SANDHILLS
Distance: 16kms return, allow 5 hours. Moderate grade.

This walk provides an opportunity to experience the unique wonders of these two massive clusters of sandhills. However, walking in the Sandhills can become extremely hot so carry ample supplies of water. Do not rely on your foot prints to guide your return walk as even light winds will remove all traces of your passing.

From the western edge of the Little Sandhills camp site, follow a disused road south through the casuarinas before turning right and walking westward to the top of the first hill. The dunes here are a brilliant white with occasional swirls of black sand.

Keep walking westward to the top of the second hill. The steep western walls of this sandhill lead down to a gully. If the walls are too steep to descend, turn left and walk along the ridge to the southern end of the gully. Climb down into the gully and up again to the top of the next ridge. From here you can see past the western beach to Crab Island and across Moreton Bay to the mainland.

The Big Sandhills are to the north. Walk diagonally in a west-nor-westerly direction, following a small finger of sand extending to the western beach. If you have walked too far north and reach the heavily vegetated northern slope of the Little Sandhills, turn left and walk steeply down through light scrub to the beach.

As you walk north along the beach, you will probably encounter armies of soldier crabs scurrying from the beach towards the shelter of mangrove flats. Hundreds of waterbirds also frequent this side of the Island. The narrow beach forms a clear division between the mangroves on the left and the casuarinas and native hibiscus (cotton trees) on the right.

Walk along the beach for about 2.5kms to a log fence at the base of the Big Sandhills. Turn right and climb straight to the top of the first sandhill, then across the ridge to the top of the next hill. Directly in front of you is the sheer western wall of a massive sandhill. Turn right and walk several hundred metres into the head of a shallow valley. Continue to the southern end of this valley past cliffs of sand flecked with red and brown pigment.

Head left and walk up and over the low point at the end of this valley into a dish shaped depression. The ironstone formations here are extremely fragile and care is required not to trample them underfoot. Some of the exposed shapes resemble the hulks of rusting ships while others look like giant rusting cauldrons.

As you continue to explore this area you will find sections where the sand has eroded leaving black, grey and white mudstone outcrops. Other sections reveal thin vein like edges of pigmented sand exposed on the surface and the stark remains of long dead trees protruding from the sand.

Stay in the Big Sandhills as long as you like, or until you run out of film, before returning via the same route to the Little Sandhills and back to the starting point.

Last reviewed: 28 January 1998

MIRAPOOL LAGOON
Distance: 1km, allow 1 hour. Easy grade.

Migratory birds roost at this site between September and April each year but there are generally some birds congregating in the area all year round.

The best way to observe the bird life at Mirapool is to leave your vehicle on the beach and walk around the edge of the tidal Lagoon. Cross the sandy strip from the beach towards the Lagoon, taking note of the location of any birds. Work you way around the edge in an anticlockwise direction, taking advantage of cover provided by vegetation adjacent to the edge of the Lagoon to observe the birds. Spend as long as you like watching and identifying the birds before returning to your vehicle. Sunrise and sunset are good times for birdwatching. Early morning reflections on the still water provide great photographic opportunities.

Last reviewed: 29 January 1998

MAP REFERENCE
Sunmap -   MOUNT TEMPEST 1:25 000
                  KOORINGAL 1:25 000
Sunmap also have a tourist map for the entire Island showing designated roads.
Tangalooma Wild Dolphin Resort supplies walking track maps for their patrons.

FACILITIES

Apart from resort style accommodation at Tangalooma Wild Dolphin Resort, there are several designated camping areas on the Island - Blue Lagoon, Eagers Creek, Comboyuro Point, The Wrecks and Ben-Ewa. These are equipped with water, toilet facilities and cold showers. Camping along the beach is also permitted. Permits for vehicles and all camp sites are required and are available from barge personnel.

Collecting firewood from the National Park is prohibited, so bring your own wood if you intend having a camp fire.

Protect the roads and beaches by deflating tyres and engaging 4WD at all times. Under no condition drive on the dunes. Check tide times.

Petrol and food supplies are available at Bulwer and Kooringal.

Whale watching is proving very popular from Cape Moreton during late winter and spring as the whales migrate to warmer waters to breed and then return to the cold Antarctic waters. Night dolphin feeding has become popular with Resort guests. Coastal wildflowers splash the Island with colour during spring.

Spring and autumn are the best times to enjoy walking but remember to carry adequate water, wear a hat and apply sunscreen.

Swimming in the many lakes is a great way to cool off in the summer.

RANGER CONTACT - (07) 3408 2710

BRIBIE ISLAND NATIONAL PARK

HISTORY

Aboriginal people lived on Bribie Island for thousands of years before European settlement. In 1800 there were between 600 to 1 000 Aborigines on the Island but the last of these had died by 1897. The Island provided a rich and varied source of food, including fruits and vegetables. Emus and kangaroos were hunted, along with a variety of reptiles. Dugong were netted in the Passage and the occasional beached whale provided an opportunity to invite neighbouring Aborigines for a feast. Shell and bone middens provide evidence of these early feasts and stone tools are still occasionally found at various locations on the Island. Scar trees have been found at Pilgrim Beach and Woorim. The Aborigines took the bark from these trees to make containers and canoes. A ceremonial bora ground has also been found on the Island.

European habitation took its toll in the form of land clearing on Bribie Island and pollution in the waterways. Conservationists struggled for decades to preserve the waterways surrounding the Island and in 1977, a Government report acknowledged the importance of conserving the natural attributes of Pumicestone Passage and its environs. The Government saw the need to limit any industrial development and to control rapidly growing residential sub-development. This would ensure changes in the tidal behaviour of the Passage were minimised, thus protecting important

159

Put yourself in the picture!

Brisbane's own island paradise

Handfeed the wild dolphins, explore the National Park, swim, snorkel, play tennis, squash, archery ... the list goes on.

- *Modern self-contained units and villas at affordable prices*
- *Day cruises to Resort daily, courtesy bus from most CBD hotels and transit centre*
- *Whale Watch Cruise - seasonal mid June to the end of October*

TANGALOOMA
Wild Dolphin Resort

For information & reservations
(07) 3268 6333
www.tangalooma.com

fishery, flora and fauna habitats.

All but one small sand mining lease had been relinquished by 1984. This allowed for the planned Environmental Park along the ocean side to be extended to the beach.

It wasn't until August 1988, that 1 940ha was gazetted as Pumicestone National Park. Queensland now had some protection for the extensive wetlands, estuarine systems, bird habitats and beachfront areas adjoining Pumicestone Passage.

However, the condition of the Passage continued to deteriorate and as late as 1990, water in the channel was proven to be '*outside Australian water quality guidelines*'.

Also in 1988, the Bicentennial Gardens, set in 60ha of natural bushland with introduced rainforest, were officially opened. The walking tracks in this area were originally constructed by volunteers but a Government grant allowed the laying of a hard surface, suitable for wheelchairs, as far as the Waterhole.

The controversial '*Turnbull's Lease*' area of 200ha was purchased by the QNPWS in 1990. A further 60ha, south of this area and known as '*The Vestibule*' was also included, bringing protection to 2 200ha of land.

Thoolara Island in Pumicestone Passage, critical for the protection of the estuarine system and water quality, plus an extensive esplanade or buffer zone were also added and by 1992 the Park totalled 2 350ha.

The Queensland Government called for public input into the management of the National, Environmental and Marine Parks of Bribie Island. Considered were the marine and freshwater wetlands, coastal sand dune communities, birdlife, fish and crustacean nurseries, recreational interest and economic values from tourism and commercial fishing. The main issues addressed were visitor numbers, fishing, dredging, canal estates, erosion control, access, camping and picnicking facilities, fire management and cultural heritage management.

In February 1997, the Government refuted claims that it intended selling pine plantation freehold land on Bribie Island and gave the people assurance that the land would be retained for public use. Much of the pine plantation is on leasehold land and is not included in the National Park estate.

Additional land, including the wildflower heathlands north of Woorim and the former Bribie Island Environmental Park have been included in the National Park which now totals 4 890ha. The name was changed to Bribie Island National Park in 1994.

FEATURES

Bribie Island, a sand island, and Pumicestone Passage, the estuary separating the Island from the mainland, forms the northern most section of Moreton Bay. The Island differs from other sand islands of Moreton Bay, in that most of the land is only a few metres above sea level.

A vast catchment area stretching from the Caloundra Bar in the north, west to the D'Aguilar Range, south to South Point and taking in Bribie Island itself, feeds nutrients as well as pollutants into Pumicestone Passage.

The park areas fronting the Passage protect tea tree forests and woodlands, that were once widespread throughout the region and support many species of plant and animal life that are now considered rare or vulnerable. Scribbly gum, forest red gum, bloodwood, brush box, black she-oaks and cypress pine, known locally as Bribie Island pine, grow in the forests. Wetlands host paperbarks, and mangroves fringe the shallow waters of the Passage providing a balanced marine environment for spawning a vast array of crustaceans and fish. Dolphins and green turtles are seen regularly in the channel, that also supports part of the Moreton Bay dugong population.

(During 1996 a female loggerhead turtle was fitted with a transmitter that sent signals to a French-United States satellite tracking system. The turtle left her feeding grounds in Moreton Bay in late 1996 and was traced to New Caledonia, where she possibly laid her eggs. She has since returned to her original feeding grounds in Moreton Bay.)

The open forests contain beach banksias and eucalypts and the heathlands are covered with wildflowers during the spring. On the ocean side, sand dunes are covered with beach spinifex and belts of casuarinas.

Ten to fifteen thousand migratory birds, including black swans, white-faced herons, sandpipers, royal spoonbills and several species of ibis and ducks, use the area as a refuge during summer months. Kingfishers, warblers, whistlers and honeyeaters are common amongst the melaleucas and mangroves. Predatory birds including sea eagles, ospreys, kites and falcons soar through the skies and nest in the Park.

Dingoes and kangaroos are common throughout the Park.

ACCESS

Several safe moorings can be found in Pumicestone Passage, making Bribie Island National Park easily accessible by boat.

If visiting the Park by car follow the Bruce Highway north of Brisbane, to Bribie Island. Cross the bridge over Pumicestone Passage and continue straight ahead on Benabrow Street to the second roundabout. The following directions are given from this roundabout.

ACCESS - BICENTENNIAL GARDENS AND WHITE PATCH AREA

0.0kms	Turn left on Sunderland Drive towards Banksia Beach.
0.8kms	Continue through the next roundabout on Sunderland Drive.
1.9kms	Entrance to the Community Arts Centre car park and the start of the Bicentennial Bushwalking Tracks.
3.4kms	Cross a canal bridge.
3.6kms	Turn right into Endeavour Drive. There is a sign pointing to *White Patch.*
4.5kms	Turn left into White Patch Esplanade. There is another sign pointing to *White Patch.*
6.7kms	*Bribie Island National Park* sign and boundary. A well sign posted 4WD track leads right towards *Gallagher Point, 3kms* and *Poverty Creek, 7kms.*

BICENTENNIAL BUSHWALKING TRACKS
Distance: 3.8kms return, allow 1.5 hours. Easy grade.

From the car park, walk straight ahead past the Rainforest Circuit, ignoring a short loop track on the left, and turn right at a young labelled brush box. Much of this area was wiped out by bushfires in 1994 and the Bribie Island Garden Club has carried out restoration. This area has not been included in the National Park. The track passes some large wallum banksias before reaching a sandy road. Turn left and walk to the Waterhole. The water is stained brown from tea tree sap. Turn right at the Waterhole and follow the sign to the *Banksia Walk*, through an area of grass trees, wallum heath and fire scarred banksias. The track turns left at a sign post, about 500m from the Waterhole.

A few metres past the sign post, take the track to the right. (The disused track straight ahead leads through a stand of paperbarks to a road but the track is often flooded.) Continue on the track to a 'T' junction and proceed straight ahead towards the Melaleuca Walk, through another area of wallum heath. Ignore a faint track to the right and follow the track past melaleucas on the left and banksias on the right until you reach a sandy road. This section of the walk is good for birdwatching. Turn right along the road and walk a few minutes to a sign posted track, leading left to *Palm Grove*. You soon descend to a grove of cabbage palms and the track swings right and gradually climbs uphill past clumps of rice flowers and dusky coral pea. Continue past the track leading left to a car park, cross the sandy road again and walk to the next track junction to complete the loop. From here, retrace your steps past the Waterhole towards the starting point.

Last reviewed: 18 November 1997

WHITE PATCH AREA
Distance: 2kms return, allow 1 hour. Easy grade.

From Poverty Point camp ground, follow the waters edge north past the mangroves for about 1km, enjoying the views across the water and looking for bird life. The prominent peaks of the Glass House Mountains are easily recognisable across Pumicestone Passage. Sunrise and sunset provide excellent photographic opportunities, however, sandflies often pose a problem unless ample quantities of insect repellent are used.

The terrain at Gallagher Point is very similar, but you could walk north, initially along an unused road for about 1km before retracing your steps to the parking area. Migratory waders and other water birds frequent this area and you could spend as long as the sandflies allow, looking for birds.

Last reviewed: 18 August 1997

ACCESS - WOORIM HEATHLANDS AND EASTERN BEACH

0.0kms	Turn right on Goodwin Drive towards Woorim.
1.1kms	Cross canal bridge.
2.7kms	Veer left into First Avenue.
3.7kms	Turn left into McMahon Street for the Woorim Heathlands walk.
6.1kms	Turn left into North Street.
7.6kms	Veer right.
7.9kms	Car park and access to Eastern Beach.

WOORIM HEATHLANDS

Distance: 14kms return, allow 5 hours. Easy grade.

The Woorim Heathlands are a favourite location for birdwatchers and wild flower enthusiasts alike. The time spent in this area and the distance covered, is only limited by your enthusiasm. To appreciate the bird life and the wildflowers, leave your vehicle at the end of the bitumen and walk along the gravel road. After about 3kms, ignore a side track to the right and continue for another 1.2kms to a second road junction and turn right. Although the walking is a bit tedious, the absence of vehicle noise allows you to identify many different species of birds, especially in spring when the wildflowers are at their best. After exploring this road, return to the junction and turn right.

Continue walking for 700m to another track junction. Turn right and explore this road for a while before returning to the junction.

Turn right again and continue through the Heathlands for another 1.7kms to the pine forest at the National Park boundary. Several low-lying sections of the road may be flooded after heavy rain but these low spots can usually be bypassed by skirting around through the scrub.

From the Park boundary, retrace your steps to your vehicle. To fully appreciate this area, it is a good idea to concentrate on one side of the road on the way north, and the other on the way back.

Last reviewed: 18 August 1997

NB. Prior to starting this walk, it would be advisable to purchase a copy of *Wildflowers of Bribie Island* by *Ian C. MacRae*, available at the Bribie Island Community Arts Centre. A bird list is also available.

EASTERN BEACH WALK

Distance: 5-10kms return, allow 4 hours. Easy grade.

If you enjoy beach walking, follow the road directions to the Eastern Beach. The National Park boundary extends to the high water line and the heathlands can be accessed from various locations along the beach. Note the relics of gun emplacements positioned in the dunes. These formed part of the protection plan for the East Coast of Australia during World War II.

Sunrise is a particularly good time to walk along the beach, especially if you are into photography. Retrace your steps along the beach to your vehicle.

Last reviewed: 18 November 1997

MAP REFERENCE
UBD Brisbane Street Directory - Maps 42 and 53

QNPWS supply a Visitor's Information sheet showing the various camping areas and locations of different sections of the Park.

The Community Arts Centre provides a map of the Bicentennial Track for a small fee.

FACILITIES
Parts of the Park may be explored by boat, but bushwalking enables you to enjoy the different aspects the Park has to offer. Visitors flock to Bribie all year round for great birdwatching and photography opportunities.   Be sure you have insect repellent, sunscreen and a hat if visiting during summer.

Picnic and camping areas are available at Poverty Creek and Gallagher Point but a 4WD is necessary to travel the roads to these sites. A permit from the Caboolture Shire Council is required to drive along the ocean beach.

Unfortunately toilet facilities are limited due to vandalism. There is no freshwater at any of the camp sites and fuel stoves are recommended for cooking. You will need to provide your own wood to utilise the limited fireplaces available.

There are various parks and picnic areas outside the National Park.

RANGER CONTACT - (07) 3408 8451

DARLING DOWNS

RAVENSBOURNE NATIONAL PARK

HISTORY

Local Aborigines used the Ravensbourne area extensively. It was considered a good stop over point for transient tribes travelling to the bunya nut feasts. You can still see evidence of areas where they dug for yams along the Rainforest Circuit.

Pit sawyers felled tall red cedar, black bean and rosewood during the 1860s and 1870s. Cedar was so plentiful that Ravensbourne was originally known as Cedar Scrub. Beef cattle and dairy farmers then utilised the cleared land. Population in the area increased and soon a community dance hall and tennis court were built on the site of Gus Beutel's picnic ground.

A 100.2ha parcel of land was proclaimed as a national park in 1922 to preserve a representative sample of rainforest and open eucalypt forest that once covered most of the area.

Late in 1994, developers proposed to construct a sand and kaolin mine near the Park's boundary. Naturally, this proposal created quite a controversy. Dust from the kaolin plant would have suffocated vegetation and had a severe impact on the fauna of the Park. Common sense prevailed and the Crows Nest Shire Council quashed the idea. Additional land purchased in 1997 increased the total area of the Park to 440ha.

FEATURES

This small scenic park located along the eastern edge of the Great Dividing Range, overlooks Toowoomba and the Lockyer Valley. Views of prominent mountains along the Scenic Rim are gained from Gus Beutel's Lookout.

Rich red soils host remnant rainforests and dense groves of piccabeen palms in the Park's west and south-west areas. Vines, ferns and staghorns thrive amongst the forest under the dense canopy. Open eucalypt forests of blackbutt, Sydney blue gum and forest red gum, along with she-oaks and wattles grow in sandy soils in the eastern section of the Park.

Birds and animals are abundant. Look for satin bowerbirds, catbirds, whipbirds, golden whistlers, wompoo fruit-doves and sooty owls in the rainforest areas. Scaly-breasted and rainbow lorikeets fly through both the rainforest and open forests. Crested pigeons and red-backed wrens make their homes in the eucalypt forests and the rare black-breasted button-quail lives along the grassy ridges.

Brushtail and ringtail possums, gliders, red-necked wallabies and swamp wallabies inhabit Ravensbourne along with many reptiles, frogs and insects. Paddymelons and bandicoots graze on the forest fringes. A colony of eastern horseshoe bats, said to be one of the most significant colonies in Queensland, and possibly Australia, inhabit the extensive area of caves beside Weller Road. It is not known how vast the cave systems are, but during earlier bushfires, smoke entering one cave poured out others, nowhere near the fire front. Many of the cave outlets are on adjoining private land.

ACCESS
Drive along the Brisbane Valley Highway to Esk, approximately 1.5 hours from Brisbane.

0.0kms	Turn left onto the Esk-Hampton Road towards Crows Nest and Toowoomba. A sign post points to *Ravensbourne National Park 33kms.*
32.1kms	Turn left at the sign, *Ravensbourne National Park 400m.* This road leads to the bottom picnic area along Scenic Drive.
32.6kms	Bottom picnic area.
33.0kms	Gus Beutel's Lookout and picnic area.

BUARABA CREEK
Distance: 6kms return, allow 2.5 hours. Moderate grade.

The walking track starts at the bottom edge of the first picnic area. Follow the track into the rainforest, ignoring the start of the Rainforest Circuit a few minutes from the picnic ground. The track passes a clump of attractive piccabeen palms in a gully before reaching another track junction. Turn left and head down some steps past a massive gum tree. Continue past the next track junction that leads to the Caves and walk downhill past hundreds of piccabeen palms. A few minutes past the next junction, the track leaves the palm forest and follows the side of a ridge through open eucalypt forest. The grassy understorey is a favourite nesting place for quails. A bush fire that raged through the Park in 1936 has scarred many of the tree trunks along the ridge.
Continue to descend via some steps and you soon re-enter the palm forest with a small creek on your left, before reaching Buaraba Creek. The Creek makes an ideal spot for a picnic. Spend as much time as you like enjoying the scenery, listening to the birds or exploring up and down the Creek before starting the climb back uphill to the picnic area.

Last reviewed: 15 July 1997

PALM CREEK CIRCUIT AND THE CAVES
Distance: 4.8kms return, allow 2 hours. Easy grade.

From the first picnic area, walk to the Rainforest Circuit track and turn right. On the right side of the track you will see several depressions in the ground caused by early Aborigines digging for yams. Continue along the track as it curves to the left, past large Sydney blue gums, to some steps. The gully to the left is filled with piccabeen palms. Turn right at the first track junction and head downhill towards the Caves. You soon leave the rainforest and reach a track junction leading straight ahead, 500m to the Caves. The fine powdery soil on the floor of the Caves makes it an ideal spot to look for different bird, animal and reptile tracks. On the way back, see how many species of plants you can identify growing from the rock face above the Caves. Five hundred metres from the Caves, veer right on the Palm Creek Circuit. The track soon re-enters the rainforest, crosses Palm Creek and starts winding uphill. Turn left at the next junction and continue uphill, past a storm damaged section. Listen to the different bird calls as you wind uphill. Take the right hand branch of the Rainforest Circuit and walk 600m back to the picnic area, past several old stumps, a reminder of the logging days.

Last reviewed: 16 July 1997

CEDAR BLOCK WALK
Distance: 500m, allow 30 minutes. Easy grade.

This short walk along a well graded track, starting from Gus Beutel's picnic area is an exceptionally good interpretative walk. Signs along the way describe the various trees and plants growing in the forest. You should identify and remember the shape of the stinging tree with its plate shaped leaves, often pitted with holes. The cunjevoi growing nearby are said to be an antidote for the painful sting inflicted by fine bristles under the leaves. You pass a massive Sydney blue gum, spared by the loggers because of its hollow trunk. Look for the fallen giant blue gum, gradually decomposing along the side of the track. Continue walking in a loop past a large red cedar, and then a native tamarind, a relative of the Asian rambutans and lychees, before returning to the picnic area.

Last reviewed: 16 July 1997

MAP REFERENCE
Sunmap - RAVENSBOURNE 1:25 000
A walking map is provided on the information sheet available from QNPWS.

FACILITIES
Camping is allowed at nearby Crows Nest National Park and Cressbrook Dam, or stay at Lake Perseverance Recreation Camp.
At Ravensbourne National Park there are two ideal family picnic areas with tables, shelter sheds, barbecues and toilets. Tank water is available. Enjoy the views from Gus Beutel's Lookout. Birdwatching is popular and any time of the year is pleasant to visit, with summer being a particularly good time to escape the lowland heat.

RANGER CONTACT - (07) 4698 1296

CROWS NEST NATIONAL PARK

HISTORY
As early as 1885, some tin was obtained from a few creeks in the Crows Nest area. A government geologist reported in 1905 that tin-bearing granite did not exist east of Perseverance Creek, but a 1945 military map shows tin sluicing on one of the side creeks.

The Crows Nest Falls section of the Park was a popular picnic spot as far back as 1905 when it was declared a recreation reserve. Diving and swimming competitions were held in the pool at the bottom of Crows Nest Falls. During the early part of the century the pool was about 22m deep.

Access to the falls prior to the 1930s would have been on horseback and possibly horse-drawn buggy. A reasonable dry weather road was constructed in the '30s. In 1934, an article in the *Crows Nest Advertiser* described Valley of Diamonds as '...a national asset...' and four years later, moves were made to have the area set aside as a national park. The newly formed Toowoomba branch of the NPAQ visited the area in 1939. They too were campaigning to have the area declared a national park but the Forestry Department soon announced that the proposed park *'would not be possible'.*

World War II intervened and it was not until 1965 that the push to have the area proclaimed a national park was taken up again.

An area of 234ha was finally set aside as Crows Nest Falls National Park in 1967, protecting a remnant stand of open eucalypt forest that is an important wildlife habitat. Over the years, extensions including a smaller area adjoining the original park and used for camping and day visitor activities have increased the Crows Nest section to 492ha.

Perseverance National Park consisting of 970ha and proclaimed in 1980 and a 49ha area set aside as Bungaree Nature Reserve were combined under the banner of Crows Nest National Park in 1989. The total area protected is now 1 511ha.

Valley of Diamonds is a significant area of the Crows Nest section of the Park. In 1982 the Queensland Place Names Board changed the name to *Nullingirra Gorge*, an Aboriginal word for *'stone'* or *'stony'*. Although the origins of the original name are uncertain (there are no diamonds in the valley), it obviously held a lot of attachment for local residents. They objected to the change, petitioned the Government and in 1983 the name officially reverted back to Valley of Diamonds. Koonin Lookout overlooks Valley of Diamonds. *'Koonin'* is the Aboriginal word for *'pine tree'.*

FEATURES
Crows Nest National Park is situated in the Great Dividing Range, just north of Toowoomba. Crows Nest Creek with its falls, cascades and rock pools is the central feature of this section of the Park. Perseverance Creek tumbles over granite boulders on its journey north from Perseverance Dam, completed in 1965. Both

creeks meet just downstream from Koonin Lookout in the Crows Nest section and form Cressbrook Creek, that eventually flows into the Brisbane River.

The Park is dominated with lichen-patterned granite boulders and features several characteristically domed outcrops. It is a contrast to the hilly country surrounding the township of Crows Nest.

An area of predominantly open eucalypt forest, it has some fine examples of forest red gum, ironbark and stringybark growing on the slopes between the picnic area and the Cascades. Other vegetation includes smooth-barked, rough-barked and broad-leafed apples and some heath areas are present. Weeping bottlebrush, river she-oak and swamp mahogany line the Creek banks, with hoop pines in the Gorge below Koonin Lookout. Bloodwoods, grey gums and kurrajongs are also common and patches of rainforest flank the swimming holes.

A variety of birds including parrots, pale-headed rosellas, rose robins, eastern yellow robins, grey thrush, blue-faced honeyeaters and noisy miners feed on the nectar and blossoms of the shrubs and trees. Kookaburras and butcherbirds frequent the picnic areas looking for an easy meal. A delightful pair of Peregrine falcons nest on the rocky outcrop, visible from Koonin Lookout.

Sugar, feathertail and greater gliders may be spotted at night as they soar between trees. Rock wallabies graze on the steeper cliffs and swamp wallabies can be seen closer to the Creeks. You may also spot platypus around the Creeks at dawn or dusk if you are patient. Brushtail possums frequent the camp ground scrounging for food. PLEASE don't feed the animals. It makes them aggressive and it's bad for their health.

ACCESS

From Brisbane, travel via Toowoomba or Esk to the township of Crows Nest on the New England Highway.

0.0kms	Turn right at the Crows Nest Police Station on Albert Street. The road junction is sign posted *Crows Nest National Park.*
5.3kms	Turn right Into a dirt road at a sign pointing to *Crows Nest Falls.*
5.7kms	Cross a grid at the National Park boundary.

CROWS NEST FALLS AND VALLEY OF DIAMONDS
Distance: 4.8kms return, allow 2 hours. Easy grade.

Start this walk from the far (southern) end of the car park. The dry sandy track winds through open eucalypt country. Look for a smooth-barked apple growing over the top of a large rock, just after the start. Turn right 500m from the start and walk 50m down some steps to the Cascades. Extreme caution is required around the Cascades as the rocks are very steep. Children should be well supervised.

From the Cascades, return to the main track and a little further on take another 50m detour to the right and visit Kauyoo Pool. *'Kauyoo'* means *'to swim'* in the dialect of the local Aboriginal tribe. This would be a good swimming hole following rain, but successive drought years have reduced the Pool to a puddle, with coarse river sand along the edges.

Once again, return to the main track from the Pool. Descend some steps and follow the Creek. Continue on the right branch at the next 'Y' junction to Crows Nest Falls. The Lookout is 25m high. The Falls make an impressive sight following heavy rain.

From the Falls, walk 50m back to the track junction and turn right towards Koonin Lookout and Valley of Diamonds. A 200m detour to the pool is worth the effort, especially if the Falls are flowing. This track descends some steps and passes through a narrow gorge before reaching the pool.

Back on the main track, continue to Koonin Lookout across a small creek, then climb back up the ridge before reaching a set of steep steps leading to the Lookout, 120m above Valley of Diamonds. A favourite spot for Peregrine falcons is on top of the breadknife shaped finger of rock on the left side of the Gorge.

On the return trip, take the right hand fork at the 'Y' junction, a few minutes after the Crows Nest Falls track. The 800m return track through eucalypt forest is much flatter than the track used on the way to the Cascades.

Last reviewed: 15 July 1997

MAP REFERENCE
Sunmap - CROWS NEST 1:25 000
Walking guide maps for Crows Nest Falls area are available from QNPWS.

FACILITIES
Caravan and camping sites are situated at Crows Nest Falls section of the National Park. The site is also equipped with picnic areas complete with barbecues (firewood provided), shelter sheds, tables, toilets and drinking water. A pleasant day can be had swimming in the rock pools if there is enough water and the day is warm. Winter can produce heavy frosts but the clear nights are great for spotlighting native animals. Spectacular wildflower displays in spring and summer provide a haven for the naturalist and photographer.

There are picnic facilities on the foreshore of Perseverance Dam. Water skiing is the only water activity allowed on the Dam and boat ramp access is provided for club members.

RANGER CONTACT - (07) 4698 1142

LAKE BROADWATER CONSERVATION PARK

Although this 1 795ha area has not been gazetted as a national park, we have included it with the Parks of the Darling Downs region. Visitors to the west are rewarded with the unique qualities of the Lake, good walking tracks and excellent camping facilities. Natural bushland contrasts with vast open farmlands. You realise the importance of Australia's primary industries as you drive through the rural areas and the township of Dalby, with its wide streets and an emphasis on agricultural facilities and services. You will also appreciate the necessity to preserve some parcels of land and wildlife for our future generations, when you experience the oasis that is Lake Broadwater Conservation Park. In this area of the Darling Downs, agriculture, recreation and conservation coexist.

For this reason we have invited you to *'take a walk'* in Broadwater Conservation Park.

HISTORY

Prior to European settlement large groups of Aboriginal people lived around the shores of the Lake. Evidence of bora rings and other archaeological finds confirm their early presence.

Early European settlers frequently camped in the area when travelling west from Jondaryan rail terminus. When the railway was extended in 1868, it was routed via Dalby because Broadwater Lake was dry and Myall Creek offered permanent water.

The area around the Lake was originally part of the large St Ruth Station until some land was resumed to form Loudoun Station. The owners of Loudoun Station purchased Lake Broadwater reserve from the Queensland Government, leaving the public with no access to the Lake. In the 1930s, the Lake Broadwater Association purchased 15ha along the western shore and lake bed and it became a popular picnic spot. This land was subsequently gifted to the QNPWS and a further 855ha was purchased by QNPWS and gazetted an environmental park in 1981.

The park now consists of Lake Broadwater Conservation Park,1 220ha and Lake Broadwater Resources Reserve, 575ha. It is popular with boating and skiing enthusiasts and an ideal spot for family gatherings.

The Dalby Lions Club erected a bird hide 100m from the turn off to the South West walking track. It is a sturdy construction about 5m from the ground and provides excellent views across the Lake. Early mornings or late afternoons are ideal for photographing or watching different water birds.

FEATURES

Lake Broadwater was once part of the Condamine flood plain. Currently, waters feeding the Lake are only caught in the adjacent grazing areas and the section surrounding the Lake. When full, the Lake covers almost 350ha and is up to 3m deep. It is the only naturally occurring body of water of its type in the drier Western Darling Downs.

The land is generally flat and soil types range from heavy black soil to light sandy loams interspersed with low gravel ridges. The floodway consist of dark alluvial silt.

Four hundred and fifty species of plants have been identified in the Park. River red gums and blue gums line the shores of the Lake. Uncommon braid fern grows in the forest with tree orchids, heath and impressive wild flowers amongst poplar box, ironbarks and bloodwoods.

Numerous water birds including ducks, cormorants, swans, jabirus, brolgas and herons flock to the semipermanent Lake. It provides an important breeding ground for up to 240 species of birds, some migrating from the Northern Hemisphere. Boats are prohibited in the area referred to as 'The Neck' as it is an important waterfowl refuge.

Eastern grey kangaroos, red-necked and swamp wallabies are common and you can occasionally see koala and echidna. The rare Dunmall's snake is one of 15 species of snake observed in the Park. Long-necked tortoises and Murray turtles live in the Lake.

ACCESS

Lake Broadwater Conservation Park is west of Dalby, via the Moonie Highway.

0.0kms	Dalby.
20.0kms	Turn left on the sign posted road to Lake Broadwater.
29.0kms	Sign to the bush camp ground.
31.0kms	Entrance to the main camp ground.

SOUTH-WEST CIRCUIT TRACK

Distance: 6.7kms return, allow 2 hours. Easy grade.

There is road access to the start of this track, but it is more pleasant to walk the extra few kilometres from the main camp ground so as not to disturb the bird life. Walk south from the camp ground on the gravel road for about 10 minutes and turn left on the sign posted road, past the Ranger's residence to the start of the walking tracks. (The bird hide is only 100m from the sign pointing to the *South-West Circuit.*)

From this sign, walk 1.2km down the road through open cleared paddocks to the start of the track. Turn right at the 'T' junction and after 50m, turn left at the track and walk in a clockwise direction past a large stand of cypress pine. The track is well marked and very flat.

The self-guiding walk helps you identify many different plants and trees from the conveniently placed markers. Look for hickory, bloodwood, bull-oak, and quinine. Continue on the track for about 15 minutes, past a fence and veer right past a good example of rusty gum. Matt rushes, ironbarks, tumble down gums, wattle, cork bark, and large Moreton Bay ash form an impressive avenue. Look for the uncommon braid fern, rough and smooth-barked apples, jasmine, myrtle and rosewood.

Hundreds of grey kangaroos will bound out of your way as you walk around the track. Continue to the track junction and follow the road back to the camp ground.

Last reviewed: 25 February 1997

CAMP GROUND TRACK
Distance: 4kms return, allow 1.5 hours. Easy grade

This is another self guiding walk, this time starting at the northern end of the main camp ground. The track follows the edge of the Lake for one kilometre to the Lake overflow. Look for an old fence paling embedded in a tree trunk.
The track swings left past an old dingo fence that was erected in the late 1860s on what was St Ruth Station. Continue past a stand of brigalow and a clump of belah to the bush camp entrance. From this point, either retrace your steps, or walk along the road back to the camp ground.

Last reviewed: 25 February 1997

MAP REFERENCE
Sunmap - DALBY 1:100 000
A map of the walking tracks is available at the self-registration booth in the Park.

FACILITIES
Toilets, cold showers, camp sites, barbecues (wood provided) and tank water are available. There are no powered sites but it is suitable for caravans. Camping is only allowed in the bush camp ground and the main camp ground.
Activities include; water sports, fishing, swimming, walking and birdwatching.
Summer is the best time to visit to enjoy the water sports, while spring, autumn and winter are best for walking.

CONTACT - (07) 4662 2922 - Wambo Shire Council

THE PALMS NATIONAL PARK

HISTORY
Early pioneers cleared the surrounding land for farming, cutting down huge hoop pines, supposedly "...*so big you could not see over their trunks once they were felled*". Luckily, this small parcel of land remained intact. Proclaimed a national park in 1950, the 12.7ha area now protects a unique stand of piccabeen palms.

FEATURES
Continual ground seepage keeps the tree ferns, piccabeen palms, bunya pines and other vegetation alive. Dense rainforest grows around the outer edge of the palms.
The Palms National Park is a recognised breeding place for the noisy pitta. Black-faced monarchs, yellow robins, rose-headed and wonga pigeons and sacred kingfishers have been sighted in the Park.
You may be lucky and find an echidna shuffling through the leaf litter.

ACCESS
Situated approximately 230km north-west of Brisbane, access is from the New England Highway, north-east of Cooyar.

0.0kms	Turn left at the Cooyar Hotel and follow the New England Highway towards Yarraman.
0.3kms	Turn right on the road sign posted *The Palms National Park 6kms*.
3.8kms	Veer left at the sign posted road to *The Palms*.
7.6kms	Turn left into the car park at The Palms National Park.

THE PALMS CIRCUIT
Distance: 500m, allow 30minutes. Easy grade.

This short graded track leaves from the car park and immediately descends into a grove of tall, slim trunked piccabeen palms. Cross the wooden bridge over the creek and follow the track as it climbs up the hill and swings right along the edge of the creek. You soon pass a large brush box on the left, then several old hoop pines and a large Moreton Bay fig, before heading down some steps and over a swampy section via a wooden bridge. As you cross another section of boardwalk you pass a massive tree with buttress roots extending towards the track. The track then emerges at the top end of the car park.

Last reviewed: 15 July 1997

MAP REFERENCE
Sunmap - THE PALMS 1:25 000

FACILITIES
Picnic tables, barbecues with wood provided and toilets make this attractive area an ideal picnic spot for families, especially during spring, summer and autumn. Tank water is available at the picnic ground.

RANGER CONTACT - (07) 4698 1296

TARONG NATIONAL PARK

HISTORY
Before European settlement the area was covered by a mixture of open eucalypt forest and dry rainforest. Areas of land surrounding the Park were cleared during the soldier settlement period (1945-46) and extensive logging and grazing disturbed much of the remaining vegetation.
Tarong Coal's open cut mine is adjacent to the Park. Before mining commenced, all topsoil was removed and stored for use in later rehabilitation. Extensive surveys

were conducted to determine what species of flora and fauna were present prior to mining. At the completion of mining, it is the intent to rehabilitate the area to a native ecosystem, rather than grazing land, as has been the norm.

Native species will be grown by *'direct seeding'* with seed collected from trees, shrubs and creepers within Tarong National Park. Other areas will be planted with tube stock of dry rainforest species. The seed of these species is either not commercially available or is an unusual shape, making it unsuitable for use in seeding equipment.

Zoologists gathered base line data relating to fauna in and around the Park and this information will assist with monitoring the return of these species to the mined sites. It is believed that in 50 to 100 years, considerable successional changes will have taken place in the regenerated area providing invaluable data on the reconstruction of different ecosystems.

Tarong National Park was gazetted in 1995. This 1 490ha Park contains several small parcels of intact riparian vegetation with only small amounts of weed and will play an important role in the rehabilitation of Tarong coal mine site.

FEATURES

The land within the Park is undulating and forms part of the catchment area of Meandu Creek. This Creek ultimately flows into the Burnett River.

The term *'riparian vegetation'* refers to that which is usually found along riverbanks, however, there is only one ephemeral creek in the Park. In woodland areas, the upper canopy is eucalypt and the mid-canopy shrub layer consists of the *Acacias*; *jacksonia, hovea and boronia.* The vegetation on Tarong is predominantly *Araucarian* (hoop pine), complex microphyll rainforest (commonly called softwood scrub) and narrow-leafed ironbark communities.

Ninety-eight bird species have been recorded including Richard's pipits, tawny grassbirds, double barred finches, several species of cuckoos, honeyeaters, robins, fantails, thornbills and flycatchers. Uncommon or rare species include the black-breasted button-quail, king quail, oriental cuckoo and Peregrine falcon.

Seventeen frog species and 38 species of reptiles have been recorded in or around the Park. Mammals include grey kangaroos, red-necked wallabies, echidnas, bandicoots and pale field rats.

ACCESS

Travel through Esk via the Brisbane Valley Highway and take the D'Aguilar Highway to Yarraman.

0.0kms	Turn left towards Toowoomba at the Yarraman Hotel.
21.0kms	Turn right towards Maidenwell.
31.0kms	Maidenwell Hotel. Continue ahead towards Nanango, 32kms.
38.8kms	Turn right at gravel road. *Tarong National Park* sign on left.
41.3kms	Road junction. The road to the right is sign posted *Ryans-Reagons*. There is a *National Park Boundary* sign on the left and a *Tarong National Park* sign on the right.

THE BIRDWATCHER'S WALK
Distance: 1km return, allow as long as you like. Easy grade.

There are no defined walking tracks in Tarong, however, the Park is becoming popular with birdwatchers. The suggested access point is at the *'Ryans–Reagons'* road junction. Walk diagonally into the Park in a west, south-westerly direction. There is some lantana infestation close to the boundary, but very little further into the Park. There are several animal tracks leading through the understorey. Continue walking until you locate what you feel is a suitable spot for birdwatching. To return to your vehicle, either retrace your steps, or turn left and head east down to the road and walk back to the starting point.

Last reviewed: 15 July 1997

MAP REFERENCE
Sunmap - YARRAMAN 1:50 000

FACILITIES
There are no facilities in the Park.

RANGER CONTACT - (07) 4668 3127

BUNYA MOUNTAINS NATIONAL PARK

HISTORY
Prior to European settlement, Aboriginal tribes from surrounding areas gathered about every three years for tribal ceremonies, corroborees, feasting and mock fighting in the Bunya Mountain area. Smoke signals were used to communicate with distant tribes and these gatherings were timed to coincide with good crops of bunya nuts. It is believed that they collected the nuts by climbing the trees with the aid of a vine. Deep scars, possibly the remains of footholds used to assist climbing, are still seen on some of the tree trunks. Young nuts were eaten raw. Older nuts were roasted and pounded into a *'cake'* that could be stored for several weeks. When roasted, bunya nuts resemble the flavour of chestnuts. They provided the main food eaten during these *'bonye bonye'* feasts.
The first European to visit the area was Andrew Petrie, Moreton Bay's Superintendent of Works. He collected samples of the *'bonye bonye'* tree in the late 1830s. These were sent to London's Kew Gardens for identification by botanist John Bidwell. Hence, the botanic name of the bunya pine is *Araucaria bidwilli.*
During the 1840s and 1850s, timber getters moved in to harvest red cedar. When this was depleted they started logging bunya pine and hoop pine.
Expansion of European settlement made it difficult for visiting Aboriginal tribes to

travel across their traditional pathways and the last big *'bonye bonye'* feast was held in 1876.The Great Bunya Sawmill was established alongside Myall Creek in 1883. Closure of the last operating sawmill was in 1945. Relics of saw milling days still remain on the Mountain.

In 1908, Bunya Mountains National Park became the second national park declared in Queensland. The original park was 9 303ha, but subsequent extensions have increased the area to 11 700ha, protecting the world's largest, and Queensland's most significant stand of bunya pine.

FEATURES

The Bunya Mountains form part of the Great Dividing Range and overlook Queensland's Darling Downs. The highest peak is Mt Kiangarow, 1 135m, and the average height of the peaks is 975m. The mountains were formed about 30 million years ago by an erupting shield volcano. Cooling basaltic lava flows produced dome shaped hills. Eroding basalt rock formed the black soils and red-brown earths of the area.

Tall moist rainforest dominated by bunya pine grows on the higher ridges. Dry rainforest with hoop pine and vine thicket grows at lower elevations and covers more than 50% of the Bunya Mountains. The bunya pine has a distinctive rounded crown and lighter, smoother bark than the hoop pine. Bunya pine cones take 18 months to develop from flower stage. Between January and March every year, massive cones, some weighing up to 7kgs develop and fall from the crown of the bunya tree. Each cone produces 50 to 100 seeds, or *'bunya nuts'*.

Vines, mosses, lichens, ferns, orchids and epiphytes grow throughout the rainforest. With the wetter and warmer conditions about 12 000 years ago, subtropical rainforest took over some areas of eucalypt forest.

Remaining areas of open eucalypt forest contain Queensland blue gum, mountain coolabah, yellow box, white box, forest red gum, and stringybark with some brigalow and belah.

Grass trees are common and on the western slopes of Mt. Kiangarow some species grow to 5m, making them the tallest grass trees in Queensland. Many of these grass trees are at least several hundred years old.

Grassy plains or *'balds'* are a prominent feature of the Mountain. It was thought that regular burning by Aboriginal people caused these balds, but more recent studies indicate that they may have been caused by climatic changes 30 000 years ago. The balds are known to have been significantly reduced in size over the last 50 years, so even if they were originally formed by climatic changes, burning by Aboriginal people probably helped to maintain their larger size. The poor soil condition of these areas has difficulty in supporting even the hardiest eucalypts.

King parrots, crimson rosellas and rainbow lorikeets are a common sight around the camp grounds. Look for satin bowerbirds, regent bowerbirds and the green catbird. It is an experience to spot the bower of a male bowerbird, with its scattered collection of blue bits and pieces. Peregrine falcons, wedge-tailed eagles and kites are often seen around grasslands and disturbed areas. Other common birds include fairy wrens, honeyeaters, robins, finches, cockatoos, owls, drongos and fantails. Listen for the sharp cry of the Paradise riflebird.

Red-necked wallabies, pademelons and swamp wallabies feed around camp grounds and road sides. Koalas live in eucalypt forests and possums and gliders can be spotted in the trees at night. The Bunya Mountain ringtail possum, a close relative of the common ringtail possum, is unique to the area.

The echidna is more difficult to locate. Goannas, lizards, skinks and geckos share the forest with many different species of frogs. The eastern tiger snake, eastern brown snake and red-bellied black snake, are only a few of the snakes found in the Park

The most pressing problem in the Park is visitors who feed the animals. This causes severe health problems for birds and wallabies. When you visit <u>any</u> national park, please resist the temptation to feed the wildlife!

ACCESS
The Bunya Mountains can be reached via Kingaroy, Dalby or Esk. If travelling from Brisbane, follow the directions as detailed below.

Travel through Esk via the Brisbane Valley Highway and take the D'Aguilar Highway to Yarraman.

0.0kms	Turn left towards Toowoomba at the Yarraman Hotel.
21.0kms	Turn right towards Maidenwell, sign posted *Bunya Mountains 35km*.
31.0kms	Turn left at the Maidenwell Hotel.
40.8kms	Gravel road starts.
48.9kms	End of dirt road.
56.7kms	'T' intersection. Turn right.
59.5kms	Turn right towards Dandabah camp ground. Continue straight ahead for Westcott and Burtons Well camping areas.

BARKERS CREEK AND SCENIC CIRCUITS
Distance: 12kms, allow 4-5 hours. Easy grade.

These walking tracks start from the Dandabah picnic area. Take the Barkers Creek track, down over Saddletree Creek and up onto its northern bank, turning left after a few hundred metres. The track climbs uphill through attractive forest past massive bunya pines. The ground cover is predominantly ferns. About 30 minutes from the start, look on the left of the track for a giant strangler fig that has totally destroyed its host plant. After passing the track to Paradise parking area, the trail descends alongside a creek filled with tree ferns and cunjevoi before reaching Paradise Falls and then Little Falls. Beware of stinging trees near Paradise Falls.

A few minutes later you leave the rainforest and reach the first bald. From here, the track again enters the rainforest before reaching a track junction. Turn left and walk to Big Falls and Barkers Creek Lookouts. The valley beyond the 122m Falls is covered with large hoop pines.

Return to the track junction and turn left. The terrain soon changes to open forest with old gnarled eucalypts and a ground cover of grasses. A further 10 minutes downhill and you reach the Scenic Circuit track. Walk left and cross a series of wooden bridges and a boardwalk as the track follows the tree fern filled creek bed. About 30 minutes later you reach a wooden platform built around a massive, forked bunya pine with large crows nest ferns clinging to its trunk. From here you continue on to Pine Gorge Lookout where you get good easterly views towards Tarong. Keep following the track and take the 80m detour to see Festoon Falls before climbing back uphill alongside the Creek to the picnic ground.

Last reviewed: 14 July 1997

MT KIANGAROW AND CHERRY PLAIN CIRCUIT
Distance: 10.7kms, allow 4 hours. Easy grade.

Start this walk 100m south of Burtons Well Picnic Ground. Just after the start, you take the right hand track towards the Mountain. The ground is covered with ferns as you enter the forest. You pass several ancient grass trees before leaving the rainforest and soon reach a grassy ridge with the tall grass trees previously described and views out to the west. A further five minutes walking through old moss-covered trees and you reach the summit. A short track leads about 20m down from the summit to a rocky ridge with good western views.
Return via the same track and turn right at the track junction towards Cherry Plain. After about five minutes the track turns sharply to the right and then left downhill. Note the vegetation change. The forest canopy closes over and the ground cover of ferns is replaced with leaf litter. You soon reach the track leading about 80m to Chinghion Lookout on the right.
Five minutes on you get good views back towards Chinghion Lookout, above the cliff face, and to Mt Kiangarow.
You are now in open eucalypt forest as you follow the western escarpment. Look for a large landslip to the right of Bottle Tree Bluff. The next track junction takes you 300m through more eucalypt forest to a lookout on the Bluff. From here, continue to the next track junction that leads back to Cherry Plain picnic area, stopping off at Cherry Plain Lookout. The north-easterly views are across to a bunya pine covered ridge. The track climbs again, passing through another clump of rainforest before reaching Cherry Plain picnic area. Turn left and follow the road 2.4km back to Burtons Well.

Last reviewed: 13 July 1997

WESTCLIFF AND WESTCOTT PLAIN TRACKS
Distance: 11.4kms, allow 4-5 hours. Easy grade.

Start this walk opposite Paradise parking area. After walking for 10 minutes you reach Little Pocket, the smallest bald on the Mountain, before entering rainforest again. This is a particularly attractive parcel of forest with large vines hanging from the canopy and a complete ground cover of ferns. It is also a favourite haunt for whip birds. As you get closer to the western cliffs the vegetation changes to open eucalypt forest and as the track swings north along the escarpment there are hundreds of grass trees. A little more than 30 minutes from the start you reach Westcliff Lookout with views out towards Dalby.

From the Lookout pass through a section of rainforest before reaching another small bald on the way to Westcott picnic area. The track leading to Cherry Plain picnic area immediately descends through rainforest and then eucalypt forest before reaching Kondaii Lookout Circuit junction. Continue on to Kondaii Lookout for views extending from the rocky bluffs on either side, down to the Kondaii Valley. From here, follow the track past a moss-covered rocky outcrop and up some steps to another track junction. Turn left towards Cherry Plain picnic area. You soon enter rainforest again and the track crosses a scree-covered slope. Note the old twisted fig tree leaning across the track. Leave the rainforest again and arrive at a 'Y' junction, turn right and head uphill, passing one more section of rainforest before reaching Cherry Plain picnic area. Then return along the road to your starting point.

Last reviewed: 14 July 1997

MAP REFERENCE
Sunmap - BUNYA MOUNTAINS 1:25 000
Walking track maps supplied by QNPWS are available from the Ranger's office and self-registration booths in the Park.

FACILITIES
There are three camping areas in the Park.
Dandabah has hot showers, toilets with wheelchair access, barbecues (firewood supplied) and picnic tables. A privately run kiosk with basic supplies and take away food is situated adjacent to the Park. There are several privately run restaurants and guest houses on the Mountain, outside the National Park.
Burtons Well camping area has bush showers, pit toilets and picnic tables.
Westcott Plain camping and picnic area is more spartan, providing only picnic tables, toilets and drinking water.
Some of the shorter walks in the Park have wheelchair access. The three walks described above can all be done in part. Carry water on all tracks.
Guided activities for park visitors are provided voluntarily by the Bunya Mountains Natural History Association.
Temperatures on the Mountain range between freezing and 3°C. Evenings and early morning can be quite cool even in summer.

RANGER CONTACT - (07) 4668 3127

THE GRANITE BELT

GIRRAWEEN NATIONAL PARK

HISTORY
During the mid 19th century, much of the current area of Girraween National Park was covered by sheep stations. Towards the end of the century, large parcels of land were divided into smaller selections for growing apples and stone fruit to supply the expanding Brisbane market. In 1932, 1 600ha were acquired for the formation of Bald Rock Creek and Castle Rock National Parks. An intervening orchard was purchased in 1966 and allowed the amalgamation of these two smaller parks into Girraween National Park. Additional land has been purchased since, and the Park now covers an area of around 11 700ha and extends to the Queensland - New South Wales border. Girraween National Park and Bald Rock National Park in NSW share a common border. Girraween, is an Aboriginal word meaning *'place of flowers'*.

FEATURES
Much of the Park consists of steeply sided granite hills and domes, large tors and boulders, balancing rocks and expansive granite outcrops. In the valleys and gullies, creeks flow over beds of granite. The landforms were caused by volcanic activity around 225 million years ago. Molten rock, heated deep below the earth's surface, penetrated older sedimentary and volcanic rocks. The submerged magma slowly crystallised and formed granite. After many years of weathering, the older rocks eroded, leaving the dramatic granite landforms that make up the unique landscape of Girraween. The erosion has been hastened by severe winter frosts, uncommon in most other parts of Queensland.
Many visitors to Girraween come in spring, solely to enjoy the spectacular displays of wildflowers unique to the Park. The plant colonies are closely allied with those of the Southern States. In the rocky areas where soil is scarce, mat-rushes, grasses, lilies and low shrubs take root in cracks and joints in the rocks. Thirty species of eucalypts have been identified amongst low dense heath, flowering wattles, pea-flowers, daisy bushes and rock roses. Because of the poor drainage, swamps containing rushes and sphagnum moss flourish near granite outcrops. Around the edges of swamps you will find heaths, sundews and terrestrial orchids. Grass trees, drumsticks and bracken fern are common and epiphytic orchids grow in moist, protected areas.
The golden wattle begins flowering in late July. September and October are the most spectacular months for flowering heath and shrubs, and in summer, flannel flowers, wattles, bottlebrush and paperbarks are in bloom.
Girraween is also home to a wide variety of bird life. Parrots, treecreepers, honeyeaters and flycatchers live among the eucalypts while robins, firetails, wrens and thornbills live in the shrubs and thickets along watercourses. You can spot wedge-tailed eagles, little eagles and Australian goshawks hunting in open grassy

areas.

Kookaburras, black cockatoos, blue wrens, crimson rosellas, yellow-rumped thornbills and red wattlebirds can all be seen without straying too far from the picnic and camping areas. In the northern end of the Park, lyrebirds and the relatively scarce turquoise parrot have been sighted.

Common brushtail possums frequent the picnic and camping areas while the less common sugar gliders and feathertail gliders can occasionally be seen. Greater gliders and ringtail possums may be spotted high in the surrounding eucalypts.

Grey wallaroos and kangaroos, red-necked and swamp wallabies inhabit the Park. The common wombat, usually found in the Southern States, has been sighted in Girraween but is rare due to the northerly position of the Park.

Red-bellied black and common brown snakes inhabit the Park and are often seen basking in the sun on open rocky areas. Frogs, skinks and lizards are active in the warmer months along swamps, creek banks and isolated pools.

The animals in Girraween are best spotted at dawn or dusk, or at night with a spotlight.

ACCESS

Girraween is approximately 260kms south-west of Brisbane. Take the Cunningham Highway west to Warwick, then the New England Highway south to Stanthorpe. You will travel through orchards, vineyards and small townships, past fruit stalls, wineries, and pottery and craft outlets to enter the unique granite strewn countryside that is Girraween National Park. The road is sealed and suitable for caravans.

0.0kms	Southern junction of the Stanthorpe by-pass.
24.0kms	Turn left from highway (sign posted).
25.9kms	T-junction at Pyramid Road. Turn left.
32.5kms	Arrive at Girraween National Park Information Centre

THE PYRAMID

Distance: 3kms return, allow 2 hours. Moderate grade.

The track starts at the picnic ground. Follow a concrete path on an exposed granite slab beside Bald Rock Creek and turn right over a concrete bridge onto the Pyramid track. After 600m, take the right hand track at a 'Y' junction and continue on the Pyramid track. After crossing a small creek, the track climbs a set of steps to the base of the Pyramid. The steep trail now follows a series of white painted markers leading up the granite dome. About one third of the way to the top you pass several trees that have taken root in a fissure in the rock. Their roots extend about 10 metres down the crack. Follow the white markers to the left, over some rocks to a channel created when a large section of granite cracked off the top layer of rock. Climb over the rocks at the top of the channel and follow the white markers as they skirt around to the left of large rocks. This section of the track is exposed and would be extremely slippery after rain. As the Second Pyramid and the Balancing Rock come into view, take the track to the right and head for the summit where you obtain 360° views of the Granite Belt. Castle Rock can be seen to the south with Sphinx Rock and Turtle Rock to the right and Mt Norman to the left.

On the descent, stop and look at the Balancing Rock and the second Pyramid before retracing your steps back to the picnic ground. After reaching the 'Y' junction, the walk can be extended by about 10 minutes by taking the Granite Arch Track which meets the Junction Track about 500m from the picnic ground. A granite arch straddles the track about 100m from the turn off.

(The Second Pyramid is steep and exposed and should only be attempted by experienced rock climbers with specialised equipment. People intending to do any rock climbing _must_ check with Ranger first.)

Last reviewed: 19 February 1997

CASTLE ROCK
Distance: 5.2kms return, allow 2 hours. Easy-moderate grade.

This is an ideal average sized walk providing excellent views. The walking track starts opposite Gunn's Cottage, or from the southern end of Castle Rock camp ground. Climb steadily until you reach the top of a ridge. The track levels out, then passes through undulating country before reaching a track junction, 1.8km from the start. Take the left sign posted track towards Mt Norman and Castle Rock. After a further 50m, turn left to Castle Rock and follow the white markers to the summit.

The track climbs steeply over some large boulders, through a cleft in the rock and out onto an smooth, exposed slab. Stay close to the high side of the rock and you will finally reach the summit, 500m from the track junction. Good 360° views are obtained from the top. You can see Bald Rock National Park to the east and Mt Norman is to the south-east. Return to the camp ground via the same track.

Last reviewed: 20 February 1997

MT NORMAN
Distance: 10.4kms return, allow 5 hours. Moderate grade.

Follow the directions to Castle Rock. From the Castle Rock track junction, continue up to the top of a ridge before descending into a gully. Mt Norman, the highest point in the Park stands at 1 267m and can be seen from the top of the ridge. Cross two small creeks and continue up to an exposed granite slab. Follow the white markers on the granite slab to the top of a cliff-line where the track turns left, and then right, before again heading straight up the exposed granite towards the summit. You soon reach a 'T' junction at the top of a ridge.

The left branch leads you to the Eye of the Needle where two tall pillars of rock appear to form a hole at the base of a single pillar. Return to the track junction and continue straight ahead. The track passes under an arch formed by large granite boulders and sidles alongside a sheer cliff, before reaching a granite ledge overlooking the valley leading to Mt Norman picnic area. You cannot climb any further up Mt Norman without considerable rock climbing experience and specialised equipment. Again, you must check with the Ranger prior to doing any rock climbing.

The walk can be extended 4km by completing a return walk to Mt Norman picnic area. Alternatively, you could arrange a car shuffle and only walk one way. The Mt Norman picnic area is accessed from Wallangarra.

To reach the picnic area from Mt Norman, follow the white markers down the southern side of the Mountain, past small gullies and depressions where mosses and sedges grow. At the bottom of the granite hill, you reach a sandy footpad leading to a 4WD track before reaching Mt Norman picnic area. From the picnic area, retrace your steps to Mt Norman and back to your starting point.

Last reviewed: 20 February 1997

TURTLE ROCK AND THE SPHINX
Distance: 7.4kms return, allow 4 hours. Moderate grade.

Follow the directions to Castle Rock. Take the right sign posted track towards Turtle Rock and The Sphinx. The track heads uphill before flattening out on the top of the ridge and climbing again to the base of the Sphinx. From the Sphinx, follow the trail for 300m to Turtle Rock. Continue on the track until you reach a gully heading towards the top of the Rock. Climb the gully for 20m and head right, up a fault line to a higher point on the Rock. From here, good views of the Sphinx are obtained. Extreme caution is required at this point and only persons with previous scrambling experience should attempt the final climb to the summit.

Last reviewed: 20 February 1997

MAP REFERENCE
CMA - WALLANGARRA 9240-II and III 1:50 000
Walking track maps are available from the Information Centre at the Park.

FACILITIES
Bald Rock Creek and Castle Rock camp grounds have hot showers, toilets, tables and barbecue fireplaces. Limited firewood is provided for cooking purposes only. Be sure to book for peak seasons.

There is wheelchair access to amenities at Castle Rock camp ground. Caravan sites are available but none have power and generators are not allowed. A coin operated public telephone is located at the Information Centre. Water is available in the camping areas, but make sure you carry your own when walking. Rubbish bins are not provided. It is your responsibility to take ALL your rubbish away with you.

No fuel or provisions are available in the Park

Visit during the spring for spectacular wildflower displays. The days are sunny and crisp and the nights are cool. Picnicking and swimming are popular pass times in the summer months. Maximum temperatures of 30°C may be experienced during summer, while in winter the minimum may drop as low as -8°C.

RANGER CONTACT - (07) 4684 5157

SUNDOWN NATIONAL PARK

HISTORY

Tin, copper and arsenic were mined in the region during the 1870s. More than 70 men were employed when the mines were at peak production, but only low grade ore was produced and mining was not a commercial success. Remnants of these early mines can still be seen from several 4WD tracks that cris-cross the Park. The area around many of these mines is still contaminated and should be avoided.

The park was originally part of Ballandean, Glenlyon and Nundubbermere stations. Parts of these stations were sub-divided into smaller blocks and cleared for grazing in the early 1900s. Some fine grade wool was produced, but most properties were uneconomical and grazing was abandoned. Evidence of salt troughs and yards still exist in some sections of the Park.

Sundown National Park was proclaimed in 1977 to preserve unique landforms of scenic beauty, atypical of those throughout Queensland, and the distinctive riverine habitat along the Severn River.

An additional 1 031ha was purchased in 1983, jointly by the QNPWS and the Queensland Water Resources Commission, as a reserve against the possibility of a dam being built to support a local irrigation project. The dam project was abandoned in favour of the Mole River area in New South Wales and this parcel of land was added to the Park in 1994. The management area now includes 12 500ha of Sundown National Park, and the Sundown Resources Reserve of 2 590ha.

FEATURES

Much of the Park consists of high rugged country between 600 to 800m above sea level, but some peaks rise to more than 1 000m. Spectacular panoramic views can be obtained from many of the steep sided gorges eroded by the Severn River. The area is known locally as *'traprock'* country, formed by deposits of ancient marine sediment. Extensive erosion and folding has exposed large areas of layered rock around the edges of the Gorge.

The flora changes from north to south due to variations in climate and soil types. The northern eucalypt forests contain stringybark, yellow box, brown box and Tenterfield woollybut.

The southern region consists mainly of ironbarks, white box, tumbledown gum and some cypress pine. Significant stands of ooline trees are preserved in this section of the Park. The ooline tree has rainforest origins dating back 10 000 years when the continent was much wetter than it is today. The only other stand of ooline to be preserved is at Tregole National Park in Western Queensland. The rivers and creeks are generally lined with river red gum, river oak, tea tree and bottlebrush.

More than 130 species of birds have been recorded in the Park. The northern section contains satin bowerbirds, lyrebirds and scarlet and rose robins. In the south, you can find spotted bowerbirds, red-capped robins, honeyeaters, white-faces and red-winged parrots. Along the river banks you will often spot herons, cormorants, azure kingfishers and black ducks.

Grey kangaroos, wallaroos, red-necked swamp wallabies, pretty-faced wallabies, gliders and possums are common in the Park. Competition with wild goats and predatory foxes has eliminated the brush-tailed rock wallaby from all but a small section at the northern end of the Park.

ACCESS - NORTHERN END

Sundown National Park is approximately 250kms south-west of Brisbane. Take the Cunningham Highway west to Warwick, then the New England Highway south to Stanthorpe.

0.0kms	Southern junction of the Stanthorpe by-pass. Drive to the township of Ballandean.
16.7kms	Turn right from highway into Curr Road, sign posted *'Golden Grove Orchard* and *Winery'.*
17.1kms	Turn left into Sundown Road, past several vineyards and boutique wineries.
21.7kms	Bitumen ends, continue on dirt road.
22.1kms	Sundown Road turns left, sign posted *'Sundown National Park'* and *'4WD vehicles'.* The road becomes quite rough from this point as you travel through cattle and sheep grazing country, parts of which are unfenced.
27.5kms	Arrive at the Park boundary. Continue through the gate to the self-registration booth and complete your camping permit if you intend bush camping.
27.8kms	Sign post pointing to *Red Rock Gorge 7kms* and *Severn River 20kms* on the left. Continue straight ahead for another 20m to the site of the old Sundown Station homestead on your left. Leave your vehicle here and commence the walk.

RED ROCK GORGE

Distance: 13kms return, allow 5 hours. Moderate grade.

From the old homestead site, follow the road downhill for five minutes to a creek crossing. You immediately experience the isolation of the country. If there is water in the creek, cross near an old chicken wire fence on the right hand side. After another 10 minutes walking you reach the remains of a wooden gate. Ignore the right hand track leading to Mt Lofty, one of the highest points in the Park, and continue straight ahead.

The road crosses several small creeks that are easily forded, even following rain. Continue along the road past large orange gums, climbing a long hill to the remains of another old gate, a clearing, and the junction of the 4WD track to Red Rock Gorge.

Follow the sign post right towards Red Rock Gorge for a further five minutes. Turn sharply left on an old vehicle track at the bottom of the hill. This track leads downhill to a clearing on the right that makes an ideal bush camp spot.

At the far end of the clearing, hop into Red Rock Creek and follow the granite slabs downstream. In this area you will most likely hear bleating and sight feral goats as they crash through the scrub. Feral pigs also live in this area.

Continue downstream, picking your way along the creek bed or the scrubby creek banks. After about 15 minutes you will reach a cliff face. It is best to skirt around to the left of the cliff, up over the granite rocks and down the grassy slope. Large carpet pythons inhabit this area.

Follow the creek for another 15 minutes until you reach the brink of Red Rock Falls. The falls drop 50m over the red granite cliff in front of you. The views over the falls to Red Rock Gorge and the Severn River Valley are spectacular, but extreme care is required, especially following rain.

To your right you will notice a viewing platform, constructed on the highest point of the cliff-line. Scramble up a faint track to your right and follow the cliff-line up and around towards the platform. This is an easy 20 minute scramble, keeping well back from the cliff face. You will reach a gravel track leading left to the viewing platform. From the platform the panorama includes the Falls and the cliff-line that you have just traversed. A smaller gorge can be seen straight ahead.

After a well earned rest, follow the gravel track up to a car park and another bush camping spot. Pit toilets are located along the road to the right.

Continue along this road for 10 minutes until you reach the junction where you walked downhill to the Creek. From here, walk uphill, retracing your steps along the road to your vehicle.

Last reviewed: 21 February 1997

ACCESS - SOUTHERN END

The Broadwater Camping area is approximately 250kms south-west of Brisbane. Take the Cunningham Highway to Warwick, then the New England Highway to Stanthorpe. Drive approximately 75kms south-west towards Glenlyon.

0.0kms	Turn left at the sign posted *Permanents Road*, towards Sundown National Park. The road is gravel from this point.
1.0kms	Cross a gravel floodway.
2.2kms	*National Park Boundary* sign.
3.7kms	Sign to camping areas.
4.2kms	Arrive at camp ground. The first grassy clearing is ideal for caravans.

OOLINE CREEK GORGE
Distance: 5kms return, allow 3 hours. Easy grade.

This walk is relatively straightforward, even for people with no previous rock hopping experience. Start from the information stand at the end of the camp ground road and follow the track as it leads above the western (left) side of the Severn River. Ignore an old footpad leading to the River soon after the start and continue on the main track. After about 15 minutes of steady walking, the track descends into Ooline Creek. Take a quick detour to Permanent Waterhole by turning right and walking towards the Severn River. The Waterhole is around 5m deep and at dawn and dusk you may spot platypus around the water's edge. This is also an ideal time to observe waterbirds.

From Permanent Waterhole, walk back to the track and rock hop up Ooline Creek. You will notice several small cascades, rock pools, and scattered sections of dry creek bed where the water flows beneath the surface, even following a considerable amount of rain. After 30-45 minutes in the Creek, the Gorge narrows and you reach another large waterhole. A 20m waterfall now blocks your progress. The bank to the right is too steep to navigate without extreme caution and should not be attempted by inexperienced scramblers. Alternatively, swim through the pool and continue exploring, but be aware, there are large leeches living in the Creek! From the waterhole, walk back down the creek and follow the track back to the camp ground.

Last reviewed: 22 February 1997

McALLISTER'S CREEK - SPLIT ROCK FALLS
Distance: 6kms return, allow 3-4 hours. Easy grade.

To start this walk, follow the track towards Ooline Creek. Take the old footpad to the right soon after the start and walk down towards the River. Continue upstream for about 100m until you reach the rapids and pick your way across the River. If the water level is too high, you may need to cross below the Broadwater. Head east at right angles to the River, crossing several dry stony creek beds until you reach an old footpad. Turn right and follow this track through a cleared paddock for 15 minutes and you will reach McAllister's Creek. It is likely to be dry here, even after rain. Rabbits were responsible for the old eroded burrows along the track, and not wombats as is often thought. Turn left into McAllister's Creek and rock hop upstream. Around McAllister's Creek you will probably spot feral goats as well as fallow deer. The deer are thought to be descendants of those released into the wild by English farmers at the turn of the century.

After 30-40 minutes of rock hopping, the gorge narrows and the rock slabs on either side project into the Creek at 45° angles, just prior to a small waterfall. Climb around the waterfall and continue upstream to where the gorge widens. You will need to watch for snakes as you pick your way through grassy patches along the sides of the Creek, especially near rock pools. Another 30-40 minutes will take you to the base of two waterfalls. Skirt around these until your progress is blocked by a tall narrow gorge at the base of Split Rock Falls.

It is possible to climb around these Falls and continue up the creek to Double Falls, but the cliff-line is steep and the traprock is crumbly and treacherous after rain. You should not proceed unless you are an experienced, confident scrambler. Take the time to rest and listen to the birds before starting the walk back to the camp ground.

Last reviewed: 23 February 1997

MAP REFERENCE
Hema –   SUNDOWN 1:50 000
CMA -   WALLANGARRA 9240-II and III 1:50 000
Walking track maps are available from the self-registration booths in the Park.

FACILITIES
NORTHERN END
Bush camping is permitted at Burrows Waterhole, where there are pit toilets, or the grassy area mentioned in the Red Rock Falls walk notes.

Vehicle access to these camping areas is by 4WD only. Conventional vehicles can reach the old Sundown homestead site to begin the Red Rock Falls walk.

Carry your own water as the condition of water in Red Rock Creek varies.

SOUTHERN END
There are camping facilities at the Broadwater.   Fireplaces and barbecues (firewood supplied), pit toilets and facilities for hot bush showers are provided. Bush camping is permitted elsewhere in the Park.

Conventional vehicles can access this area.

The best time to visit is between May and September when warm, clear days and cold, frosty nights ensure walking is comfortable. Summer is very hot with daytime temperatures soaring to 40°C. Swimming and canoeing is possible in some of the waterholes.

No food or petrol supplies are available in the Park so visitors must be self sufficient.

For visitors to the southern end of the Park there is a small general store with fuel, ice, smallgoods etc., at Glenlyon Dam.

RANGER CONTACT - (02) 6737 5235

THE BRIGALOW BELT

WONDUL RANGE NATIONAL PARK

HISTORY

Declared in 1993, Wondul Range National Park provides protection for the poorly conserved Brigalow Belt.   In announcing the State Government's decision to protect the 3 555ha area, the then Environment and Heritage Minister stated *"...the extent to which brigalow has been cleared represents one of this country's most irresponsible environmental acts."*

To the average person the Park may not appear very striking as it does not house majestic rainforests, idyllic streams or craggy mountains, but protection of the undisturbed brigalow scrub, of which there is very little in the Park, was vital to ensure that natural biodiversity was not lost.

FEATURES

Small sandstone cliffs, sandy pink soils and clay soils all support different types of flora and fauna. The most dominant tree growing along the ridges is the smooth-barked apple. Although worthless in the commercial sense, the smooth-barked apple does house a host of reptiles, birds, insects and mammals. Note the long streams of red sap flowing to the ground where branches have broken from these trees. Other flora to note in the Park include several species of ironbark, wattle and cypress pine along with the brigalow, Queensland blue gum, grey box, tumbledown gum, zamia palms, wild pineapple, Queensland peppermint, native cherry, she-oaks, bull-oaks and wild may.

Black cockatoos, yellow-tailed black cockatoos, spotted and striated pardolates and wedge-tailed eagles are a few of the birds likely to be encountered.

Several different wallabies including, red-necked and swamp wallabies have been recorded in the Park and brush-tailed rock wallabies have been recorded in the surrounding area.

ACCESS

Travel on the Gore Highway to Millmerran, 48kms south-west of Toowoomba. Continue through town to the Teepee Rest Area.

0.0kms	Teepee Rest Area. Drive towards Goondiwindi.
20.0kms	Cross a grid and turn sharply left into Road 11, then turn right into Road 128. Continue ahead ignoring all roads to the right.
29.8kms	Road ends at the National Park boundary. Turn left on the side road through an old gate and follow the firebreak road along the fence.
32.3kms	An old vehicle track turns off to the right. Park here to commence the walk.

THE OLD ROAD WALK
Distance: 16kms return, allow 5 hours. Easy grade.

Experience Wondul Range National Park by walking along the 4WD track that bisects the Park from east to west.
Follow the sandy track through tall eucalypts for about 1km to an earth dam usually containing water, on the right side of the road. Low flowering heaths grow around the edge of the dam. About 2.5kms from the start the road passes a low ridge on the right with some interesting sandstone caves. Leave the track and walk 50m to the ridge and explore these small caves. The sandy soil on the floor of the caves displays evidence of habitation by small animals. The terrain from here is varied with grey gums, ironbarks, acacias and wattles lining the gradually descending road.
Continue following the road and after another 5.5kms you reach the sign posted western boundary of the Park. There is a firebreak around the perimeter of the Park, but it is easier to retrace your steps back to the starting point. There are few discernible features that would make navigation easy, along any other route.

Last reviewed: 17 April 1997

MAP REFERENCE
Sunmap - INGLEWOOD 1:100 000

FACILITIES
There are no camping or picnic facilities in this park. Carry your own drinking water.

RANGER CONTACT - (07) 4661 3710

BENDIDEE NATIONAL PARK

HISTORY
Brigalow, which can grow to 25m in height, once grew in a belt 1 100kms long between Narrabri in New South Wales and Collinsville in Queensland. Land surrounding Bendidee National Park was initially cleared with an axe - a slow and tedious process. Prickly pear infestation also slowed progress. By the 1950s, mechanisation hastened the clearing and in seven years between 1954 and 1960, it is estimated that more than 1 000 000ha were cleared.
Changing attitudes towards conservation and preservation of remnant stands of vegetation saw this 931ha parcel of brigalow scrub being declared a national park in 1979.

FEATURES
Like most of the country in this section of the Brigalow Belt, Bendidee National Park is relatively flat with gilgai soils dominating. The large depressions or *'melon holes'* hold water for long periods and support a wide variety of wildlife. Following rain, the area becomes very swampy.

The vegetation is predominantly brigalow/belah forest, with some poplar box and cypress pine and there is very little ground cover.

Some commonly seen birds include brush turkeys, pigeons, doves, galahs, black cockatoos, kookaburras, robins and honeyeaters.   Kangaroos, wallabies and possums inhabit in the Park.

ACCESS
Bendidee National Park can be reached by following the Cunningham Highway west from Inglewood to Yelarbon.

0.0kms	Yelarbon.
19.0kms	Turn right towards Wyaga, sign posted *Milmerran 121kms.*
32.8kms	Bitumen road ends.
37.8kms	Turn left into Tenomby Road and drive west to a grid. The grid marks the western boundary of the Park.

SWAMP TRAIL
Distance: 2-3kms, allow 1 hour, or as long as you want bird watching. Easy grade.

Apply a liberal amount of insect repellent and walk about 100m east along the road from the grid and then head north into the Park. The low ground vegetation common to this brigalow scrub area makes navigation relatively simple. Once inside the Park boundary, walk in a north-easterly direction. Following rain, your progress is constantly blocked by swampy depressions in any other direction. Linger alongside any of the waterholes to spot and listen to the birds. To return to your starting point, turn right and keep walking south until you reach the road, then head back to your vehicle.

Last reviewed: 24 February 1997

NB. This was following a period of local flooding. During August 1997, the Park and the surrounding area was reported to be *'dry'.*

MAP REFERENCE
Sunmap - GOONDIWINDI 1:250 000

FACILITIES
There are no facilities at all in this park. Birdwatching is the main attraction. Mosquitos can make visits unpleasant in summer.

RANGER CONTACT - (07) 4661 3710

SOUTHWOOD NATIONAL PARK

HISTORY

As with much of South-Western Queensland, Alan Cunningham was the first European explorer to visit the area. Stock routes were established along the Moonie and Weir Rivers during the mid 1800s and towards the end of the century, large parcels of land were subdivided for farming. The only limitation on the size of *'selections'* was the owners ability to clear and stock the properties, but these conditions were rarely policed. The park was originally surveyed for grazing land in 1870, but unlike most of the surrounding land, it was never cleared.

Prickly pear was introduced as a garden shrub in some of the cleared areas, but discarded clippings flourished and soon the plant became a pest. Many properties were abandoned prior to the First World War because the cost of controlling the pear was too great. A moth, *Cactoblastis* whose larva ate the plant, was introduced to biologically control the spread of the pear in 1926 and by 1934 it had eradicated most of the noxious plant, and farming resumed. The National Park, like all those in the Brigalow Belt is now surrounded by cleared farmlands and the moth and the pear are said to be in a state of equilibrium.

Australia's first commercial oil field was established in the Moonie district in the early 1960s. Today, oil reserves are almost depleted but exploration continues and many gas fields have been discovered and capped for later use.

Southwood National Park consists of 7 120ha and was gazetted in 1970 to preserve a *'remnant'* stand of one of the last remaining examples of vegetation communities originally found throughout the area. It is part of the region originally known as Wild Horse Paradise.

FEATURES

The region surrounding much of the brigalow belt is relatively flat with poor drainage. Gilgai soils dominate the area forming deep depressions, or *'melon holes'*, which are characteristic of the terrain. This soil consists of mounds and depressions often up to two metres deep. During dry periods, the topsoils crumble and fall into deep cracks. Following rain, the soil swells and pushes the surface upwards. A dry crust is then formed on the top layer.

Swampy areas supporting brigalow and belah dominate the heavy clay soils. This vegetation is interspersed with cypress pine and eucalypts growing in the lighter sandy soils. Sandlewood, false sandlewood, wilga, black tea tree, limebush, and fuchia bush form the under story. Ground cover is generally sparse, with brigalow grasses being the main species. Wildflowers flourish in the spring, especially following good rains.

Water retained in the swamps and gilgais provides a refuge for numerous species of local and migratory birds. Birds that have adapted to the drier western areas are common in the Park. Emus, doves, pigeons, cockatoos, parrots, rosellas, babblers, thornbills and honeyeaters are just a few species you are likely to see. Birds whose habitat is primarily the coastal ranges, ie. brush turkey, pale-headed rosella, superb blue wren, pied currawong and noisy miner, have also been identified in the Park. This shows the complexity of the area and is a further reason to protect the remaining representative samples of brigalow country.

Koalas live among the eucalypts. Kangaroos, wallabies, wallaroos, possums and gliders inhabit the brigalow, along with amphibians and reptiles.

ACCESS
To reach this park, travel west on the Moonie Highway to Moonie.

0.0kms	Moonie.
21.0kms	Park boundary on the right.
29.0kms	Turn right into Fabians Road. There is no sign post, but this road is 50m past the road to *'Milgarra'*, a property on the left.
29.8kms	Turn right into camping area.

NB. The dirt road into the camping area becomes very boggy after rain. The top crust of the road appears to be firm, but once this crust is broken, vehicles can become hopelessly bogged in the gilgai soil. Do not attempt to drive further than the camping area.

CAMPGROUND TRAIL
Distance: 2-4kms return, allow 1-2 hours. Easy grade.

If you are to enjoy exploring this remnant stand of vegetation during the summer months, especially following rain, first coat yourself with copious quantities of insect repellent.

Walk along the track to the camping area. Continue on in a north-easterly direction for 30-45 minutes. Find a suitable spot to sit and attempt to identify some of the 92 species of birds that have been recorded in the Park. Spend as long as you like and enjoy the solitude, then retrace your steps to your vehicle.

Last reviewed: 25 February 1997

MAP REFERENCE
Sunmap - SURAT 1:250 000

FACILITIES
There are no facilities at all in this National Park. Bush camping is only permitted in the designated area. A permit is required from the Department of Environment. Carry your own water.

RANGER CONTACT - (07) 4661 3710

ALTON NATIONAL PARK

HISTORY
Like all the Parks in the Brigalow Belt, Alton was once surrounded by brigalow scrub. When the surrounding area was cleared for grazing land, this small section was left intact.

Early settlers originally preferred the open forest and grassland, but as these areas became settled, selectors were forced to clear the dense brigalow scrub. They soon found that after clearing, brigalow scrub was superior to open forests.

This was the start of broad acre clearing that saw the estimated area of brigalow and allied communities in Queensland fall from 9 300 000ha in 1953, when a tally of the remaining brigalow was completed, to only 4 730 000ha in 1962 when the next survey was completed.

Alton National Park, was proclaimed in 1973 and protects a 558ha sandplain, with vegetation communities unique to the Brigalow Belt.

FEATURES
Sandplains in Alton National Park rise gently to low ridges supporting a ground cover of heath and hummock grasses. Other vegetation includes small tea trees, smooth-barked apple, poplar box, silver-leafed ironbark and white cypress pine. Grass trees are also common. With the exception of the north-west corner, there is very little brigalow in this park, despite its location in the Brigalow Belt South, Biogeographic Region.

The area is alive with blooms in spring and is becoming a popular destination for wild flower enthusiasts, with many Western Queensland *'wildflower'* trips including Alton on the itinerary.

ACCESS
Alton National Park is located west of Moonie.

0.0kms	Moonie.
104.0kms	Continue past the cross roads of Ula Ula and Kooroon Roads.
108.0kms	*Alton National Park* sign and Ula Ula Creek crossing.
111.0kms	Turn left into Fairymount Oilfield Road.
112.3kms	Leave vehicle on National Park side of the grid.

SAND TRAIL
Distance: 2-4kms return, allow 1-2 hours. Easy grade.

Once again there are no walking tracks in the Park but navigation is relatively simple. Access is gained by walking east along the boundary fence. As you walk along the fence you will identify many different animal tracks in the sandy soil. Look for kangaroo, emu, dingo, echidna and mosquito. There are several places where kangaroos have left the Park and hopped under the fence to enter the adjoining land, and visa versa. After walking along the fence for about 30 minutes, locate any one of the animal tracks and head north into the Park. Spend as much time in the Park as you like, exploring the different types of vegetation, enjoying the wildflowers or identifying the various birds of the area. To return to your vehicle, walk southwards until you locate the fence, turn right and walk back to your car.

Last reviewed: 25 February 1997

MAP REFERENCE
Sunmap - SURAT 1:250 000

FACILITIES
There are no facilities at all in this National Park. Ensure you have adequate supplies of water, a hat and sunscreen, particularly if you visit the Park during summer.

RANGER CONTACT - (07) 4622 4266

ERRINGIBBA NATIONAL PARK

HISTORY
Mr David Gordon AM donated the 877ha area of Erringibba National Park to the Queensland Government. It was part of his property *'Myall Park'*. The National Park section, declared in August 1990, had been preserved by Mr Gordon in its natural state since 1928 and conserves a variety of brigalow, belah, yapunyah, silver-leafed ironbark and poplar box vegetation. The area has never been cleared, despite Government pressure to comply with lessee requirements and it has only been lightly grazed to minimise the risk of fire. According to Mr Gordon, the only timber ever cut from the area was *"...a few yapunyah logs, used for fence posts around the Park."*

Mr Gordon, a renowned botanist, collected seeds and cuttings from all over Australia and has cultivated them on a 90ha section of his grazing property since 1941. Particular emphasis was placed on propagating rare and endangered species that were threatened in their natural environment, but would grow in the harsh conditions of Western Queensland.

This section of Myall Park has been recognised as a Botanic Garden since 1985, and is the only botanic garden in the unique brigalow zone. The seed bank at the garden houses seeds from thousands of plants, some that have since become extinct. Botanists from over the world visit the gardens. Samples of black bean seed from the bank were personally collected by the Keeper of the Herbarium at London's Kew Gardens and are being used in research for a cure for AIDS.

Mr Gordon propagated the hybrid grevilleas; *'Robyn Gordon'*, *'Sandra Gordon'* and *'Merinda Gordon'*. These plants have become a commercial success and are sold in many nurseries throughout Australia. The three original, naturally occurring hybrid grevilleas still flourish in Myall Park Botanic Garden, alongside their parent trees. They are named after his three daughters.

He was responsible for saving the pink form of *Nympaea gigantea*, a waterlily now extinct in its natural environment. Many of the waterlilies in the botanic garden come from tropical Australia.

The Myall Botanic Gardens are not part of Erringibba National Park but are worth a visit to understand the devotion and foresight of one of Australia's great botanists. Among his many credits is the Member of the Order of Australia, bestowed on Mr Gordon in 1987 for his services to horticulture and conservation.

FEATURES

Erringibba National Park, situated south-east of Glenmorgan township conserves the district's last substantial undisturbed area of brigalow, belah and yapunyah scrub.

As with the other parks in the Brigalow Belt, large melon holes are formed in the gilgai soil, retaining water for long periods and providing a haven for bird life.

Many types of open forest bird life including quails, noisy miners, Rufous whistlers, eastern yellow robins, western warblers, bar-shouldered doves, sacred kingfishers, yellow-rumped thornbills, diamond firetails, striated pardolates, superb blue wrens, black faced cuckoo shrikes, willie wagtails and several species of honeyeaters and finches have been identified around the Park.

Koalas inhabit the eucalypts, and large goannas, and smaller frilled necked lizards and geckos scurry before you as they make their way to their homes in the many old tree hollows.

ACCESS

From Dalby take the Moonie Highway, then turn right on the Surat Development Road towards Tara. From Tara follow the signs another 85kms to Glenmorgan. The road is bitumen all the way. Just prior to the township and railway line, turn left into Windermere Road.

0.0kms	Windermere Road (gravel).
2.9kms	*Erringibba National Park* sign. This is the north-western corner of the Park. The road runs parallel to the western boundary. Leave your vehicles by the locked gate.

ONE MAN'S DREAM

Distance: 8kms, allow 2-3 hours. Easy grade.

From the gate at the north west corner of the Park, walk along the fire-break towards the southern boundary. The terrain consists of undulating sandy soil, dominated by brigalow, belah and yapunyah scrub. Half way along the western boundary, the fence veers left and then right again. The fire break is about 10m wide and well maintained.   Take the time to walk into the scrub and note the spongy gilgai soils.   There is a stand of younger brigalow about 3m tall growing in a patch just before the southern border.

The southern border fence is finally reached, about 2.4kms from the start.   As you turn left and follow the fence, note the difference between the original vegetation of the Park, and that growing in the cleared paddock to the right.

After walking for a further five minutes, follow one of the animal trails into the Park for about 30m, turn right and continue walking east, parallel to the southern boundary.   Look for hollows in the tree trunks, especially the yapunyah.   These hollows provide homes for birds and gliders.   When you reach an old road about one kilometre from the south-west corner of the Park, turn left and follow the road as it winds towards the northern boundary.   If conditions are right, you will see open cracks in the soil, some up to a metre deep.   The melon holes on either side of the old road are also obvious.   This road passes through the centre of one of the last substantial undisturbed areas of brigalow, belah and yapunyah scrub in the district. Look for geckos, lizards and monitors as you head through the scrub.   When you reach the northern boundary of the Park, turn left and follow the fence-line back to your vehicle.

Last reviewed: 6 December 1997

Authors note.   *'One Man's Dream'* is the title of the biography of Mr David Gordon AM.   The book is available from the Myall Park Visitors Centre.

It was a great privilege for us to discuss with Mr Gordon, then aged 98, the history of Erringibba National Park and his *'plans for the future'*.

MAP REFERENCE
Sunmap – SURAT 1:250 000

FACILITIES
There are no visitor facilities or walking tracks in the National Park, but walking and birdwatching are permitted.   Carry adequate water supplies, wear a hat and apply sunscreen and insect repellent.

Cottage and camping facilities are available at the Myall Park Botanic Gardens Bushland Retreat. For information, phone (07) 4665 6798 or (07) 4665 6734.

RANGER CONTACT - (07) 4661 3710

THE MULGA LANDS

THRUSHTON NATIONAL PARK

HISTORY

Initially part of a large grazing property, the area contained within Thrushton National Park was subdivided as a *'soldiers settlement'* block following the First World War. The homestead, originally the Dunkeld Hotel, was relocated during the 1920s. By the time it was shifted to its current site, most of the exterior wall lining had been lost. The current vertically lapped timber was all pit sawn on site from local pine. With no permanent water, a bore was sunk on the adjacent property and a bore drain was used to provide water for Thrushton. This bore drain extended for almost 60kms from the bore.

Thrushton lies within the Mulga Lands Bio-geographic Region that makes up around 12% of Queensland. This park and Idalia National Park were the first to be proclaimed in the Mulga Lands Region and were declared by Prince Philip, the International President of the World Wide Fund for Nature, in November 1990. The park now protects an area of 25 652ha.

Visitors to the nearby town of Bollon can usually find koalas high in the eucalypts along the banks of Wallam Creek. The trees behind the tennis courts is a favourite haunt. These animals have become so used to living in the area that they will sometimes be found in the school yard, with the occasional foray into the local hotel grounds.

FEATURES

Much of Thrushton National Park is made up of sandy plains and levees containing large stands of *'soft'* mulga. The creeks are lined with poplar box, river red gum and coolabah. Other species include forest gum, silver leafed ironbark, brigalow and belah. Spinifex and wildflower heaths grow along the levees and sand plains.

Around 220 species of birds have been identified including emus, cockatoos, honeyeaters, finches and kingfishers. Fifteen birds of prey and 10 species of ducks have been recorded in the Park.

Mammals found in the Park include eight species of kangaroos, echidnas and a large population of koalas. Feral dogs were originally a problem in the area, but they have now been eradicated. Some dingoes still live in the Park.

ACCESS

Travel west from St. George on the Balonne Highway for 94.8kms and turn right into a dirt road (14.2kms east of Bollon).

0.0kms	Start of dirt road.
1.5kms	Turn left.
17.2kms	Having driven through six gateways, you arrive at another gate, just west of the south-west corner of the Park. Continue through this gate and three more gateways.

33.0kms	Cross-roads at the division of the top and bottom paddocks. To reach the site of the old homestead, turn right here.
36.4kms	'Y' junction. Keep right. Drive through two more gates.
43.0kms	Turn right through gate into Thrushton National Park.
45.2kms	'Y' junction. Take left branch.
46.1kms	Site of old homestead. All buildings on the property are totally protected. Do not enter fenced off areas.

To reach Neabul Creek, turn left at the **33.0km** crossroads.

42.7kms	Neabul Creek crossing.

NB. Please leave all gates as you find them.

NEABUL CREEK WALK
Distance: 5–6kms return, allow 2 hours. Easy grade.

From the creek crossing, walk to the right in a north-easterly direction up the creek. The creek bed is generally dry and sandy. Following floods or heavy rain, large amounts of sand are shifted and redeposited in different parts of the creek bed, so conditions are likely to vary considerably from year to year.

After about fifteen minutes of steady walking, you reach a sweeping left-hand bend in the creek. The exposed rocky creek bed is a stark contrast to the surrounding sandy terrain. At this section of the creek you are likely to find the remains of small crustaceans washed downstream in recent floods.

Continue upstream, ignoring several dry gullies leading into the creek from the left. The eucalypts here are home to a large koala population. Continue to explore the area around the creek bed for as long as you like, before returning to your vehicle.

Last reviewed: 15 April 1997

MAP REFERENCE
Sunmap - HOMEBOIN 1:250 000

FACILITIES
There are no facilities in the Park. Bush camping is permitted in the top block, but there is no permanent water. The Park is isolated and all visitors need to be self-sufficient. There are lots of great opportunities for photographers interested in capturing the wild flowers in spring, and the bird life. Do not attempt to drive over bore drains. Apart from getting bogged, you will damage the drain.

RANGER CONTACT - (076) 226 466

TREGOLE NATIONAL PARK

HISTORY
This relatively new national park in semi-arid South-Western Queensland was originally used for grazing land. Much of the area surrounding the Park received significant broad acre clearing. Tregole is situated in an area where the Mulga Lands and the Brigalow Belt Biogeographic Regions meet. Fragile and diverse semi-arid ecosystems are conserved within its boundaries. The park protects relatively pure stands of ooline, a tree species previously thought to be only found in Sundown National Park and the Moolayember section of Carnarvon National Park. This 7 580ha park was proclaimed in February 1995.

FEATURES
Much of the terrain consists of siltstones and weathered mudstones. Loamy red soils are common and cracking clays dominate the plains and alluvial plains.
Significant stands of ooline are preserved in the south-eastern section of the Park. The ooline has rainforest origins dating back 10 000 years when the continent was much wetter than it is today. It is both unusual and unique for ooline to survive in the hot dry climate of the area. The relatively rare black orchid grows in the ooline forest and produces particularly beautiful flowers when in bloom. Other easily identified species include belah, brigalow, mulga, poplar box, red ash, bottle trees and mountain yapunyah. Mitchell grass plains make up the northern section of the Park.

ACCESS
Drive west on the Warrego Highway, 89kms west of Mitchell (or 177kms west of Roma) to Morven.

0.0kms	Morven. Turn left at the Morven Hotel Motel into Victoria Street/Nebine Road. A large sign directing visitors to *Tregole National Park* has been erected near the hotel.
10.7kms	Park boundary. Note the massive ooline tree on your left as you turn right and cross a grid into the day use area.

TREGOLE CIRCUIT TRACK
Distance: 2.1kms, allow 1 hour. Easy grade.

This walk starts from the parking area. Follow the signs as the track heads left (east) past the picnic table to a fence. Locate species marker number 16 and look up the tree to find a clump of black orchid. The track continues around in a loop, to a set of steps leading to a ridge. There is a good stand of red ash and ooline on the left. About 15 minutes from the start you reach another picnic table. The track climbs slowly to the top of a low ridge and you encounter a large stand of *Acalypha eremorum*. Follow the track as it turns right again over some small boulders on a sandy ridge. The track may occasionally be overgrown with summer grasses, producing some navigational difficulties. Continue following the track as it curves around to the right until you reach a large bottle tree near the end of the walk. Continue on to your vehicle.

Last reviewed: 7 April 1997

MAP REFERENCE
Sunmap - MITCHELL 1:250 000
A self guiding track map, along with a plant identification list is available from the Department of Environment at Charleville.

FACILITIES
Picnic tables and pit toilets are situated in the Park. There is no water, so carry your own when walking.
The weather is mild in autumn and spring. Spring is the best time to see the black orchid in flower.

RANGER CONTACT - (07) 4654 1255

MARIALA NATIONAL PARK

HISTORY
Mariala National Park is a 28 300ha reserve situated in the Mulga Country of South-Western Queensland. Formerly a grazing property, Mariala was gazetted as a national park in May 1992 to protect significant areas of mulga lands, scarps and gorges. For many years prior to receiving national park status, the area was a scientific reserve. It was used to study the effects of environmental conditions and destocking on native pasture composition, and regeneration. Relics of European pastoral industry are also contained within the Park.

FEATURES
The red soil floodplains, scarps and gorges of the Park provide a home for over 300 species of plants, some of which are not well represented in other Queensland National Parks. A rare low-lying spiny shrub called by its scientific name, *Rhapidaspora bonneyana*, grows in Mariala. Mulga, mountain yapunyah and Dawson gum are significant in most areas of the Park.
Galahs, wagtails, green parrots and whistling kites gather around abandoned dams, particularly during early morning and dusk.
Very large red and grey kangaroos and wallaroos, some standing as tall as two metres, feed on the grasses of the flood plains. The Department of Environment has established a breeding and release program for the yellow-footed rock wallaby, a vulnerable species living in the northern section of the Park. Koalas have also been recorded at Mariala.

ACCESS
Travel west on the Warrego Highway to Charleville.

0.0kms	Take the Adavale turn off on the western side of Charleville and travel across the plain where Ross and Keith Smith touched down on their first historic flight to England in 1922.
30.0kms	Start of gravel road – watch for emus grazing beside the road.
39.0kms	Small section of bitumen road through mulga plain country.
46.0kms	Bitumen strip at a bridge over Middle Creek.
50.0kms	Another sealed section passes an abandoned farm site on the left.
66.0kms	Veer left at sign post pointing to *Adavale 118kms*. Continue past a homestead on the right and a further sign, *Adavale 115kms*.
69.0kms	Cross the Langlo River and continue past Lake Dartmouth.
127.0kms	*Mariala National Park* sign and park boundary.
131.0kms	Earth dam on the left. Turn in here. You may camp at the rear of the dam.

NUMBER 3 BORE TRACK
Distance: 20kms return, allow 8 hours. Easy grade.

If you enjoy walking along old country roads, then this is the walk for you. Even if you don't have the time to visit Number 3 Bore, just amble through the mulga lands and red flood plains along an old 4WD track. You may even elect to drive along the road, park your vehicle and then get out and walk for a while. Either way you will appreciate the azure blue skies and feel the remoteness of Western Queensland. If walking from the dam, locate an old cattle trough at the rear of the dam and walk due south for about a100m, through long grass to join up with the road.

After about 1.5kms, power lines cross the road. Take note of the unusual caterpillar nests suspended from the trees along the way. Pick up a long stick. It will be handy to remove the sticky, yellow spider webs that cross your path.

About 5kms from the power lines you will pass Mogera Tank, an earth dam, on your right. Even following the floods of March 1997, this dam did not hold much water at the time of writing. After another hour you will reach a road veering off to the left. Ignore this and continue due south, past the remains of an old gate and stock holding yard, with 5 strands of wire connecting the 2.5m posts.

Continue along the main road, ignoring the road junction to the right, for about another kilometre and you will reach the remains of an old windmill, tank stands, cooking fire and animal troughs. Water from the Great Artesian Basin was once channelled to the property, but successive years of drought rendered the area dry. The dry bore drains run parallel to the road.

Continue south about a hundred metres past the windmill to the start of a small gorge. Use any remaining time you have to explore the gorge as it meanders its way towards an unnamed creek. The pink, yellow, mauve and tan colours of the rocks in the gorge are a striking contrast to the red country you have just walked through.

To return to your vehicle or camp site, simply retrace your steps. Remember to allow yourself enough time for the return trip.

Last reviewed: 9 April 1997

MAP REFERENCE
Sunmap - ADAVALE 1:250 000
The park is on the border of four 1:100 000 maps.
Sunmap - ADAVALE, AMBATHALA, LAKE DARTMOUTH and GUMBARDO

FACILITIES
There are no facilities in this National Park, and camping is for self sufficient visitors only. Ensure you have adequate water supplies.

Dramatic sunrises and sunsets can be seen during autumn and winter. Winter nights can become extremely cold. Wildflowers are at their peak during spring.

RANGER CONTACT - (07) 4654 1255

CULGOA FLOODPLAIN NATIONAL PARK

HISTORY
Abutting the New South Wales border, Culgoa Floodplain National Park covers an area of 46 856ha. Originally a sheep and cattle grazing property, Culgoa boasted the last *'ten stand'* shearing shed to be erected in Queensland. The park now plays a significant role in the regeneration of natural bushland in Queensland's west. The Ranger in Charge encourages neighbouring farmers to participate in land regeneration and erosion prevention trials. Visitors to the Park soon appreciate the logic behind the preservation of Culgoa's vegetation types, in a region that is rapidly being cleared for cultivation.

Programs for unemployed youth, conducted by the Youth Conservation Core, have resulted in more than 3kms of fencing being erected within the Park, along with other maintenance and improvement projects. Children from nearby Goodooga school are encouraged to visit the Park regularly to learn about local conservation and heritage issues, from the forward thinking Ranger.

Feral animal eradication programs are being undertaken in an effort to return the Park to its natural state. Culgoa Floodplain National Park was proclaimed in 1993 and is an area where conservation, education and scientific goals can coexist.

FEATURES
Part of the Great Artesian Basin lies only 525m below Culgoa. This is the largest artesian basin in the world and occupies around 1.75 million square kilometres,

about two thirds of which are in Queensland. Because of the relatively shallow bore depth, water flowing to the surface is warm, but much cooler than in other areas of the country where it often exceeds boiling point. Bore drains are used tochannel water to different sections of the property. The Culgoa River does not flow through the Park, but its vast floodplains host a variety of native flora and wildlife. Claypans throughout the Park retain water following floods. The clay soils of the flat alluvial plains support stands of gidgee, brigalow, mulga and eucalypt woodlands.

In Culgoa, the gidgee, that produces a pungent smell before rain, is almost at its eastern limit of distribution in Queensland. Undisturbed stands of brigalow grow beside paddocks that were previously cleared for grazing. It is interesting to note the regrowth of brigalow in these paddocks, after a decade of no grazing. Emu bush growth is proving to be a problem as it grows up around new brigalow. Mulga, poplar box and scattered sandalwood shrubs dominate low hills. Never-fail grass covers the ground around black box and salt bush in areas that are subject to flooding. Spiny lignum, kangaroo grass, yarrapunyah, and beefwood are also prevalent.

Culgoa is a relatively new national park and while birdwatchers have visited the Park and recorded many species, not much was known about the ground animals until September 1996, when the Department of Environment began work in this area. The results have been pleasing and about 20 mammals have now been recorded. Red, eastern grey and western grey kangaroos are quite obvious to the visitor, and recently several species of marsupial mice have been encountered.

Of the 140 species of birds recorded in the Park some of the most spectacular include Major Mitchell cockatoos, Australian ringnecks, blue bonnets, and red-winged, red-rumped and mulga parrots. Emus, brown falcons, crested pigeons, galahs, grey-crowned babblers, apostlebirds, white-winged choughs and little crows are common. Pallid cuckoos and red-backed kingfishers are seasonal visitors to the territory. Australia's six species of woodswallow reside in the Park. Some birdwatchers are rewarded with sightings of splendid, variegated and white-winged fairy-wrens, southern whitefaces, crimson chats, red-capped and hooded robins, crested bellbirds, ground cuckoo-shrikes, spotted bowerbirds and plum-headed finches. Look for the white-browed treecreeper in the mulga regions. The flower of the mistletoe tree feeds the rare painted honeyeater, one of 10 species of honeyeaters in the Park. Pacific black ducks, grey teals, little pied cormorants, white-faced and white-necked herons, great egrets and straw-necked ibis inhabit the waterholes, lagoons and dams at Culgoa.

Western bearded dragons are a common sight, sunning themselves on fallen logs and fence posts. Shingleback lizards and sand goannas enjoy the warmer months in the Park. Bynoe's gecko is one of seven gecko varieties and Boulenger's skink is one of at least a dozen skink types at Culgoa. Watch out for the king brown and the mulga snake.

Large numbers of frogs are evident following rain. Burrowing types include the barking and spotted marsh frogs, ornate burrowing frogs and salmon-striped frogs.

Tree frogs include the green tree frog, emerald-spotted tree frog and naked tree frog.

If you take the time to look around Culgoa Floodplain National Park, you will be rewarded with a fine sample of Western Queensland's flora and fauna.

ACCESS

Culgoa Floodplain National Park can be accessed from Dirranbandi in Queensland's far west, via Goondiwindi or St George. Follow the bitumen road to Hebel, a small settlement with an interesting hotel. Murals have been painted on the pub by a *'local'* from Lightning Ridge. Top up with fuel at the hotel and enjoy a cool drink in the bar as you talk to the locals and view the memorabilia that has taken years to collect. From Hebel cross into New South Wales and travel 40km along the gravel road to Goodooga.

0.0kms	Goodooga. Turn right at the sign post reading *Brenda 18kms* and *Weilmoringle 84kms*.
21.9kms	Cross grid.
22.8kms	Take the left fork sign posted *Byra 7kms*.
27.9kms	Ignore the road to the left and continue straight ahead.
29.6kms	Cross another grid at the entrance to the Park. Turn left and drive the short distance to the original homestead, now used as the Ranger's residence.

NB. The dirt road is suitable for caravans when dry, but a dusty trip is likely to be encountered.

There are plans to develop a *'drive through tour'* suitable for 4WD vehicles to allow visitors to view different sections of the Park. Although there are no recognised walking tracks, walkers can visit the remains of the *'ten stand'* shearing shed situated near the homestead and take the short stroll described below. Additional areas suitable for walking may be opened to the public after the drive through route is finalised. Consult the Ranger in Charge for current information.

BYRA LAGOON TRACK

Distance: Approximately 2kms, allow 1 hour. Easy grade.

Park your vehicle near the Ranger's homestead and walk east along an old road towards the Lagoon. After a few hundred metres, the road crosses an open swampy area that is generally dry, unless there have been recent rains. Within about 30 minutes you should reach the edge of the Lagoon. Water backs up into the Lagoon from the Culgoa River. At the edge of the Lagoon, turn left and head in a northerly direction, picking your way through the swampy grass until you locate a dry, stony creek bed. The homestead can be seen off to the left. Skirt around the thick undergrowth close to the Lagoon and walk through the paddock until you reach an old road, then head back down towards the edge of the Lagoon. Much of this area of the Park is covered with buffel grass, an introduced South African species. The grass provides good feed for cattle, but is out of place within a national park where attempts are being made to restore the area to its original condition. A small camp site has been cleared near the Lagoon. This is likely to be the location for any future expansion of camping facilities in the Park. Several brolgas live around the Lagoon and may be seen at early morning and late afternoon.

Last reviewed: 16 April 1997

MAP REFERENCE
Sunmap - DIRRANBANDI 1:250 000

FACILITIES
Bush camping is permitted only at the Lagoon and by prior arrangement with the Ranger. Campers must be self sufficient and carry their own water and supplies. The best time to visit is during the cooler months. The wildflowers bloom across the plains during early spring, making a spectacular sight.

RANGER CONTACT - (076) 250942 - Culgoa
(076) 226466 - Roma

CURRAWINYA NATIONAL PARK

HISTORY
Discoveries of artefacts and relics dating back nearly 14 000 years are evidence that Aboriginal people occupied the area around Currawinya National Park, long before it became a sheep grazing property in the 1860s. It is still possible to discover signs of their passing, and of early European settlement. The remains of the old homestead, *'Caiwarro'* are located in the north-eastern section of the Park. Remember, all archaeological sites and artefacts are protected in national parks.
This 151 300ha park, Queensland's eighth largest, was proclaimed in 1991 to protect the archaeological sites, mulga lands, lakes, claypans and saltpans surrounding one of Queensland's most extensive inland waterbird habitats. Destocking of the Park has assisted regeneration of native flora.
About 2 000 people now visit the Park each year.

FEATURES
A semi-arid landscape contrasts with the rivers and the freshwater and salt lakes in the Park. Lake Numalla is the largest freshwater lake, and Lake Wyara is the largest saline lake in Currawinya National Park. Whilst Lake Numalla is regarded as a *'permanent'* lake, it has dried out three times this century. Lake Wyara often dries out during drought periods, leaving a giant saltpan.
Although the Lakes are separated by only a few kilometres of sand dunes, they are

unique in that they have completely different drainage systems. Many temporary lakes are formed between the dunes and in the claypans after steady rain.

The soils surrounding the Park are usually deficient in nitrogen and phosphorous, making the Mulga Lands one of the most fragile of Queensland's diverse Biogeographic Regions.

Mulga, with its characteristic dark fissured bark and silver-grey foliage, forms tall scrub lands in sections of Currawinya National Park. It also dominates the sand plains of the Park.

Other common trees include poplar box, beefwood, emu apple, leopardwood, whitewood and black box. The banks of the Paroo River are lined with yapunyah, coolibah and river red gums. The gidgee tree produces a pungent aroma before and during rains. Lake Wyara is fringed by salt tolerant species of low-lying shrubs.

Both types of lakes support different varieties of waterbirds, with up to 200 000 visiting the area some seasons. Migratory waders visit as they travel through inland Australia.

Lake Wyara generally has the greater population. Small waders and plant-eating waterbirds feed in the waters. Many species of duck including the rare freckled duck, Australia's rarest, share the Lake with black swans, coots, swamp hens and grebes. Sandpipers, godwits, glossy ibis, Pacific herons, dotterels and stilts feed on the numerous invertebrates that live in the Lake. Safe breeding grounds for avocets, silver gulls, Caspian terns and Australian pelicans are found on some of the Lakes' islands. If Lake Wyara becomes dry, most birds disperse to other suitable habitats that may be hundreds of kilometres away, generally outside the Park.

The large waders and fish eating birds frequent Lake Numalla. These include egrets, herons, cormorants, ibis, plovers and brolgas.

The Lakes are also an important drought refuge for terrestrial birds and other animals.

Emus, red kangaroos and eastern grey kangaroos are easily spotted throughout the Park. Less common are the darker western grey kangaroos and wallaroos.

ACCESS
Travel west from Brisbane to Cunnamulla, and then to Eulo.

0.0kms	Eulo
4.7kms	Turn left at the sign posted gravel road to Hungerford.
23.6kms	Section of bitumen as you pass over the flood plains.
26.5kms	Gravel road continues over grids numbered 1 to 12.
59.4kms	*National Park* boundary sign.
70.3kms	Sign to the left points to the ruins of the old Caiwarro homestead site. (Some bush camping is allowed along the Paroo River, reached from this route.)
101.5kms	Sign pointing right to *Currawinya.* The homestead is the site of the Ranger's Information Centre and residence. You need to call in here and register for camping.

105.1kms   Turn right at signs to the *Camp Ground* and *Thargomindah.*
105.4kms   Turn left into Ten Mile Bore camp ground.

NB. Parts of the Park are closed to visitors. Vehicles must keep to designated roads. Some roads pass through pastoral properties, so take care to leave gates as they are found. The roads are unsealed and impassable in wet weather so 4WD vehicles are recommended. Please observe 40km/hour speed limit on the Park's narrow roads. It is important to remain with your vehicle if it breaks down. A vehicle is much easier to locate than people.

LAKES NUMALLA AND WYARA

The sign posted road to *Lakes Numalla (28kms)* and *Wyara (33.5kms)* starts from Ten Mile Bore camp ground. After 27.5kms you reach an intersection. The road straight ahead leads 500m to Lake Numalla car park. The road to the left leads 6kms to Lake Wyara car park.

Authors note. The Ranger in Charge of Currawinya National Park supplied these amended road directions in December 1997, prior to publishing. They refer to a *'new'* road, under construction at that time and due for completion around March 1998.

This park has recently been zoned and areas have been designated as either; *'Intensive Use'*, *'Common Use'*, *'Dispersed Use'* or *'Minimum Use'*.

Zone maps and interpretive information will be positioned at sites near the car parks. Much of the area is fragile, so be sure to stay on the walking tracks and follow the signs at all times.

LAKE NUMALLA

Distance: 4-5kms return, allow 1.5 hours, plus birdwatching time. Easy grade.

From the car park, follow the walking track to the edge of the Lake. There is a picnic table at the Lake's shore that makes a good spot to watch the sunrise or sunset. Turn right and walk south along the Lake, skirting around a small clump of trees that provide reasonable cover for birdwatching. Continue past low red sand dunes, heading back towards the Lake. Keep walking for about 1 to 1.5kms, enjoying this beautiful outback oasis before returning to the car park.

The second part of the walk continues for about 800m north of the car park, along a road closed to vehicle access. Follow this down to a picnic table on the Lake's edge. From here, you will get another opportunity to view the bird life, or capture the serenity of the Lake on film. The sun rising over the Lake adds a golden hue to the plants on the shoreline.

Last reviewed: 13 April 1997

LAKE WYARA
Distance: 2kms return, allow 1 hour. Easy grade.

Because of the soil types around this Lake, rainfall and high water levels make the area very boggy, so walking tracks and access roads may be closed.
Follow the track from the car park to the Lake paying particular attention to the interpretive signs. The sand around the edge of the Lake is crusted with salt and crumbles underfoot.
Once again, spend as much time as you like appreciating the harshness of the terrain and observing the birdlife. There is very little cover along the edge of the Lake, but you could hide in the scrub and spot the birds with a pair of binoculars.
Take a short stroll along the edge of the Lake before retracing your steps back to the starting point.

Last reviewed: 13 April 1997

THE GRANITES
Distance: Approximately 4km return, allow 2 hours. Easy grade.

From Ten Mile Bore camp ground, travel towards Thargomindah for 10kms, before turning right towards the Granites car park. Due to the fragile nature of soils in the area, the original road has been closed and access to the Granites is on foot. The site of the car park was still to be determined at the time of publication, but the Granites are 2.1kms from the Thargomindah Road turn off.
A walking track is currently being constructed, but if it is not complete at the time of your visit, follow the original road to the base of the Granites.
The Granites are an interesting rock formation with large tors and boulders, not unlike those found in Girraween National Park. They are a stark contrast to the rest of the Park. From the base of the Granites, head straight up to the top of the formation in a north-easterly direction. The grandeur of the Australian outback can be experienced from here.
To return to the base of the Granites, walk down in a north-westerly direction skirting around the base of the rocks. Retrace your steps to the starting point.

Last reviewed: 13 April 1997
NB. Before heading off on any walk in Western Queensland, ensure you have adequate supplies of water, a hat and sunscreen. The area is remote and the terrain is harsh. Sudden storms could isolate you from your vehicle and/or camp site without warning.

MAP REFERENCE
Sunmap - EULO 1:250 000
A Visitor Information Sheet is supplied by QNPWS.

FACILITIES

Camping at the Park is for self sufficient visitors only. Tank water is available here, but may be unreliable and unsuitable for drinking, so it's best to carry your own. There are no food or petrol supplies inside the Park. Limited food and fuel can be purchased at Hungerford, 16kms south of Ten Mile Bore camp ground, and Eulo, 105kms north. However, it is recommended that enough supplies to last four to five days be carried, in case you become stranded.

Camping is not permitted at Lakes Numalla and Wyara, in order to protect their fragile environment.

Birdwatching, photography, walking and stargazing on clear nights are all enjoyable activities at Currawinya.

Paddle and row boats are only allowed on designated areas of Lake Numalla. Leave power boats at home.

The cooler months are the best time to explore Currawinya National Park. Summer is very hot with days exceeding 40°C. More than half the average rainfall of 295mm falls during this time. Winter temperatures average about 19°C but the nights, that are ideal for stargazing, can drop to -5°C.

RANGER CONTACT - (07) 4655 4001

LAKE BINDEGOLLY NATIONAL PARK

HISTORY

Lake Bindegolly National Park was an essential part of a network of 14 reserves originally identified by the Mulga Lands Biogeographic Study. None of this land was protected until Idalia, Thrushton and Currawinya National Parks were declared in the late 1990s and early 1991. Lake Bindegolly National Park, 11 930ha, followed in December 1991. The network of parks conserves 92% of the major vegetation types and most of the landforms associated with these vegetation types. Lake Bindegolly is also one of the most important inland wetland systems within South-West Queensland.

FEATURES

Most of the Park is relatively flat with salt plains and flood plains draining into one of three lakes within the Park. Lakes Bindegolly and Toomaroo are saline whilst Lake Hutchinson is freshwater.   The samphire flats around the Lakes are particularly fragile and would be damaged if vehicles were allowed in the Park. Fifteen of the 91 unique land systems within the Western Mulga Country are found within Bindegolly.

Lake Bindegolly National Park conserves one of only two known areas where the *Acacia ammophila* grows. The other small stand lies west of Adavale and is not protected in a national park.   Mulga open shrubland and low woodland, gidgee woodland and samphire herbfields dominate the area, but local QNPWS staff have identified around 200 different species of plants within the Park

The Lakes within the Park provide an important feeding and breeding ground for waterbirds. Freckled ducks, pelicans, swans and a variety of waders can be found on the Lakes. More than 150 different birds have been recorded within the Park boundary including, herons, ibises, brolgas, bustards, quails, cuckoos, owls, hawks and kingfishers.Red and grey kangaroos are common and other native mammals include echidnas, dunnarts, wallaroos and several species of bats. The Park is also home to many types of skinks, geckos, lizards, dragons, goannas and snakes.

ACCESS

Sixty seven kilometres west of Cunnamulla is the township of Eulo, the gateway to Lake Bindegolly and Currawinya National Parks. Drive west from Eulo on the Bulloo Development Road, towards Thargomindah.

0.0kms	Eulo.
86.0kms	Turn right, just before the bridge sign posted *Lake Bindegolly.*
86.3kms	Turn right into the old road, then left under the power lines and continue ahead.
88.3kms	Park boundary and locked gate. Pedestrian access only from this point.

LAKE BINDEGOLLY

Distance: 7-8kms, allow 2 hours, plus birdwatching time. Easy grade.

Start walking along the service road at the Park boundary. After about a kilometre, you reach a tagged *Acacia ammophila* on the right side of the track. The taller shrubs give way to the herbgrass plains and the Lake can be seen off to the left. The service road soon veers left and heads towards a clump of small trees on the shore of the Lake.

When you reach a cross road, continue straight ahead to the shore of the Lake. Emus run out of your way as you head towards the Lake. Turn left and follow the shoreline in a general south-westerly direction.

There is no cover in which to '*hide*' along the shore of the Lake. (If you want to observe the birds at dusk, it may be better to wait near the small clump of trees, then retrace your steps back along the road to your starting point, especially if you are not confident walking back across the plain after dusk.)

After about 2kms of steady walking, turn left and head due east back towards the starting point. The ground here is covered in low herbgrasses and the salt plains crumble underfoot as you head for home. When you reach the road, look for either foot prints or tyre tracks to determine whether you should turn right or left to reach your vehicle.

If you have continued around the Lake in a southerly direction, you will soon reach a point where the southern tail of Lake Bindegolly heads east. Follow the shoreline east at this point and you will reach the road leading to the Park boundary.

No defined walking trails exist in the Park, but the Department of Environment intends to erect directional signs, roughly along the route of the walk described. It is extremely important to carry adequate supplies of water.

Last reviewed: 11 April 1997

MAP REFERENCE
Sunmap - EULO 1:250 000

FACILITIES
No camping is allowed in the Park. Camping is permitted along the stock route, south of the Bulloo Development Road, opposite the access road to the Park. There are no amenities or water available here. Caravans have easy access.

Spring and autumn are the best times to visit the Park. Extremes of temperatures occur in winter and summer months. (-1°C to 20°C in winter and 23°C to 45°C in summer.) In fact, summertime temperatures regularly reach the mid 40°s with the area often recording the highest temperatures in the state.

RANGER CONTACT - (07) 4655 3173

REFERENCE MATERIAL

The following reference material has been used in the production of this book.

100 Walks in South Queensland. Groom and Gynther.

All in a Day's Walk. Graham Churchett.

Bushwalking in South-East Queensland. Ross and Heather Buchanan.

Camping in Queensland. QNPWS.

Discover National Parks Around Brisbane. QNPWS.

Discovering Binna Burra on Foot. Thomas Lackner.

Nature Conservation (Protected Areas) Regulation 1994. Queensland Government.

The Conondales. Bushwalking and Recreation. Cheryl Seabrook.

Vegetation on Moreton Island. Helen Horton.

Wild Australia. Reader's Digest.

Wildflowers of Bribie Island. Ian MacRae.

Wild Places of Greater Brisbane. Stephen Poole and others.

Secrets of the Scenic Rim. Robert Rankin.

Slater Field Guide to Australian Birds, Peter, Pat and Raoul Slater.

Along with:

Various *Visitor Information Sheets, Park Guides, Brochures* and *National Park Management Plans,* produced by the Department of Environment.

The vast *Archives* of the National Parks Association of Queensland and many editions of N.P.A. News.

ADVERTISERS INDEX